MW00331492

Contemporary Issues in Digital Marketing

Contemporary Issues in Digital Marketing
New Paradigms, Perspectives and Practices

John Branch, Marcus Collins
and Eldad Sotnick-Yogev

LIBRI
PUBLISHING

First published in 2018 by Libri Publishing

Copyright © Libri Publishing

Authors retain copyright of individual chapters.

The right of John Branch, Marcus Collins and Eldad Sotnick-Yogev
to be identified as the editors of this work has been asserted in
accordance with the Copyright, Designs and Patents Act, 1988.

ISBN 978-1-911450-23-8

All rights reserved. No part of this publication may be reproduced,
stored in any retrieval system or transmitted in any form or by any
means, electronic, mechanical, photocopying, recording or otherwise, without the prior written permission of the copyright holder
for which application should be addressed in the first instance
to the publishers. No liability shall be attached to the author,
the copyright holder or the publishers for loss or damage of any
nature suffered as a result of reliance on the reproduction of any
of the contents of this publication or any errors or omissions in its
contents.

A CIP catalogue record for this book is available from The British
Library

Design by Carnegie Book Production

Cover Design by Hunter Langston and Scott Taylor

Printed by Lightning Source

Libri Publishing
Brunel House
Volunteer Way
Faringdon
Oxfordshire
SN7 7YR

Tel: +44 (0)845 873 3837

www.libripublishing.co.uk

Contents

Figures

Tables

Chapter 1

New Paradigms, Perspectives and Practices

John Branch, Marcus Collins and Eldad Sotnick-Yogev

Jeff Goldblum, *Jurassic Park* and Digital Dinosaurs

Jeff Goldblum has played many characters during his distinguished forty-plus-year acting career. Certainly, his first professional cinematic job, portraying Freak #1 in 1974's *Death Wish*, might not be particularly memorable. But who can forget Michael Gold in *The Big Chill* (a movie whose setting, somewhat coincidentally, was the University of Michigan)? Or what about Seth Brundle in *The Fly*, a role which won Jeff Goldblum several guild awards?

More recently, however, Goldblum has become a household name – more of a household face actually – as chaos theorist Dr. Ian Malcolm in the four Jurassic Park movies from 1993, 1997, 2001 and 2015. (A fifth instalment is scheduled for a 2018 release.) Based on novels by best-selling writer Michael Crichton, the movies centre on the catastrophic attempt to create an amusement park (Jurassic Park) which features cloned dinosaurs. The stunning computer-generated visual graphics, the human fascination with these awe-inspiring creatures and the nostalgic nod to the 1933 classic *King Kong* have made the movies one of the most beloved and financially successful movie franchises in cinematic history.

From a more philosophical perspective, however, the Jurassic Park movies, which at first glance appear to be intellectually light fare, belie a more cerebral undercurrent. Indeed, amidst all the dinosaur action chases are fundamental ontological questions about human existence, human experience and human evolution. Consider the following exchange between Goldblum's Dr. Ian Malcolm and two other characters:

> Malcolm: If there is one thing the history of evolution has taught us it's that Life will not be contained. Life breaks free, it expands to new territories and crashes through barriers, painfully, maybe even dangerously, but, uh... well, there it is.
>
> Hammond: There it is.
>
> Henry Wu: You're implying that a group composed entirely of female animals will... breed?
>
> Malcolm: No, I'm, I'm simply saying that Life, uh... finds a way.

And so it is with technology... or maybe, Technology, with a capital 'T'. That is to say, Technology, like Life, will find a way; it will also not be contained. To paraphrase Dr. Ian Malcolm, Technology breaks free; it expands to new territories and crashes through barriers, painfully, maybe even dangerously. In other words, Technology evolves through the sometimes wrenching replacement of existing versions – that which Schumpeter (1975) called "creative destruction".

Now, the specific technology which is the subject of this anthology, and which is part and parcel of this broader Technological evolution, is digital marketing. 'Digital', when used as an adjective, refers to a series of 1s and 0s. Accordingly, a digital signal is a signal which is composed of 1s and 0s. A digital watch is a watch whose timing is actuated by 1s and 0s, not balance springs and escapements.

It follows, therefore, that digital marketing – by definition – is marketing which is expressed in a series of 1s and 0s. Stated this way, the term 'digital marketing' is meaningless, nonsense, a load of rubbish. And as such, digital marketing could be written off as nothing more than a buzzword, a catchphrase, the *soupe du jour*.

A more mindful reflection on the term 'digital marketing', however, leads to a different and more nuanced understanding of the phenomenon. We suggest that digital marketing ought to be viewed as marketing which employs – harnesses, leverages, exploits – digital technologies. Ponder those pesky pop-ups on your favourite newsfeed site and you realise that they are promotional advertisements on digital media. How about those (Orwellian) text messages which you might receive when walking past the GAP, tempting you with personalised discounts on a new pair of jeans? Or consider Bank of America's mobile-telephone deposit application which allows customers to deposit cheques straight into their accounts using their mobile-telephone cameras, thereby freeing them of long queues, tedious deposit slips and all the other hassles of traditional face-to-face and even drive-thru banking.

Viewing digital marketing this way extends the boundaries of digital marketing beyond the street-level notion that marketing=advertising. That is to say, digital marketing is not only digital communications. On the contrary, digital marketing can and ought to include all types of marketing activities, from marketing research, to the STPs, to the other three 'P's of the marketing mix. Consider Klout, for example, a company which developed an algorithm to assign a word-of-mouth score according to a person's influence on various websites.

Viewing digital marketing this way also intimates that any digital technology, although important, is subordinate to marketing. Indeed, despite the moniker, it is marketing first, digital second. Consequently, one conclusion which might be drawn is that the essence of marketing has changed little, if any, over time, despite the rapid advances of Technology. In other words, marketing – the act of going to market with a product to exchange for money with a customer – remains the same, irrespective of any digital technology which is employed in service of going to market.

This foregrounding of marketing instead of digital also reminds us that human behaviour is very slow to change, even in the face of rapid advances in Technology. A digital technology often encourages a behaviour, making it more prevalent and more frequent, but it rarely alters that behaviour. Digital readers, for example, enable people to read in more locations, and perhaps even to read more books. But the act of reading remains the same.

So, if the essence of marketing is fundamentally the same, and if human behaviour is relatively static over time, then why all the fuss about digital marketing? Why indeed? The answer to us is simple – that digital technologies transform the market, thereby presenting marketers with many new opportunities (and simultaneously many new challenges) that point to new marketing practices: new research modes, new product designs, new pricing models and so on.

A market, from an economics perspective, is the site of an exchange (between a company and the customer). It is the place where buyers and sellers come together. It is the nexus of supply and demand. But to many marketers (because we love alliterative models), a market is comprised of customers, the company, competitors, collaborators and the context. In this model, both the company and competitors make up the industry. Collaborators are those entities which help the company go to market. And the context is the business environment.

Using this model of a market, therefore, it ought to be obvious that digital technologies have indeed transformed the market. Beginning with customers, they now have new choices for their media, for example, and their preferences for which media to use have changed. They rely on different influencers in their purchase decisions. They have different expectations from the industry. Consider the immediacy with which customers now expect their complaints to be resolved. According to the Lithium-commissioned study by Millward Brown Digital (2013), 53% of people expect a company to respond to Tweet demands in less than an hour.

Digital technologies have likewise transformed industries, and in turn the nature of competition within these industries. Where oh where is Blockbuster these days, once the darling of the media industry? Hilton Hotels and Resorts faces trouble as its room count is surpassed by the number of listings on Airbnb. And how about Uber, which, without owning a single vehicle, is disrupting the entire transportation industry, and whose market capitalisation is greater than that of both Ford and General Motors?

And it is plain to see that digital technologies have also transformed both collaborators and the context. Companies can issue coupons with the assistance of digital promotional 'agents' like Groupon, for example. Retailing and sales transactions can be outsourced to the likes of Amazon and Alibaba. And society no longer views the online search for a mate as vulgar and inappropriate.

As stated previously, however, all these market transformations which have resulted from digital technologies present marketers with many new opportunities (and simultaneously many new challenges) which point to new marketing practices. And therein lies the rub. Many companies are unprepared to seize these opportunities because they lack the requisite skills in digital marketing. Worse still are those companies whose future depends on developing these skills in digital marketing in order to overcome the many new challenges which the transformations present. If not careful, these companies might go the way of their Jurassic brethren, becoming, in a very Darwinian sense, digital dinosaurs.

It is not surprising, therefore, that companies around the world are scrambling to up their digital competencies. Nestlé, for example, was one of the first high-profile global corporations to implement a reverse-mentoring program for members of the C-suite. Under the leadership of Pete Blackshaw, Vice President of Digital and Social, the 150-year-old FMCG company has tapped young 'digital natives' to educate the older generation of Nestlé executives. "It's such an unbelievable experience because it's not only understanding the digital world it's also understanding different perspectives from different generations," explained Guillame-Grabisch, Chief Executive of the company's German division, reflecting on her experience of being mentored by a twenty-something employee.

It will take more than chats over coffee, however, to avoid

becoming a digital dinosaur. Indeed, the opportunities and challenges which are presented by the market transformations necessitate a more sophisticated grasp of the basic and evolving nature of digital marketing. They point to the need for robust theories on digital marketing – theories which can help explicate consumer behaviours in the digital age. And they require the development of specific digital marketing practices to facilitate the execution of digital marketing. Voilà, the inspiration for this anthology!

The Symposium

This anthology is the product of a symposium, the format of which is based on a model from John's colleague Claus Nygaard from Copenhagen Business School. About 10 years ago, Claus noted that professors (and practitioners) often attend conferences at which they present their research in a 10–20 minute session, receive a few comments then 'head to the bar for a drink'. The conferences can be very expensive and they rarely lead to any tangible output. He proposed an alternative, therefore, which returns to that ancient Greek format – the symposium – at which co-creation is key and which generates a physical product for the participants.

So, about six months prior to a symposium, a call for chapter proposals which has a relatively tightly focused theme is announced on various electronic mailing lists. Authors submit chapter proposals accordingly, which are then double-blind reviewed. If a chapter proposal is accepted, its author is given four months to complete it. The whole chapter is then double-blind reviewed and, if it is accepted, the author is invited to attend the symposium. There, all authors revise their own chapters, work together to develop each other's chapters and collaborate to assemble an anthology which, a few months later, is sent to the publisher.

For this anthology, the theme was digital marketing. As the call for chapter proposals made plain, we now live in the digital age. Indeed, there are more than three billion people connected to the Internet. For every 100 people on the planet, there are 96 mobile-telephone subscriptions. And more and more of our everyday objects – cuddly toys, cars, even kettles – have been connected to create an 'Internet of things'.

It is no surprise, therefore, that companies are eager to harness this digital world. Marketers, in particular, hope that so-called digital marketing will allow them to gain new customer insights, refine customer segmentation, and communicate to customers more efficiently and effectively. They anticipate that the digital age will offer possibilities for new product innovation, advanced methods for engaging customers and original vehicles for creating brand communities.

Despite the pervasiveness of digital technologies, however, digital marketing is seemingly still in its infancy. To begin, what exactly is digital marketing? The term is bandied about but its meaning – its scope, outline, boundary and limits – is far from concise. Second, digital marketing is still very atheoretical. To date, it has largely been based on assumptions, guesswork and conjecture. And third, digital marketing is conducted ad hoc, with few (if any) standardised policies, practices or procedures.

For this anthology, therefore, the editors sought chapters which explored digital marketing. They welcomed chapters from professors and practitioners alike, and they were open to any methodological tradition. Specifically, the editors were guided by the three broad but interrelated themes which were identified above. These were:

1. Conceptual: What is digital marketing? Are there different types? How is it situated within marketing more broadly? Answering these types of questions will sharpen the definition of digital marketing. Proposals were evaluated, therefore, on their contribution to our understanding of the *nature* of digital marketing.

2. Theoretical: How does digital marketing work? What are its effects? Can it be controlled? Answering these types of questions will raise the significance of digital marketing. Proposals were evaluated, therefore, on their contribution to our understanding of the *mechanisms* of digital marketing.

3. Practical: How is digital marketing conducted? What are its different channels? In which contexts does it work? Answering

these types of questions will increase the application of digital marketing. Proposals were evaluated, therefore, on their contribution to our understanding of the *function* of digital marketing.

The call for chapter proposals resulted in more than 30 submissions from around the world which covered an array of different aspects of digital marketing. The subsequent review and re-submission process served to whittle these down to the 15 chapters which follow in this anthology. The symposium at which the chapters were revised and the anthology was assembled was held in October 2016 at the University of Michigan in Ann Arbor. In addition to the academic symposium activities, authors strolled the campus of the University of Michigan, seeing, among other things, the spot at which President John F. Kennedy announced the American Peace Corps program. We enjoyed Michigan's culinary delights, including a Lebanese feast, chocolate-covered cherries and nibbles from Ann Arbor's 'famous' Zingerman's Deli. And we watched the home team, Wolverines, beat the visiting Illinois Illini in American football at Michigan Stadium – a.k.a. *The Big House* – the nation's largest and the world's third-largest stadium.

The Editors and Digital Marketing

As editors, of course, we bring our own perspectives to the role, which are based on our own experiences in and with digital marketing. We have our own philosophical assumptions about human nature which, in turn, influence our views about the appropriateness of digital marketing. And of course, we have our own career paths which have dictated our engagement with digital marketing.

John

It is often said that today's children make up the first generation of 'digital natives'. Indeed, in their new book, *Born Digital: Understanding the First Generation of Digital Natives*, authors John Palfrey and Urs Gasser argue that these children were raised – to paraphrase the age-old saying – with a silver device in their hands. And consequently, the authors claim, they constitute a new generation which has its own unique worldview, its own specific behavioural patterns and even its own distinctive philosophical life approach.

At almost 50, I would definitely be considered too old by Palfrey and Gasser to be part of this generation. But I suggest – perhaps in a very Generation X self-centred way – that it is my age peers and I who are the true digital children. Huh? My reasoning is simple. We lived through the digital revolution. We witnessed first-hand the launch of all the new-fangled digital products. We listened and watched in awe as digital technology transformed our lives.

My first memory of digital technology is of a digital bedside clock which I received as a gift for my 10th birthday (the year was 1977). The clock's inner workings were actually analogue – an electric motor which flipped a rolodex-like system of numerical segments which, in turn, constructed the appropriate digits. But the switch from a traditional clock with hour and minute hands to that digital clock was a harbinger of things to come. I can still hear that characteristic click as one of the numerical segments flipped over.

A year later, Coleco launched a handheld electronic football game which was called 'Electronic Quarterback'. Compared to the lifelike graphics of today's Playstation and Xbox games, its red LED 'players', which only moved in vertical and horizontal patterns down the screen, were absolutely Stone Age. But I was enthralled, and admittedly envious because two of my hockey teammates, Scott Kwiecen and Billy Vivian, both had the game and I did not.

The early 1980s also gave rise to the video-game parlour – those slightly seedy places with slightly seedier teenagers who, my mother assured me, were there to "sell marijuana cigarettes". Despite her warning, I could not resist the temptation of the sounds, the lights, the action of the parlour and of course such memorable games as 'Joust', 'Asteroids' and my favourite, 'Galaga'.

In 1982, *Tron* hit the movie theatres. We hockey players scoffed at their headgear, which anyone who had ever played the game could easily tell were simply Cooper brand helmets under all the Wham-coloured fluorescent optics. But the movie seemed to capture perfectly the digital zeitgeist of the time. Indeed, digital calculators had become commonplace, digital watches were all the rage and futuristic digital typefaces were employed indiscriminately in order to convey the brave new (digital) world.

It was probably 1983, however, which represented the most important digital moment of my life. Rob Shearer, a friend in secondary school, invited me to his house to listen to Rush's *Moving Pictures* on his new compact-disc player. Rob had worked many hours to save enough to buy it. In fact, it was the first commercially available compact-disc player, and it cost him approximately 2,000 USD.

But I had never heard anything so magical, so pure, so sonically blissful. I had only recently turned 15 and was starting to develop my musical tastes. (Ah yes, the formative secondary-school years!) I had an eight-track player for my father's old Howlin' Wolf collection. I had some vinyl recordings (I still have them in a milk crate in the basement) but had started to switch to cassettes. Hearing Geddy Lee belt out 'Tom Sawyer' on Rob's compact-disc player was like a punch in the gut. Never again would I be satisfied with the crackle and pop of a needle in a groove. How could I bear the background hiss of a magnetic tape?

And perhaps it is this sense of wonder which distinguishes me and my age peers from the so-called digital natives of today's generation. Our wide-eyed, gob-smacked sense of reverence for all those digital products stands in stark contrast with the taken-for-granted-ness with which digital natives treat the announcement of a new iPhone, the launch of a new app or the release of a new edition of 'Grand Theft Auto'.

It is also because of my history with digital (and a healthy dose of scientist's scepticism) that I still harbour a high degree of doubt about the sweeping claims which are made about its potential as societal saviour, lifestyle liberator, educational emancipator and so on. That is to say, I view digital as just that – a language of 1s and 0s which can be used to represent, store and communicate information. And as such, digital has not changed things so dramatically. On the contrary, the concept of time is no different because it can be displayed as digits rather than rotating hands – or even more apropos, because the passing of time is triggered by a quartz-regulated, digitally encoded signal rather than a continuously running analogue motor. I listen to and enjoy the same music – 1980s hits will never go out of style – irrespective of the recording medium and playback method. And I watch movies and television programming in the same way, whatever the visual conversion systems which operate behind (or in front of) the projection screen.

Or do I? Am I underestimating the power of digital? Is it simply an innocuous technology which, like steam power, magnetic recording and silver film, will one day also fill the dustbin of history? Or has digital already transformed (and will continue to transform) life as we know it. It is this tension, I suppose – this philosophical conundrum – which motivates my intellectual interest in digital marketing. The Scrooge McDuck in me scoffs at digital, maintaining that marketing is marketing is marketing. Indeed, we did not create a new version of marketing when bus shelters became available to advertisers, so why do we now have digital marketing? But the other part of me recognises that something more meaningful might be going on – that digital has transfigured many of our quotidian activities. One thing is certain, however – my compact-disc collection takes up a huge amount of space in my office!

Marcus

I am a child of the 1980s. Michael Jackson, MTV, *Beverly Hills Cop*, Atari, Bart Simpson, Saturday-morning cartoons and just about every other '80s artefact which you can name brings back fond memories of my formative years. While this decade laid the foundation of my love affair with contemporary culture, it was the '90s which introduced me to the digital revolution. I bypassed typewriters and wrote school papers on the RadioShack-issued Tandy 1000 which my mother gave my brother Eugene and me in the winter of 1990. I bought my first compact disc in the spring of 1991: Boyz II

Men's *Cooleyhighharmony*. I surfed the Internet for the first time, via Internet Explorer, as a high-school sophomore in 1994 at the University of Michigan's Summer Engineering Academy. I got my first email address as a college freshman, which drastically decreased my handwritten-letter output, despite having a long-distance girlfriend at the time. And that was just the beginning. GeoCities-built websites became my source of new music discovery. Google aided my research studies and often times distracted me from it. AOL Instant Messenger helped me to stay connected to my friends, while BlackPlanet helped me find new ones. By that time, I was completely immersed in the 'digital world'. But before it ended, the decade had one last discovery for me: MIDI.

MIDI, short for Musical Instrument Digital Interface, is the technology – the digital language – which enables individual electronic musical instruments, computers and other related devices to connect and communicate with one another. With MIDI, an electronic keyboard can sync with a drum machine, for example, and relay their shared performance to a computer for recording purposes. Music, therefore, can be endlessly edited, thereby empowering songwriters to produce full compositions in 'digital space'... and without the need for a band. With MIDI, I found myself exploring a new world of musical possibilities.

This exploration completely changed the trajectory of my career. Although I studied material science engineering in college, I spent most of my undergraduate hours writing and producing music with MIDI-enabled digital/electronic instruments. Indeed, after graduation I went straight into the music business, co-founding a record label and artist-development start-up. I was making music for a living... albeit modestly. I produced all the tracks for the company's debut album release entirely in my bedroom studio, which kept overheads extremely low. The company was one of the early independent record labels to get music onto iTunes and, thanks to music commerce aggregates like CD Baby, the sale of products advanced without the need to press additional CD inventory. I used the company's website to generate leads and leveraged an email CRM system to distribute communications to fans and supporters. No doubt, the digital revolution afforded me great opportunity both as an artist and an entrepreneur.

The ubiquity of digital technology also removed barriers for amateur music-makers to create. Programs like Fruity Loops and Cakewalk reduced the financial barrier which expensive recording studios once erected. Creativity was 'democratised'. Meanwhile, as the Internet continued to proliferate, the growth of communities of people online ballooned. Out of this came the benefit of collective intelligence where people began to share their learnings of these new music-creation tools with others in the community through vehicles like YouTube. As a result, amateur music-makers learned from each other, thereby reducing the perception that a lengthy apprenticeship was necessary for success.

Before the advent of digital technology, music-makers also required access to radio in order to distribute their art. And radio airplay, unfortunately, was strictly reserved for, and to a large degree controlled by, major record labels. Likewise, very few music-makers could afford to produce music videos. And even if they could, the production quality was low and access to MTV was limited. The growing Internet removed the intermediaries and the gatekeepers, thereby allowing these new, non-major-record-label-affiliated music-makers, like me, to reach music fans directly.

These changes also had a massive impact on the music business. The digital-medium shift from compact discs to compressed files (MP3s) made the Internet the most effective vehicle for distributing and discovering music. Consumers (perhaps surprisingly) accepted the varying quality of MP3s; indeed, sonic quality ceased being a discriminating factor for music fans, which levelled the playing field for amateur musicians and producers. Consequently, there was an influx of content in the market – from amateur creators to superstars with reduced latency between album releases. And so music fans found themselves, for the first time ever, with more supply of music than time to consume it. This in turn reduced the half-life of songs... it created a kind of 'dopamine cycle' in which listeners spent less time experiencing specific content. Ironically, the same technology which opened my eyes to a potential career in music – which helped me realise my dreams – was the same technology which brought those same dreams to a screeching halt.

The digital revolution forever changed the business of how music is created, discovered, and sold. There were winners and losers, much like in almost every other industry in which technologies have infused themselves. With all these changes and their subsequent implications, the need for the business community to understand these technologies better is more important than ever.

Eldad

Like John, I also grew up with Coleco 'Electronic Quarterback' and was convinced that my skills acquired moving red LEDs on the screen would translate directly to an NFL career. Six years later, however, and with no football contract in hand, the first Macintosh was launched... and I was hooked. Indeed, I saw at first hand the tremendous shift from red LEDs to the first GUI (graphical user interface), and I immediately became fascinated with technology and its impact on society.

Recall that one of the main innovations which Apple introduced was the mouse. (The original Macintosh had no arrow keys and the CTRL function was also added later.) With the mouse came a new sense of control, a power, an elegance. Basic GOTO commands gave way to a more interactive experience. And this juxtaposition between the primitive coding which I was being taught in school and the purposeful interactions on the first Mac was the thing which sparked my love for the computer.

But for me, the Macintosh was a true game-changer not because of its features, nor because of its transformational GUI, but because it became a fixture in my classroom *and* my home. It became ubiquitous. And that was a radical departure from the time when the computer was an almost coveted entity, available only to a privileged few in a 'nerdy' after-school computer club.

When the online world opened up – officially launched 11 August 1991 with Tim Berners-Lee's posting on the alt.hypertext newsgroup – I was quick to explore this new digital universe. For me, it represented a powerful combination of Technology, Digital and Society. Two specific experiences from when I was living in Tel Aviv, Israel capture this Venn diagram. The first experience occurred in 1999, when my friends in California asked me about Google. "Have you seen this new search engine?" I instantly recognised the superior trawling skills of Google, although to be fair, I did not understand how or why Google was better in finding the information which my queries sought. But my previous foray into coding suggested to me that they were definitely onto something. Consequently, I began reading voraciously about search-engine optimisation (SEO) and six months later I tried my hand at building a few poorly constructed websites (my coding skills never were any good), as an experiment to test if I could get them higher in the search results. Success came as an increasing number of people visited the websites to view items which I was trying to sell. So when Google launched Adwords in 2000, my passion for both digital technology and marketing spiked. As a former English Literature major, an avid American sports fan who sponged the statistics, and a firm believer in capitalism, that ability to bid on keywords in an auction and see the results immediately was pure bliss.

The second experience which captures the powerful combination of Technology, Digital and Society occurred in one of the small markets/bazaars in Tel Aviv's centre. A young lady was on her handheld mobile flip-phone (itself a relatively new innovation), chatting with her friend while browsing through a rack of dresses. Suddenly her voice rose sharply and she screamed, "Oh, I found two! Which one do you think will look better on me?" In my mind, I scoffed at the silliness of the question. How could someone on the other end of a telephone be able to answer that question? Two weeks later the first mobile phone with a built-in camera was released in the country. And we all know the impact which this mash-up has had on society: the Arab Spring, YouTube influencers/millionaires and selfies, to name only three.

Those two experiences in Israel led to my return to the United States, where I would pursue my MBA, the goal of which was to launch my career into this digital world. And it did. What started as an intellectual pursuit concerned with how search results get generated and can be influenced became a hobby, and ultimately developed into a wonderful and passionate career. And to this day, when orchestrating a digital campaign, I still get a thrill about the three elements: technology, digital and society. Indeed, I believe that much of the success of the digital campaigns in which I have participated is based on considerations of how these three elements fuse together and create, almost alchemically, the right message communicated to the right people, at the right time, in the right channel.

One other major influence which has shaped my digital world-view was the 'Cluetrain Manifesto', a collaborative web (not a book) publication by Rick Levine, Christopher Locke, Doc Searls and David Weinberger. Think back to what an oddity web publishing seemed at the time! Now something like this might very well be crowdfunded, another digital innovation.

The authors originally examined the impact of the Internet on marketing, especially with respect to the growing movement of online 'conversations' which consumers were beginning to have in niche forums and chatrooms but which companies had yet to comprehend. Their purpose was to highlight how and why established marketing techniques were seemingly made obsolete by these new realities. They developed 95 Theses (or propositions) which were grouped into eight categories:

1. Theses 1–6: Markets are conversations (social media, influencer marketing, affiliate networks)

2. Thesis 7: Hyperlinks subvert hierarchy (SEO, DSPs, SSPs)

3. Theses 8–13: Connection between the new markets and companies (social media, PPC, programmatic advertising, influencer marketing)

4. Theses 14–25: Organisations entering the marketplace (agencies and consultants)

5. Theses 26–40: Marketing and organisational response

6. Theses 41–52: Intranets and the impact to organisation control and structure

7. Theses 53–71: Connecting the Internet marketplace with corporate intranets

8. Theses 72–95: New market expectations.

Re-visiting these 95 theses, I am amazed at their foresight, because nearly every grouping which they put forward has become its own area of specialisation in digital marketing or digital transformation. Indeed, whole industries have evolved on both the technological and marketing fronts... social media, influencer marketing, affiliate networks, SEO, DSPs, SSPs, PPC, programmatic, agencies, consultants, authors, speakers, journalists and the never ending array of events. It is difficult to keep them all straight – which perhaps hints at the reason for the success of Lumascapes from LUMA Partners which attempt to make sense of the very complicated ecosystem.

More importantly, the 95 theses provoke marketers to confront the massive changes in marketing which have resulted from digital. In theses 1–7, for example, marketers face some very inconvenient truths – that the conversations have outpaced the companies and that, in the words of Cluetrain's authors, "the customer service rep wields far more power and influence than the well-oiled front-office PR machine". And do not forget, these words were published long before YouTube uploaded its first video (February 2005), Twitter broadcast its first tweet (March 2006) or, perhaps most pointedly, the case of 'United Broke My Guitar'.

New Paradigms, Perspectives and Practices

A significant challenge when producing an anthology is developing a framework for 'curating' its chapters, even when they all share a common theme. During the symposium, therefore, together we attempted to tease out the many different characteristics of the 15 chapters and subsequently offered up various structuring frameworks, including:

- Macro versus mesh versus micro;

- Context, company and content;

- Conceptual, theoretical and practical; and

- A 2×2 with strategy versus tactics and theory versus practice.

In the end, however, we settled on a relatively simple structure: new paradigms, perspectives and practices. We do not suggest that the 15 chapters each fit neatly into only one of these buckets, but instead that the three terms capture the primary motifs of those chapters. The first five chapters, therefore, discuss at their core the ways in which digital represents new paradigms. The next five chapters provide new perspectives on marketing in the face of these new paradigms. And the final five chapters offer up new practices in response to the new perspectives.

The Anthology, Chapter by Chapter

Chapter 2 by Laura Sawyer introduces an ecosystem view of digital. It begins by exploring the ubiquity of digital connectivity and the multiple, intersecting contexts in which businesses and consumers are entwined today. It then illuminates the shifts in perspective and behaviour required for companies and brands to thrive in an age of deep interconnection and interdependence. Chapter 2 continues by identifying effective marketing strategies and practices which are enabling companies and brands to thrive in the digital ecosystem. Finally, it explores how organisations can institutionalise an ecosystem orientation. The key lesson from Chapter 2 is that effective marketing in the digital age requires a fundamental paradigm shift, and, consequently, a new manifestation of the shift in practice.

Chapter 3 by Marcus Collins and John Branch examines the power of the network in digital marketing. It begins by demonstrating that digital technology, when it leads to a shift in medium, does not change the underlying human behaviour, only its prevalence and frequency. It then argues that the power of digital technology occurs when it leads to a network. Finally, it demonstrates the power of the network with two examples: Waze and Amazon. The key lesson from Chapter 3 is that the power of digital technology is in the network.

Chapter 4, also by Marcus Collins and John Branch, explores the digital marketing context. It begins by discussing defaults – the pre-established factors in a digital space. It then investigates the semiotics (the meanings) of digital 'signs and symbols'. Chapter 4 continues by examining the placement, or spacial arrangement, in a digital space. Finally, it underlines the importance of cultural nuances in the digital marketing context. The key lesson from Chapter 4 is that when it comes to digital marketing, context matters.

Chapter 5 by Jon Bond argues that marketing must move beyond communication to 'marketing as a service'. It begins by tracing the origins of mass marketing. It then demonstrates the power of brand influencers. Chapter 5 continues by highlighting how marketing can not only communicate to customers but also help them. Finally, it challenges the fundamental nature of marketing. The key lesson from Chapter 5 is that marketing is most powerful when customers do not think of it as marketing.

Chapter 6 by Thamer Ahmad Baazeem illustrates the challenge of implementing digital marketing in emerging markets. It begins by underlining the importance of the differences between mature and emerging markets. It then narrows the focus to emerging markets, elucidating how culture and religion impinge on the execution of digital marketing. Chapter 6 continues by emphasising the issue of trust-building in the creation of effective digital marketing strategies for emerging markets. Finally, it identifies how divergence in the usage of information technology influences the implementation of digital marketing in emerging markets. The key lesson from Chapter 6 is that, despite the homogenisation effects of globalisation, there remain differences in culture, religion, trust-building and the usage of information technology which ought to be considered when implementing digital marketing strategies in emerging markets.

Chapter 7 by Tom van Laer and Ian Lurie creates a recipe for a virtuous digital marketing cycle. It begins by defining digital marketing as a polite, empirically measurable, two-way conversation in an effort to exchange 'something'. It then introduces marketers to the digital marketing cycle. Finally, it overviews tools in a stage-by-stage guide for implementing the seven stages of the digital marketing cycle: 1. know thyself, 2. know the room, 3. dress appropriately, 4. tell stories, 5. make a connection, 6. brag modestly and 7. observe and adjust. The key lesson from Chapter 7 is that tying the seven stages together realises concrete goals for marketers and their organisations.

Chapter 8 by Andrew Zarick introduces a framework for building communities of influence online and in-person. It begins by exploring the deterioration of social capital in real-life communities due to the rise of television. It then traces the evolution of the media landscape. Chapter 8 continues by highlighting how social platforms now have larger audiences than major media networks. Finally, it discusses how to exploit this new media dynamic.

Chapter 9 by Stephanie Leishman, Frédéric Brunel and Barbara Bickart presents a conceptual model of voice in social media. It begins by identifying and defining the layers which make up the 'vocal stack' in social media: vocal quality, meaning and identity. It then describes how individual vocal stacks contribute to collective voice. Finally, it examines implications of this model of vocal stack for managing a company's social-media voice. The key lesson from Chapter 9 is that social media can be conceptualised as a set of individual vocal stacks which must engage with, and take part in, the collective voice.

Chapter 10 by David Fossas presents a framework for marketers to harness the full value of their organisation's brand. It begins by providing historical context to, and a lexicon for, discussing brands. It then proposes a new definition of brand in the context of our modern digital world, in which social media gives a voice and influence to an organisations' stakeholders. Finally, it introduces the Shared Brand Framework, in which control and influence over the perception of a brand is shared by the organisation and its stakeholders. The key lesson from Chapter 10 is that marketers must align stakeholders through shared purpose, experiences and culture, in order to capitalise on the full potential value of the brand.

Chapter 11 by Shalonda Hunter presents an overview of the relationship between organisational design and digital technology, and shows how the two work to preserve the competitive advantage and continual growth of both new and established companies and brands. Drawing on the benefits of a newly introduced framework, the Hunter Model™, the chapter answers the following questions: (1) given that employee attraction and retention are organisational challenges, ought organisations to focus more on capabilities? And (2) ought organisations to lead with strategy or digital technology goals?

Chapter 12 by Bryan Pedersen illuminates the utility marketing opportunity which social and digital media provide today. It begins by outlining the abundance of digital messages which consumers receive on a daily basis – from friends, family and brands alike. It then offers a number of ways for creating an alternative to smaller and more frequent digital messages. Finally, it provides a funda-mental list of considerations in launching a social utility program, creating value for both the consumer and the brand. The key lesson from Chapter 12 is that, amid the profusion of *pushed* digital messages, it is possible to *pull* consumers in by providing them with authentic value and social utility.

Chapter 13 by Yotam Shmargad and Jameson Watts presents a framework to guide organisations as they interact with consumers through social media. It begins by outlining this framework, called *ideological capital*, and distinguishing it from *social capital*, which social scientists use to study interactions between people. It then provides a primer on network analysis and describes how organi-sations can collect and analyse social-network data. Finally, it discusses how organisations can use social-network data to implement digital strategies which are built for the connected consumer. The key lesson from Chapter 13 is that organisa-tions need not necessarily aim to be *social* when interacting with consumers online, but instead ought to produce and disseminate content which aligns with their beliefs and values.

Chapter 14 by Deborah Goldring explores the strategy of content marketing. It begins by reviewing the historical develop-ment of content marketing and then discusses the key elements of effective digital marketing content grounded in marketing theory. Finally, it speculates on how digital marketing content is evolving to leverage new marketing strategies. The key lesson from Chapter 14 is that content marketing as a strategy is evolving as technology and marketing practices more broadly evolve.

Chapter 15 by Ed Suwanjindar explores the intersection of social media and digital media within the music industry. It begins by showcasing how music artists are harnessing the power of their audiences on social-networking platforms, in order to drive consumption of their recorded music. It then presents the role which technology companies play in fostering the dynamic between the music artists on their social-networking platforms and the business of digital media. Finally, it examines how this affects customers and fans, whether or not social media brings them closer to the artists whom they love, and if this relationship is purely voyeuristic or commercial or both. The key lesson from Chapter 15 is that social media and digital media are increasingly working together in the context of the music industry.

Chapter 16 by Francesco Rocchi and Eric Watson introduces digital marketing managers to the intricacies of creating an international website, through real-life success stories. It begins by discussing how technology has changed the trade-off between standardisation and localisation. It then delves into the linguistic and cultural aspects of website localisation, suggesting solutions to critical challenges in serving multiple markets online. Finally, it shows how technological needs are different for international websites, both because of differences among countries and regardless of them. The key lesson from Chapter 16 is that an often-overlooked necessity for websites is not only to adapt culturally, but also technologically, to different international markets.

In Summary

Richard Attenborough was famous long before his character John Hammond uttered the catchphrase "Welcome to Jurassic Park". But his toothy grin and Santa-like features became well known to a new generation of movie fans when he took on the role of Hammond – the lovable mad-scientist founder of Jurassic Park. Channelling our inner Attenborough, we conclude this introductory chapter with a hearty "Welcome to contemporary issues in digital marketing"… minus the mauling from a massive megalosaurus! We hope that you might discover within the pages of this anthology (as was the intention of Jurassic Park) a sense of wonder about digital marketing, some level of entertainment and even a few practical takeaways to help guide your own marketing practice.

References

Luma Partners (no date) "Painstakingly Compiling Sector Landscapes ('LUMAscapes') to Organize What Can Be a Very Confusing Ecosystem." Retrieved from: http://www.lumapartners.com/resource-center/lumascapes-2/

Millward Brown Digital (2013) "Consumers Will Punish Brands That Fail to Respond on Twitter Quickly." Retrieved from: http://www.lithium.com/company/news-room/press-releases/2013/consumers-will-punish-brands-that-fail-to-respond-on-twitter-quickly

Palfrey, J., and U. Gasser (2010) *Born Digital: Understanding the First Generation of Digital Natives*. New York, USA: Basic Books.

Schumpeter, J.A. (1975 [1942]) *Capitalism, Socialism, and Democracy*. New York, USA: Harper & Row.

About the Authors

John Branch is Clinical Assistant Professor of Business Administration at the Stephen M. Ross School of Business and Faculty Associate at the Center for Russian, East European and European Studies, both of the University of Michigan. John is also Visiting Fellow at Wolfson College, University of Cambridge in Cambridge, England. John recently finished a second doctoral degree, his dissertation of which focused on international higher education. In his spare time, John enjoys woodworking and restoring antique sports cars. Contact him on email at jdbranch@umich.edu.

Marcus Collins is a culturally curious thinker with an affinity for understanding the cognitive drivers and environmental factors which impact human behaviour. He is a Golden Apple Award nominated faculty member at the Ross School of Business at the University of Michigan and leads the Social Engagement practice at Doner Advertising. Marcus was recognised as one of *Ad Age*'s 2016 '40 Under 40' bright young minds who are reinventing and reshaping marketing's future. He is a proud Detroit native, loving father and devoted husband. Learn more at www.marctothec.com.

Eldad Sotnick-Yogev is an experienced strategic marketer who has worked with such companies as Ford, Jaguar/Land Rover, NBA, Fitbit, Zurich Insurance and Eurostar, helping to steer their global digital and performance marketing strategies and analytics across paid, owned and earned media channels. He has been published in Drum Magazine, WARC and within the WPP Reading Room, and has spoken on AdTech panels. Eldad enjoys cooking, hiking and travel... which is a good part of the reason why he lives in London with his wife and two children. Contact him on email at eldad.yogev@gmail.com.

Chapter 2
Systems Marketing

Laura Sawyer

Introduction

"When one tugs at a single thing in nature, he finds it attached to the rest of the world."

John Muir

Nothing exists in isolation. This is a simple truth often forgotten as we endeavour to create order, delineate one thing from another and reduce problems to manageable proportions. The human tendency to fragment the world is particularly evident in business and marketing, where companies and brands routinely segment consumers and markets, pit themselves against similar companies and brands within compartmentalised market spaces, and delineate products and services based on specific points of difference. I firmly believe that the digital world cannot be navigated in this way because it is a complex, open and distributed system, based on interconnection and interdependence. It is, in short, an ecosystem, and to thrive in an ecosystem, businesses must think and act like an ecosystem. They must mindfully build bridges of connection, leverage multiple resources, embrace diversity and contribute to the greater whole.

Stitch by stitch, the world is being woven together into a single tapestry. Today, there are 13.5 billion connected devices on earth and, by 2020, that number is expected to climb to a staggering 50 billion (Fort, 2014). Even more remarkable, it is estimated that by 2025 every person on the planet will have access to the Internet (Kelly, 2016). Simultaneously, global issues, like climate change and volatile global markets, are contributing to a growing awareness that we are all inhabitants of an undivided planet. This convergence of humanity and technology, the growing prevalence of digital connectivity and the rise of global consciousness are collectively disturbing real and perceived boundaries of all kinds, creating new vehicles for communication and connection, and providing remarkable opportunities for companies and brands to break free from their current confines.

In this chapter, I introduce and argue for an ecosystemic view of digital by: exploring the near-ubiquity of digital connectivity and the multiple, intersecting contexts in which businesses and consumers are entwined today; illuminating the shifts in perspective and behaviour required for companies and brands to thrive in an age of deep interconnection and interdependence; identifying effective marketing strategies and practices that enable companies and brands to contribute to and benefit from the digital ecosystem; and finally, exploring how organisations can institutionalise an ecosystemic orientation.

Context Setting

Digital technologies and trends are like waves on the ocean. They rise and fall away, creating ripple effects of different magnitude. Scanning digital's surface, however, tells us little about its depths or the forces that govern its behaviours. Understanding this requires an understanding of context. Many companies and brands today recognise the need for 'contextual awareness' in marketing to better understand shifting consumer values and needs, and to increase the timeliness and relevance of the advertising and content they distribute. This term commonly refers to the use of data, mobile devices and sensor technology to discern the user's current interests and location (Afshar, 2016). For me, however, thinking and acting contextually has a broader scope, taking into account historical, political and social contexts; the climate and environments in which business is conducted; and the multiple influences that are shaping the values, expectations and needs of consumers today.

Digital in Context

"With its hundred billion nerve cells, with their hundred trillion interconnections, the human brain is the most complex phenomenon in the known universe – always, of course, excepting the interaction of some six billion such brains and their owners within the socio-technological culture of our planetary ecosystem!"

Steven Rose

I began my career at BBDO, on advertising's famed Madison Avenue, in an era when clever tag lines and highly produced television spots were powerful enough to build brand awareness, sales and even brand loyalty. Looking back, I am stunned by how dramatically the industry – and marketing more broadly – has shape-shifted and evolved since then, in large part due to the advent of digital technology. While I no longer work in advertising's trenches, my day job as an educator, helping executives and organisations to comprehend and navigate the digital world, keeps me close to the front lines. The most common complaints I hear when working with marketing professionals are a sense of being overwhelmed, mental exhaustion and the haunting fear of being left behind. I certainly sympathise, but I also firmly believe that it is possible to navigate the digital world successfully by looking beneath the day-to-day clamour and clutter, and aligning with digital's deeper structure and evolution.

The explosion of smart devices and sensors, increasing computing power and connectivity, rapid expansion of cloud technology, proliferation of data and advancements in artificial intelligence, *in combination*, are rapidly creating a digital ecosystem within which we are all, for better or worse, inextricably immersed. Simultaneously, the explosion of content, channels, social platforms, messaging and mobile connectivity are continuously multiplying threads of connection and further entangling us within them. Increasingly, there is no digital world 'out there', and the divides between virtual and physical worlds will further dissolve as we engage with more organic interfaces, become immersed in virtual and augmented realities, and begin wearing and even implanting sensors and smart devices on our bodies.

While this level of digital embodiment will likely be confined for some time to technologically advanced countries, universal digital connectivity is rapidly approaching. As previously noted, *Wired* co-founder Kevin Kelly, in his book *The Inevitable* (2016), calculates that by the year 2025 every person on earth will have access to the Internet. This prediction and its implications for humanity are mind numbing, but his statement that "Everyone will be on it. Or in it. Or, simply, everyone will be it" (p.293) is even more so because it suggests a level of global embedded-ness that has, until now, seemed incomprehensible to most individuals and businesses.

Unearthing the patterns of organisation that underlie the surface phenomena of digital reveals the power and primacy of networks. Joshua Ramo's book, *The Seventh Sense* (2016), looks at this from historical and geopolitical perspectives, arguing that it is imperative for leaders today to develop a new instinct, a seventh sense, based on deeply understanding networks. While some of Rama's geopolitical concerns might not yet be of paramount concern to marketers, his argument that networks are the primary drivers of power and communication today ought to be (see Chapter 3 by Collins and Branch).

I first gained an understanding of digital networks in 2011, when facilitating a Digital Acceleration Master Class for the school Hyper Island. These classes are designed to help advertising, marketing and business executives to better understand and navigate the digital landscape. A colleague, Mark Commerford, who helped shape Hyper Island's executive curriculum, invited participants to reframe digital, first by listing all things digital (digital strategy, digital media, digital photography, digital relationships, etc.), then by replacing the descriptor 'digital' with 'network' for each, and finally by exploring how that shift changes understanding of what digital is and how it works. For me, this shift in perspective was profound, and this exercise remains an unfailingly powerful element of Hyper Island Master Classes, because it cuts through the surface clutter and artificial divides of digital. Suddenly, by virtue of seeing digital as the connective tissue between people and things, we can see that it is fundamentally about relationship and community, not about specific technologies, trends and tactics.

The Consumer in Context

"If old consumers were assumed to be passive, then new consumers are active. If old consumers were predictable and stayed where you told them, then new consumers are migratory, showing a declining loyalty to networks or media. If old consumers were isolated individuals, then new consumers are more socially connected. If the work of media consumers was once silent and invisible, then new consumers are now noisy and public."

Henry Jenkins

More than ever before in human history, technology is enabling people to bridge geographical, ideological and social boundaries, self-organise and share goods and services. People are engaging in and contributing generously to ad-hoc networks, answering one another's questions, populating open encyclopaedias and creating content of all kinds. Increasing digital connectivity is amplifying and accelerating these trends by enabling expression of these human impulses on a global scale.

Even so, growing political and social tensions, born of conflict, economic inequality and security concerns, are fuelling opposing movements: some factions press for greater openness, transparency and distribution of resources; others seek a return to greater privacy, protectionism and localism. Thomas Friedman (2016) has characterised this as an ideological clash between web and wall people, and we are seeing this tension being played out politically in both Europe and the United States. Simultaneously, consumers are moving away from public or semi-public social platforms, like Facebook and Twitter, to more closed ones, like Snapchat, WeChat, Slack and Messenger. This shift might reflect a growing hunger for privacy and safety (essentially wall people desires).

Rapid technological advancement, easy access to information and goods, and the conveniences afforded by new digital services are also radically reshaping consumer behaviours and expectations. Marketing strategies and practices which have long served companies and brands are becoming less effective, as consumers adopt new ways to consume and create media, avoid advertising and determine for themselves the usefulness of companies, brands and products. Simultaneously, corporate misdeeds and self-serving marketing practices have eroded consumer trust in, and loyalty to, brands, to the point where most people would not care if they disappeared tomorrow (Havas, 2016).

It is expected that generational shifts in consumer expectations and core values will continue to drive these trends, as consumers increasingly choose brands and make purchase decisions not just on value but on *their* values. While this is already evident among Millennials, it is by no means confined to them. Increasingly, consumers across generations are looking for companies and brands which mirror their values and act responsibly (Havas, 2016).

Further, Generation Z children, who have never known a pre-Internet world, have been conditioned, almost from birth, to see the world and act in ways which are unique to the digital age. For them, ubiquitous connectivity and immediate access to information are utterly natural, and they move much more fluidly between digital and physical worlds. In turn, their expectations of products are fluid, meaning that this generation is less likely to compartmentalise and remain loyal to isolated products and brands, focusing instead on whether their immediate needs are being met, on the quality of experience they receive and on the value the product adds.

Interbrand CEO, Jez Frampton (InterbrandGroup, 2012), has characterised this era as the 'Age of You' and marketers are scurrying to develop new methods for market segmentation, targeting, hyper personalisation, automation and one-to-one marketing, to better understand consumers and atomise content to meet individual desires. While responding to changing consumer expectations, needs and behaviours is undoubtedly of value, I believe that the trend toward increased segmentation and hyper-personalisation also risks myopathy. It reflects and perpetuates a mechanistic orientation that breaks digital down to individual parts, while losing sight of the whole they collectively comprise.

New Vision, New Reality

"Consider this: all the ants on the planet, taken together, have a biomass greater than that of humans. Ants have been incredibly industrious for millions of years. Yet their productiveness nourishes plants, animals, and soil. Human industry has been in full swing for little over a century, yet it has brought about a decline in almost every ecosystem on the planet. Nature does not have a design problem."

William McDonough

Jean Piaget considered the goal of education to be "to create men and women who are capable of doing new things, not simply of repeating what other generations have done – men and women who are creative, inventive, and discoverers" (1976, p.3). Navigating the complex and dynamic digital world requires these capabilities and a willingness to question some funda-mental twentieth-century business paradigms. Primary among these are the individualistic view of companies and brands as separate entities, acting in sole pursuit of self-interest; the agri-cultural view that organic systems and wilderness need to be controlled, managed and contained; the reductionist belief that complex systems can be completely understood in terms of their parts or components; and the Darwinian belief that businesses must pit themselves against other similar businesses in order to survive. I see these deeply ingrained views as outdated, incom-patible with the structures and patterns of the digital ecosystem, and profoundly limiting. Conversely, understanding digital as a unified ecosystem and acting in accordance with that opens up whole new worlds of possibility.

When working with executives and marketers seeking to advance their understanding of, and capabilities within, the digital sphere, I often present an image of the Internet (see Figure 2.1). It is a snapshot of the World Wide Web, constructed from visualised data, which reveals the dense and complex web of connections which comprise the global digital ecosystem. For me, this image captures, simply and elegantly, the inherent structure and nature of digital and, for that matter, the universe. It is not a machine, comprised of separate, disconnected mechanisms; it is an organic, integrated and coherent ecosystem.

Seeing digital as a cohesive and indivisible whole, rather than as an ensemble of separate things, leads, in turn, to seeing business as an integral part of that and to seeing companies and brands *not* as independent, self-contained agents acting upon the system, but rather as insiders working in sync with other players in alignment with the greater needs of the system as a whole. For many traditional companies, this requires a dramatic shift in orientation and behaviour (see Table 2.1).

Table 2.1. Systemic Shift

From (Industrial System)	To (Ecosystem)
Fragmentation	Holism
Ego-centredness	Eco-centredness
Control	Spontaneity, responsiveness and trust
One-way knowledge distribution	Collective intelligence and co-creation
Isolated self-interest	Shared objectives/community building
Excessive competition	Partnership and cooperation

This orientation reflects a way of seeing and being in the world that is consistent with systems thinking. Systems thinkers (Capra, 1996; Senge, 1990; Sharmer and Kaufer, 2013) seek to understand the patterns of organisation which underlie surface structures. These patterns exist in organisms, social systems, families, communities and ecosystems, linking both animate and inanimate elements together to form intricate webs of connection and continual exchange of matter and energy. In this view, phenomena are seen as nodes, situated within networks or systems in which the value lies more in the interrelationships and interdependencies between nodes than in the nodes themselves.

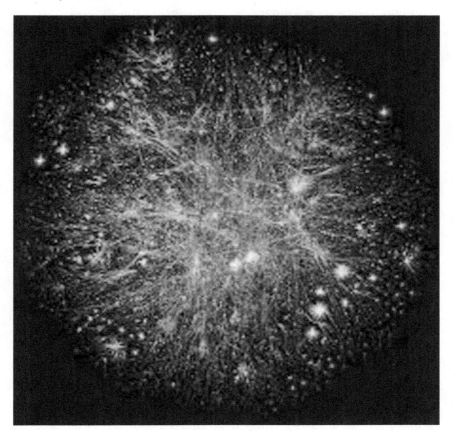

Figure 2.1. Image of the Internet
Source: Opte Project, 2014

By looking beneath digital's surface trends and technologies, marketers can observe the human patterns of organisation which are its foundation (and operating system), seeing themselves as nodes within a broader, fuller and more comprehensive whole.

This, in turn, can lead to fundamental shifts in business and marketing practices.

Walking the Walk

While adopting an ecosystemic view is a vital first step in understanding digital-age dynamics, the rubber meets the road in applying that to business. Here, I shall look at several strategies and behaviours of highly successful companies, brands and institutions which have both adopted an ecosystemic orientation and translated it into practice. Interestingly, most of the companies and brands which are highlighted here are cut from traditional cloth. They are not technology companies; and yet I consider them to be digital companies because they are willing to transcend the confines of twentieth-century business values and practices.

Building an Ecosystem

"There's an interdependence between flowers and bees. Where there are no flowers there are no bees, and where there are no bees, there are no flowers. They are really one organism. And so in the same way, everything in nature depends on everything else."

Allan Watts

Perhaps the greatest story of a large, traditional company shifting gears, embracing an ecosystem mindset and behaviours, and reaping its rewards is captured in LEGO's journey. After a crisis period during which the company bordered on bankruptcy, LEGO pivoted and gradually regained market dominance, initially through internal changes, and over time, by building its own open, inclusive and adaptive ecosystem. Recognising that the company had lost its way through poor product choices and a failure to understand its core customer base, LEGO consolidated its product lines, promoted managers who knew the customers intimately (because they had grown up playing LEGO) and hired

AFOLs (adult fans of LEGO) as designers. An equally important step was relaxing control over the product's uses, inviting LEGO fans everywhere to use LEGO products in creative, educational and social ways. And they have... in droves. A quick online search for LEGO fans offers a window into this ecosystem and culture, comprised of clubs, informational websites, educational initiatives, sub-cultures centred around specific product lines and gatherings, ranging from local MeetUp groups to large-scale Universal Builders conferences, held every month at locations around the world.

LEGO's success has also been fuelled by its willingness and ability to transcend the confines of category and brand, while remaining true to its overarching mission, "inspiring and developing children through play and learning". Focusing on learning and play, rather than simply selling more plastic bricks, has enabled LEGO to venture successfully into new industries, including the film and theme park industries. In doing so, it engages its customers across multiple touch points with a consistent brand purpose and value.

LEGO has also torn down barriers between the company and its competitors, by creating partnerships which serve the interests of all. Of particular note are its partnerships with Disney and Minecraft. While strategic partnerships between companies and brands are not new, it is worth considering the significance of each in the context of the digital ecosystem. As noted previously, children of the digital age are growing up with different perspectives and expectations than prior generations. Adults have awareness and assumptions about how business works and what separates companies and brands; young children do not. Their movement across brands and experiences is fluid. They expect to find LEGO in Disney stores and Disney themes in LEGO sets. LEGO's partnership with Minecraft also reflects an understanding that children do not separate their physical and digital worlds. Play is play, and being able to move seamlessly between Minecraft as a computer game and Minecraft bricks makes perfect sense. Another interesting aspect of the Minecraft partnership has been LEGO's willingness to validate and promote breaking down structures as much as building them, something that is central to the Minecraft ethos and experience (CNBC, 2016). This willingness is suggestive of a greater willingness on the part of LEGO to break down barriers of its own.

LEGO's willingness to transcend category and brand, and to situate itself in broader contests is also evident in LEGO education, the LEGO foundation and LEGO's sustainability commitments. All of these entities and efforts reflect LEGO's concern for broader societal and environmental needs, and a sincere desire to make a positive impact.

LEGO has emerged as the world's largest toy company by making smart, strategic decisions and by deliberately becoming more distributed, open, adaptive and contextually aware. By loosening the reigns of control, developing community, transcending boundaries of category and brand, partnering with others and making meaningful social contributions, LEGO has taken an ecosystem approach to business. Consequently, it is reaping the rewards. While LEGO does have a digital strategy and digital capabilities in the traditional sense (e-commerce, online content and activities, etc.), its success is fuelled by the entire ecosystem which it has cultivated and activated, both online and offline. Turning back the clock, who would have bet on LEGO, a manufacturer of plastic bricks, not only surviving but thriving in the digital age?

Self-Disruption

> "It is not the strongest of the species that survive, nor the most intelligent, but the one most responsive to change."
>
> Charles Darwin

'Disruption', a term used often by Clayton Christensen (1997) in his book *The Innovator's Dilemma*, has since entered the lexicon as representative of an era increasingly defined by large institutions being toppled by once-fringe digital companies which are rooted in different business models and market spaces. Traditional companies today have witnessed the demise of other Goliaths and are scurrying to develop agile business practices and digital business transformation strategies as the means of staving off a similar fate. Arguably, the greatest necessity and opportunity for traditional companies today is to challenge basic assumptions about why businesses exist and which, if any, lines actually divide market spaces and industries.

As technology and, more specifically, digital platforms become increasingly more central to how companies reach and serve consumers, opportunities are exploding for companies to transcend real and perceived boundaries. As companies and brands move in this direction, brand purpose and market space become more broad and porous. A good example of this is Ford Motor Company which is partnering with technology companies, governments and innovators globally to solve the growing problem of traffic congestion in major cities. Recognising that simply putting more cars on the road is antithetical to this aim, Ford is working with a wide cross-section of companies, developers, inventors and city governments to advance transportation systems, facilitate mobility and, by extension, improve quality of life in major cities. In doing so, it is broadening its self-definition and positioning from a car and truck manufacturer to a mobility company (McKinsey, 2014). On this trajectory, it is conceivable that Ford Motor Company (arguably the creator of industrial-era parameters and practices) will evolve into a digital service company, focused on facilitating human mobility of all kinds.

Several ecosystemic principles are central to Ford's strategy, including the pursuit of a broad and inclusive mission, a shift away from isolationist practices to openness and partnership, an evolution from product centricity to human centricity, and the willingness to transcend industry boundaries and definitions of market space.

Open Source

"Sustainable change, after all, depends not upon compliance with external mandates or blind adherence to regulation, but rather upon the pursuit of the greater good."

Douglas B. Reed

Just as Ford Motor Company is working with multiple stakeholders and across industries to advance mobility, so is Tesla breaking down barriers to advance the development of alternative-energy vehicles. Popular media often cast Tesla CEO, Elon Musk, as Iron Man, a loner hero bent on singlehandedly saving the world from destruction. In actuality, however, Musk recognises that greater power lies in knowledge sharing and collective endeavour, and he leverages these to advance both his own interests and those of society as a whole. Perhaps the greatest example of this is his decision to open source Tesla patterns.

Viewed from the perspective of traditional, protectionist business models and practices, the decision to willingly give up trade secrets and competitive advantage might seem like madness, but a broader, more contextual look reveals the underlying logic and wisdom of this move. Musk recognises that sharing ideas helps speed up innovation, thereby creating greater opportunities for all. Open sourcing is also entirely consistent with Tesla's mission to "accelerate the advent of sustainable transport by bringing compelling mass market electric cars to market as soon as possible." Accelerating the development of electric vehicles broadly helps build the momentum and overall infrastructure which will enable electric cars to reach critical mass more quickly. And if Musk's bet pays off, everyone will win. Indeed, the credibility and value of Tesla will increase as it grows with the market, the switch to alternative energy vehicles will accelerate and a model will be established to spark even more disruptive changes in transportation. Along the way, the Tesla brand will also likely gain strength by conveying to consumers that the company is open and genuinely committed to serving the greater good, and Tesla will become more attractive to employees seeking to work in an open, adaptive and socially conscious environment. Regardless of whether all of these outcomes are achieved, there are important lessons to be learned here for companies seeking to thrive in the digital ecosystem. Adopting an ecosystemic view and business practices can serve companies better than building walls and going it alone.

Acting Responsibly

> "The reductionist measure of yield is to agricultural systems what GDP is to economic systems. It is time to move from measuring yield of commodities, to health and well-being of ecosystems and communities. Industrial agriculture has roots in war. Ecological agriculture allows us to make peace with the earth, soil, and the society."
>
> Vandana Shiva

As the Tesla story reflects, ecosystem approaches enable the self-interest of each party to be achieved so that it complements rather than defeats the interests of others. In recent years there has been a marked increase in socially conscious start-ups, like Warby Parker and TOMS Shoes, whose business models are based on doing well and doing good. These companies recognise that business and people do not just interact, but interconnect and interdepend, and thus are inter-responsible. Simultaneously, we are seeing genuine commitment on the part of traditional, large-scale corporations to act in environmentally and socially responsible ways. As the following example illustrates, CSR initiatives are moving from the wings to centre stage, as critical components of global business strategies.

In 2013, L'Oréal CEO, Jean Paul Agon (following Unilever's lead), announced L'Oréal's Beauty to All sustainability commitment, promising to reduce its environmental footprint by 60% by 2020. The initiative will also ensure that every L'Oréal product has a social or environmental benefit and that everyone in the L'Oréal ecosystem, including employees, suppliers and people in underprivileged communities, contributes to, and benefits from, sustainable practices. Independent assessment of L'Oréal's fulfilment of this commitment reveals that it is ahead of schedule.

One interesting aspect of this initiative is the catalyst that motivated it: a business goal to double the number of L'Oréal customers from one billion to two billion worldwide. When announcing L'Oréal's sustainability commitment, Agon spoke of a "new model of economic development" which echoes the shift from egosystem to ecosystem economics advocated by MIT economist, Otto Scharmer. This model also reflects growing consumer demand for corporate responsibility. As Agon admits, "We don't really have a choice. This is going to be *the* new area of choice for consumers... The performance of a company in sustainability will definitely be an issue of competitiveness, and I am a competitive person, so I think we will compare well with others."

Interestingly, L'Oréal's aggressive growth ambitions and competitive spirit are not divorced from the interests of the greater whole. In fact, it is through care for the entire ecosystem that L'Oréal will fuel its continued growth. Again, this challenges traditional assumptions about the roles and responsibilities of companies, and ushers in a new era in which consumers will increasingly expect companies to demonstrate greater awareness of, and concern for, the environments in which they operate.

Leveraging Stakeholders and Networks

"Trust is essential for our social wellbeing. Without trusting the good will of others we retreat into bureaucracy, rules and demands for more law and order. Trust is based on positive experiences with other people and it grows with use. We need to trust that others are going to be basically reasonable beings."

Eva Cox

Every time I fly in and out of cities and view them from a higher elevation, I am struck by the intergalactic structure of roadways and power lines, connecting and expanding outward in dendritic patterns. These connections intimate the increasingly more complex layer of digital networks which weave together the fabric of cities, connecting people and devices of all kinds to one another. Cities are rapidly becoming smarter through the connection of parking spaces, garbage cans, street lights, green spaces and, of course, cars, personal computers, tablets and telephones. As previously noted, 13.5 billion devices are connected to the

Internet today and that number is expected to climb to 50 billion by 2020, opening whole new realms of possibility for companies (Forth, 2014).

Business often bemoans the inefficiency and ineffectiveness of government institutions, believing – sometimes justifiably – that the private sector works faster and smarter than public institutions. Interestingly, however, many municipalities and governmental institutions today are leading the way in building digital infrastructures, leveraging networks and engaging community to become more efficient and to improve the lives of citizens (McKinsey, 2014). Their successes demonstrate, in very real and quantifiable ways, the power and economic value of these practices. One example, the Open 311 initiative, is an ecosystem of cities which are building a common infrastructure for people to get better connected to government and their communities. Through Open 311 platforms and applications, residents in Boston, Chicago, Toronto, Helsinki and other cities are able to report potholes, missed garbage collections, unsafe construction sites and other neighbourhood issues. And the initiative is growing. These systems build bridges of connection between people, communities and institutions, generating higher levels of participation and engagement, good will and efficiency.

Cities also lead the way in widespread deployment of connected devices, networks of data-generating instruments which are serving the common good, by enabling smart infrastructure, utilities and transportation. Using analytics, officials utilise the data which are gathered to improve quality of life by reducing traffic congestion and parking occupancy. Barcelona is at the forefront of this practice, with a smart-city program which has reduced municipal water consumption by 25% and electric consumption by 30%, generating 95 million USD in annual savings. Sorrell (2015) estimates that cities will save 17 billion USD a year in energy bills by 2019 through the installation of smart streetlights and devices like parking and garbage sensors. McKinsey Global Institute estimates that by 2025 cities will save up to 1.7 trillion USD per year in delivering services, if they deploy new digital systems on a large scale (Walt, 2015).

Engaging customers and community stakeholders requires

a relinquishing of centralised control, a willingness to trust in people, and adoption of a test and learn culture which values progress over perfection. Excellent examples of this are Sweden's 2012 @Sweden experiment, which entrusted the nation's Twitter account to a different citizen every week, and the 2016 Sweden's Number campaign, which created a single telephone number for Sweden, as a country, connecting callers from all over the world with random Swedes who had been given no guidance or training on what to say (or not to say) when answering the telephone. Enabling the people of Sweden to represent their country in this way reflects a radical trust in people, belief in collective endeavour, and commitment to the progressive values for which Sweden stands.

Far from lagging behind the private sector, government initiatives like these are breaking new ground and creating new standards. Marketers seeking to advance their own interests *and* improve the lives of their customers ought to sit up and take note. Engaging customers and other stakeholders in pursuit of mutually beneficial goals also builds stronger relationships between brands and customers, thereby strengthening brand value (see Chapter 10 by Fossas).

Future Mindedness

> "Innovation opportunities do not come with the tempest but with the rustling of the breeze."

> Peter Drucker

Perhaps the greatest dilemma for business and for marketers today is born of the tension between trying to anticipate what is coming (and building strategies to prepare for that), while simultaneously responding, in real time, to the unexpected. Time horizons of predictability are shrinking before our eyes and the certainties we could rely on, and plan around, in previous ages are dissolving.

What business leaders and marketers commonly dub 'agile' practices are akin to the adaptive behaviours which are innate in nature. We can learn from nature's coping mechanisms, observing how ecosystems manage and reallocate resources in response to change, and also their ability to create new life which is viable under new environmental conditions. For companies, the latter requires close attention and timely response to what is emerging, and a conscious, purposeful search for opportunities. Peter Drucker (1985) identified the principles of systematic innovation, advocating an approach which is based on a rigorous and ongoing process of looking, asking and listening, coupled with a keen awareness of context. Arguably, this disciplined approach to innovation is more vital for companies today than even before.

The fashion industry is particularly adept at anticipating and responding quickly to shifting consumer tastes and behaviours, and at situating these in social and cultural contexts. A recent example of connecting the dots in this way has been the creation of 'athleisure' wear, an athletic style of clothing that is fashionable enough to wear all day. This rapidly growing trend is attributed to several intersecting factors: an increase in the popularity of yoga wear, technological advancements in fabrics, the desire for comfortable attire and the convenience of being able to wear one set of clothes across different activities. While these variables, in combination, help to explain the emergence of athleisure wear, what is of greater interest to me is the prediction that this trend will continue to grow based on changes in where and how people will work in the future. As digital technology and connectivity enable more people to work remotely, the demand for traditional office attire will decrease, while demand for more versatile and comfortable clothes will increase. Observing macro shifts like this and thinking systemically enables fashion manufacturers not only to respond to changing consumer wants and needs, but to develop new trends in anticipation of future desires and needs.

The same opportunities exist for companies in other industries which want to stay ahead of the curve. Through careful observation and ecosystemic thinking, companies can keep their finger continuously on the pulse of change, as a *practice*. As Drucker recognised, adopting this kind of systematic, disciplined approach to looking, asking and listening is central to innovation of all kinds.

Relationship Building through Value Exchange

"Competing against each other leaves little space for reciprocity and the growth of social capital. Running against another in a race may benefit our speed, but jointly organising the sports day produces cooperation and trust. There are many situations where cooperation and reciprocity are more effective than competition. Civic virtues come from building on what we have in common rather than by using our differences to create in-groups, out-groups and fear driven competition."

Eva Cox

As previously stated, relationships are primary in ecosystems. They are the backbone, glue and mechanism via which individual elements contribute to the whole and keep a system, whether that be a family, community or online network, healthy. In traditional marketing, however, relationship building is often neglected in favour of transactional business strategies based on short-term sales goals and return on investment.

An excellent example of network-based relationship building by a brand has been the creation and evolution of the Nike+ platform, which enables runners to interact and contribute to the ecosystem through interaction and voluntary sharing of personal data. Nike adds strength and value to those communities through its platform and devices, the compilation of data from other sources and the effective use of analytics to make that data relevant and useful. More recently, Nike integrated these into the Nike+ Run Club app and a Nike+ Apple Watch which enable runners to track runs, get personalised coaching and connect with other runners to share information and compete. Essentially, Nike has created an environment for value creation and value exchange, rooted in reciprocity, co-creation and community building (Ramaswamy and Ozcan, 2014).

Interestingly, Nike is also applying a reciprocal, community-minded approach to its bricks-and-mortar business by opening stores in inner cities. These stores reflect Nike's willingness to invest in relationship and community building on the ground. By opening stores in economically challenged areas, hiring at least 80% of staff from within a five-mile radius and requiring all staff to give back to the local community, Nike is building meaningful, mutually beneficial relationships between the brand and its customers.

Omnichannel Marketing

Advances in user system design and integration, advances in data analytics and the proliferation of connected devices are making it possible for companies to create cohesive and consistent messaging and brand experiences for their consumers across devices, locations and contexts. Omni-channel marketing, while still in the early stages of development and execution, holds great promise because it addresses the reality that consumers do not compartmentalise their experiences by brand, platform, device or context; and because it seeks to create a unified experience for them over time and across multiple touch points.

Perhaps the greatest psychological leap required of companies seeking to develop true omni-channel capabilities is letting go of the notion of 'my' customer to see instead through the eyes of the customer. Increasingly customers want (and will expect) a shopping experience which is continuous and consistent. They want information which is timely and relevant, and which will help them make informed purchase decisions. They want to consider different brand and product options, and to compare prices. They want to transition between their online and physical experiences seamlessly, and the look, feel and quality of those experiences to be consistently high. True omni-channel marketers will take all of this into account. It will require the breaking down of boundaries between products and brands, and the adoption of practices which are genuinely consumer centric (Christensen, 1997). Leaders in this arena, including Starbucks, Disney and Virgin, recognise the importance of this and are already reaping the rewards (Agius, 2015).

Storytelling with a Purpose

"Any technology must be inextricably linked with human purpose – with a great story that uplifts the entire user experience."

David Sable

The most coveted prize for marketers seeking recognition for creative and effective campaigns is the Cannes Lion. A look at recent Cannes winners in digital categories tells its own story about what people care about and respond to. The most successful campaigns, as measured by creativity and effectiveness (number of shares, impact on business, etc.), almost without exception, create and leverage networks, and serve a higher purpose than selling goods and services. These campaigns use great storytelling to create emotional connection with consumers. They tap into the human desire to connect and co-create, to transcend isolated self-interest and to participate in human endeavours which serve the greater good. A few examples, among many, are Burger King's 'McWhopper for Peace' campaign, proposing a temporary truce with McDonald's in the interest of promoting world peace; the Argentine Breast Cancer campaign, 'Man Boobs', which uses an overweight man to model self-breast examination; and Unilever's 'Free the Kids: Dirt is Good' campaign, encouraging children to set down electronics and go outdoors.

This last example is one of the most powerful and effective global campaigns today because it speaks to an issue which is important to parents across the globe, engages with consumers emotionally through powerful storytelling and integrates multiple platforms to engage, empower and activate stakeholders. The most recent commercials, shot in an American prison, capture inmates' responses when informed that on average children spend less time outdoors than a prison inmate. Their shocked, sad and incredulous responses communicate powerfully how deeply troubling this statistic is. Beyond the campaign itself – which has been highly effective in spreading awareness and engagement – Unilever has leveraged the power of networks and partnerships through the creation of The Wild Network. This network provides tools, inspiration, knowledge and support for parents, schools and communities to help all children lead playful, nature-rich, outdoor lives. While Unilever and its Persil brand are clearly in the business of selling products, they also demonstrate, through the campaign's many dimensions and related programs, a sincere commitment to building a healthier world, based on human connection and connection to nature. This integrative campaign epitomises an ecosystemic approach to advertising, using powerful storytelling which speaks to a shared human experience, and connects emotionally with consumers, serving a bigger goal than product sales alone and utilising digital platforms to engage consumers and leverage the power of networks. While other examples in this chapter share some of these qualities, it is worth noting that Persil is a detergent, argu- ably a product and category which falls on the opposite end of the spectrum from ecosystemic sensibility, at least as it relates to the environment. It is also worth noting that detergents typically compete with other detergents based on product efficacy claims. Persil has transcended the confines of traditional advertising, in a category which is often bound by conformity, and found a path to connecting with and uniting consumers in pursuit of a greater purpose.

Being Digital from the Inside Out

"You are bigger than your present situation."

Curtis Tyrone Jones

Developing the mindset, ethos and practices required for marketing successfully in the digital universe begins at home. For many industrial-era companies, the digital age requires some fundamental changes in organisational structure, culture and behaviours. Here, I shall explore a few of these.

Tear Down Walls

As previously discussed, human beings build walls of all kinds. We create structures, systems and laws to manage complexity and conflict, and we entrench ourselves in ideological camps so that we can avoid ambiguity, paradox and confrontation with people and ideas which make us uncomfortable. The most common fences which are shared by traditional organisations are geographical and functional silos, encouraging fiefdoms which operate independently of one another, each with its own incentives and goals. From a systems perspective, of course, this makes no sense. Particularly problematic is the separation of digital from other marketing and business functions. If you take one piece of marketing advice from this chapter, let it be this: tear down this wall! Permeating your entire organisation with a digital mindset and orientation before embarking on any new initiative or campaign will help weave threads of connection between functions and ensure that consumers experience continuity and consistency at every touch point.

Marketing organisations in these complex times also require individuals within them who understand, and can effectively leverage, digital technology, see the big picture and span disciplines. Competition to find and retain this kind of talent is fierce. Out-of-touch instructors and departmental divides within traditional educational institutions make it difficult for colleges and universities to prepare students for success in a world which will not sit still or stay inside the lines. Some schools, including Hyper Island and Singularity University, are helping professionals and executives to navigate constant change effectively, but more than ever before professionals need to learn on the job through real-world experience and continuing education.

One of the most gratifying professional experiences I have been involved with has been the design and execution of SapientNitro's CMTOu University. CMTOu is a highly integrative leadership development program for senior technologists which melds the rigour of an executive MBA program with opportunities to tackle complex, real-world marketing and business challenges. CMTOu graduates emerge with greater depth and breadth of technological knowledge, understanding of the marketing technology landscape and its workings, command of business models and processes, and the consultative skills which are required to help companies navigate digital business transformation. Importantly, equal emphasis is placed on the development of the participants' relational abilities through immersive learning experiences, reflection, team and cohort-based activities, and opportunities to develop storytelling, presentation and communication skills. Programs like these are rare because they require vision, strong leadership and a significant investment of time and resources. As the world of business continues to become more technologically mediated and multi-faceted, however, companies will need to develop cross-disciplinary talent of this kind.

Build Culture

> "If you get the culture right, most of the other stuff will just take care of itself."

> Tone Hseih

Just as consumers are gravitating toward companies and brands which reflect their values, so are workers becoming more discriminating in where they work, how they work and why they work. In my own training and consulting, I commonly hear executives bemoaning the expectations of Millennials, characterising the entire generation as impatient, spoiled and entitled. Are they? Or are they simply more evolved? Greater transparency and access to information are enabling employees and prospective hires of any generation to be more discerning and selective. In turn, a company's integrity, mission and culture are becoming more vital to its sustained health.

Glassdoor, a website which allows employees to review companies and their management anonymously, offers an interesting window into this growing phenomenon. With few exceptions, the top-ranked places to work on Glassdoor are mission-driven companies which place a high value on company culture. An excellent example of this is Airbnb, ranked the #1 Best Place to

Work in 2016. Airbnb's mission is to create a world in which you can belong anywhere and its employee-experience mission is to create a work environment in which anyone can belong. Airbnb is, both internally and externally, an open, expansive and inclusive community, and a facilitator of human connection. This seamless continuity between the company's mission and internal culture undoubtedly contributes to the company's enormous success as one of the fastest-growing companies of the digital age and as a beloved organisation.

Of course, most companies were not founded on this kind of ecosystemic ethos and many do not have missions greater than selling goods and services. Similarly, many traditional companies pay little attention to company culture. This does not, however, prevent companies from deliberately cultivating open and inclusive cultures and practices.

Be Inclusive

> "It is essential to employ, trust, and reward those whose perspective, ability, and judgment are radically different from yours. It is also rare, for it requires uncommon humility, tolerance, and wisdom."
>
> Dee Hock

In the same ways that biodiversity feeds and enriches complex ecosystems, diversity of people and ideas feeds the health of organisations, especially in a world which is becoming increasingly pluralistic and multi-cultural. Abundant research demonstrates that diverse organisations, boards and teams are better performing, and generate higher profit than homogeneous ones (Dizikes, 2014; Hunt, et al., 2015). In an interview with *USA Today*, Sheryl Sandberg, Facebook COO and author of *Lean In*, speaks to the importance of increasing diversity in the technology sector, stating that "endless data show that diverse teams make better decisions. We are building products that people with very diverse backgrounds use, and I think we all want our company makeup to reflect the makeup of the people who use our products." This is equally true for companies in other industries, and for marketers seeking to be relevant in a landscape which is no longer compartmentalised by the market segments and demographic categories of old. Marketers and the organisations which they inhabit need to step outside of what is comfortable and familiar, invite fresh ways of seeing and solving problems, and embody diversity.

A recent spate of racism and sexism cases in major advertising and communications companies has forced out some very powerful leaders, including JWT CEO, Gustavo Martinez, Saatchi and Saatchi chairman, Kevin Roberts, and Fox News CEO, Roger Aires. Hopefully, this will trigger a tidal shift toward greater diversity and inclusion. In a 2016 blog post published by Quartz, Minnie Ingersoll (2016) asserts that the pervasive gender gap in technology is a product of corporate cultures which reward aggressiveness, domineering behaviours and certainty. I particularly like the solution she proposes: "We should start by firing the assholes: the people who make others feel small, shut down constructive debates, and generally create miserable environments."

Welcoming diverse people and perspectives requires open-mindedness and self-awareness on the parts of leadership, and it involves humility. In contrast to arrogance and authority, humility invites respect for alternative points of view, and willingness to change course. These qualities and practices cultivate leaders and organisations which are flexible, adaptive and open... characteristics and capabilities which are prerequisites for long-term success in the digital ecosystem.

Bring Yourself to Work

> "The world and all its wisdom is but a booby, blundering school-boy that needs management and could be managed, if men and women would be human beings instead of just business men, or plumbers, or army officers, or commuters, or educators, or authors, or clubwomen, or traveling salesmen, or Socialists, or Republicans, or Salvation Army leaders, or wearers of cloths."
>
> Sinclair Lewis

Throughout this chapter, I have written about marketing as a professional discipline which is made up of marketing professionals. Obviously, outside of their day jobs, marketers are also consumers – although this is often forgotten when they get to work. I regularly work with executives who consider themselves out of place and out of date in the digital marketing world because they have internalised the message that digital is the domain of young people, digital natives, techies or Millennials. And this is affirmed in offices, where digital teams are cordoned off in departments of their own. When I ask these executives to consider how they view and use digital technology outside of work, many realise that they are early adopters of technology and are more digitally savvy than they imagined.

Not surprisingly, failure of marketing people to integrate their personal and professional selves shows up in inhuman marketing strategies, tactics and behaviours. Marcus Collins (see chapters 1, 3, and 4) shines a light on this, asking why marketers abandon their private-life understanding of human behaviour and social norms when they get to work. And he is correct. Why do marketers forget that consumers are people like them? Why do they view and treat prospects as targets? Why do they interrupt them and talk *at* them, especially in digital environments that are purpose-built for dialogue? The solution, or at least a good starting point, seems obvious to me – when crafting marketing strategies and tactics, marketers need to start with one simple question: would I welcome this?

The compartmentalisation of our professional and personal selves is yet another example of a mindset which sees the world, and even ourselves, as fragmented. A more ecosystemic view invites greater integration, empathy and cross-fertilisation of knowledge, skills and insights.

Conclusion

Navigating the digital age requires a fundamental shift in perception from seeing people, brands and organisations as separate entities to seeing people, brands and organisations ecosystemically. This requires moving beyond industrial and agricultural mindsets in which we imagine we can shape and control the world around us, to a more holistic, responsive and cooperative orientation, ethos and behaviours. As this chapter has illustrated, this shift is already well underway, and the adoption of ecosystemic strategies and practices is contributing to the success of many companies. Even so, the human tendencies to fragment the world, build barriers and fight for survival through excessive competition remain deeply entrenched in business culture.

Thriving in the digital age requires an understanding of context, the ability to connect the dots between disparate phenomena and responsiveness to what is emerging. While these capabilities are vital today, they will be even more critical in the coming years. Technologies and capabilities like robotics, artificial intelligence and virtual reality are poised to disrupt business, marketing and day-to-day human life in ways that are difficult to imagine and predict. As these develop and the pace of change continues to accelerate, many companies will be tossed about like rafts in a violent sea. More than ever before, companies will need a means of rising above the fray, seeing the big picture and making choices which serve both their own interests and the interests of the greater whole. Companies which recognise the power of diversity, openness, collaboration, collective endeavour and relationship building will forge creative partnerships, build and leverage networks, place the needs of consumers first and build organisations which reflect this orientation and these behaviours. Paradoxically, they will emerge the winners by lowering their guard, taming the desire to win at all costs and by adopting an ethos of genuine care and concern for the greater whole.

References

Afshar, V. (2016) "2016 – The Year of Connected Customer." *Huffington Post*. TheHuffingtonPost.com, 18 December.

Agius, A. (2015) "7 Inspiring Examples of Omni-Channel User Experiences." *7 Inspiring Examples of Omni-Channel User Experiences*. Hubspot.com, 8 June.

Branman, M. (2016) "Place Your Bets: BMW Is Running One Heck of an Innovation Race." *Digital Trends*. Digitaltrends.com, 24 October.

Capra, F. (1996) *The Web of Life: A New Scientific Understanding of Living Systems*. New York: Anchor.

Christensen, C. (1997) *The Innovator's Dilemma: When New Technologies Cause Great Firms to Fail*. Boston: Harvard Business School.

CNBC (2016) "CNBC Transcript: Interview with Julia Goldin, Chief Marketing Officer at Lego." Interview, https://www.facebook.com/CNBC, Carolyn Roth, 11 November.

Dizikes, P. (2014) "Study: Workplace Diversity Can Help the Bottom Line." *MIT News*, 7 October.

Drucker, P. (1985) *Innovation and Entrepreneurship: Practices and Principles*. New York: Harper & Row.

Forth, P. (2014) "Technology Disruption Meets the Change Monster... who Wins?" *YouTube*. TED Institute, 22 December.

InterbrandGroup (2012) "Jez Frampton: Spotlight, Building Unbeatable Brands." *YouTube*, 4 April.

Friedman, T. (2016) "Web People vs. Wall People." *New York Times*, 20 July.

Golob, U., M. Lah and Z. Jancic (2008) "Value Orientations and Consumer Expectations of Corporate Social Responsibility." *Journal of Marketing Communications* 14, 2: pp.83–96.

Havas Worldwide Follow (2016) "Project: Superbrand (Havas Worldwide)." *Project: Superbrand (Havas Worldwide)*. LinkedIn, 20 January.

Hewlett, S., M. Marshall and L. Sherbin (2014) "How Diversity Can Drive Innovation." *Harvard Business Review*, 31 July.

Hunt, V., D. Layton and S. Prince (2015) "Why Diversity Matters." *McKinsey and Company*. McKinsey.com, January.

@harvardbiz (2016) "Know Your Customers." *Harvard Business Review*, 24 August.

Ingersoll, M. (2016) "Silicon Valley's Gender Gap Problem Is Really a Culture Problem." *Quartz*, 7 April.

Kelly, K. (2016) *The Inevitable: Understanding the 12 Technological Forces That Will Shape Our Future*. New York: Viking.

Living Services (2016) Accenture Digital, 15 September.

McKinsey (2014) "Bill Ford Charts a Course for the Future." *McKinsey Quarterly*. McKinsey and Company, October.

Perrin, A. (2015) "One-fifth of Americans Report Going Online 'Almost Constantly'." *Pew Research Center RSS*, 8 December.

PersilUK. (2016) "Free the Kids – Dirt Is Good." *YouTube*, 21 March.

Piaget, J. (1976) *The Child and Reality*. New York: Penguin.

Ramaswamy, V., and F. Gouillart (2010) *The Power of Co-Creation: Build It with Them to Boost Growth, Productivity, and Profits*. New York: Free.

Ramaswamy, V., and K. Ozcan (2014) *The Co-creation Paradigm*. Palo Alto: Stanford Publishing.

Ramo, J. (2016) *The Seventh Sense: Power, Fortune, and Survival in the Age of Networks*. New York: Little Brown.

Reeves, J. (2010) "Consumers Overwhelmingly Want CSR." *Forbes*, 15 December.

Scharmer, C, and K. Kaufer (2013) *Leading from the Emerging Future: From Ego-system to Ecosystem Economies*. San Francisco: Berrett-Koehler.

Senge, P. (1990) *The Fifth Discipline: The Art and Practice of the Learning Organization*. New York: Doubleday/Currency.

Sorrell, S. (2015) *Smart Cities*. Retrieved from: https://www.juniperresearch.com/researchstore/iot-m2m/smart-cities/strategies-forecasts-in-energy-transport-lighting

Walt, V. (2015) "Barcelona: The Most Wired City in the World." *Fortune Barcelona The Most Wired City in the World Comments*. Fortune.com, 28 July.

About the Author

Laura Sawyer, Ph.D., is an adult educator, learning designer, facilitator and coach, specialising in transformative learning and adaptation. She partners extensively with the Swedish school, Hyper Island, helping executives and corporations to develop digital capabilities and navigate change. More fundamentally, Laura's passion is expanding human consciousness. She is fascinated by quantum physics, the supernatural and exceptional human capabilities because they challenge limited thinking and offer windows into unbounded possibility. She welcomes new connections and challenges. Find her on LinkedIn at Laura Sawyer, Ph.D. Contact her on email at lsawyer4@gmail.com.

Chapter 3

And She Told Two Friends – The Power of the Network in Digital Marketing

Marcus Collins and John Branch

A Global Village – or a Digital World?

"Well, there they are. Our new electronic media. Or, our new gadget. You push a button and the world is yours. You know how they say the world is getting smaller, well, it's thanks to these that it is. Everywhere is now our own neighborhood. We know what it's like to go on safari in Kenya, or to have an audience with the Pope, to order a cognac in a Paris cafe. But not only is the world getting smaller, it's becoming more available and more familiar to our minds and to our emotions. The world is now a global village. A global village."

Alan Millar (1960)

You could be forgiven for thinking that these words allude to the global village which has resulted from today's digital transformation. Indeed, the ubiquity of digital technologies has expanded without limits every facet of our contemporary lives: the way in which we socialise, the timing and nature of the work which we undertake, the provenance of the entertainment which we digest. Everything is more international as a result of 0s and 1s. The global village is seemingly also a digital world.

These words, however, were spoken by television host Alan Millar in the introduction to an interview with Canadian media theorist Marshall McLuhan in the year 1960. In grainy black and white, standing before rotary telephones and cathode-ray-tube-driven furniture-sized televisions, Millar calmly and convincingly foreshadowed the claims which McLuhan would make later in the interview that new technology – new media – have erased temporal and spatial boundaries, thereby giving rise to a 'global village'.

Today's digital world and McLuhan's global village, however, are not the only revolutions in human history. On the contrary, human history is dotted with technological inventions which have given rise to new forms of social organisation. Consider agriculture, for example, which, along with the domestication of animals and aided by new planting and harvesting tools, transportation means and irrigation techniques, disrupted the previous 'hunter-gatherer' mode of existence.

Centuries later, in the late 1700s, the so-called Industrial Revolution unleashed sweeping changes in society. Eli Whitney's cotton gin, for example, then the weaving machine, attracted workers from the countryside to settle in cities, transforming the complexion of cities such as Manchester, England, and also the nature of the workday, housing and family structure. And in the next 100-odd years, humans invented the telegraph and the printing press, which re-shaped communication. They harnessed steam power, which amplified manufacturing and altered their spatial boundaries. And eventually they pioneered petroleum distillate (and the combustion engine), which changed city-scapes, vacations and, er, almost everything else.

Digital technologies, however, appear to have the power to eclipse any changes which we have witnessed in the past. Indeed, the Internet already generates more information in a few years than was accumulated in the preceding millennia. And imagine a future of autonomous vehicles, drone-delivered groceries and shared devices. Thrill at the thought of enhanced and augmented museum visits or tourism-site excursions. Drool over a closet full of clothes which have been custom made from measurements which were calculated from photographs on your mobile telephone. Bob Dylan might have captured it best with his 1964 hit 'The Times They Are A-Changing'.

The purpose of this chapter is to examine wherein lays the power in digital marketing. It begins by demonstrating that digital technology, when it leads to a shift in medium, does not change the underlying human behaviour, only its ubiquity and frequency. It then argues that the power of digital technology occurs when it leads to a network. Finally, it demonstrates the power of the network with two examples: Waze and Amazon.

Manners (or is it Media?) Maketh the Man

Shortly after that CBC interview in 1960, Marshall McLuhan published his book *Understanding Media: The Extensions of Man*, which gave rise to the phrase 'the medium is the message'. The philosophical idea in this phrase is that the medium through which the message is communicated becomes as important to the meaning of the message as the message itself. Indeed, the message and the medium exist in a kind of symbiosis, together conveying meaning to the receiver. It is not unlike the notion that the mode of transportation – plane, train or automobile – contributes to any journey... perhaps even usurping the journey itself in some instances.

It could be argued, using a similar logic, that the recent changes in society which we have witnessed are due to shifts in media. Indeed, there seems to be a popular narrative that claims that the things which were previously analogue in nature are now digital, and consequently that the world is an entirely new place. Consider music, for example.

In the late 1800s, Thomas Edison introduced the phonograph, which in a very short period of time became the primary medium by which music was stored. This device took vibrations from sound waves and impressed them upon a rotating material – wax or tinfoil, for example. The phonograph could, in the reverse, transduce the impressions in the material into corresponding sound waves for human listening pleasure. A decade or so later, this technology evolved into the phonograph record, which used vinyl as the material for the recording medium, which in turn made listening to different musical recordings easier and exchangeable. The 'record' went on to become the dominant medium for music for almost a century, until tape took over in the 1970s.

Tape, in its various guises – eight-track, cassettes and reel-to-reel – stores sound as magnetic patterns on plastic tape and, like the record, replays the original audio event by transducing these magnetic patterns into electrical signals, which are subsequently converted to sound with the help of an audio amplifier and loudspeakers. Eight-track tape improved the sound quality of records and, perhaps more importantly, made recorded music more portable. This portability was increased further with the cassette format, the adoption of which was heightened with the ubiquity of cassette players in automobiles and the popularity of portable cassette players. Who can forget the 'boom boxes' of the 1980s?

Perhaps the greatest benefit of the cassette, however, was its ability to record, thereby allowing people to curate their own music compilations. Indeed, people could record music from the radio, from other cassettes or from live concerts, a feat which was impossible with the record. For amateur musicians and budding rockstars, the cassette was a boon, allowing them to capture their own musical performances for playback and promotion.

Technology made a giant leap forward from tape to the compact disc (CD for short). The CD is a 12 cm plastic disc which stores music in digital form as 1s and 0s which are 'burned' into the disc as hills and troughs. Sound is reproduced with a combination of three things: 1. a laser which 'reads' the 1s and 0s from the hills and troughs; 2. a digital-to-analogue converter (DAC) which, as suggested by the term, converts a stream of 1s and 0s into an analogue electrical signal; and 3. an amplifier-and-loudspeaker set-up which transduces the analogue signal into sound waves.

The CD removed many of the pain points of tape (and the record). Tape often gets caught in a player, stretches or even breaks. To access specific points on a tape is slow and tedious.

And most tape players required the user to remove and reverse the tape in order to enjoy the second half of the recording. More importantly, however, the CD offered an immeasurable sonic improvement over tape (and the record). Indeed, the so-called signal-to-noise ratio (the aural distance between the intended sound and the background sound) was vastly improved. And with the advent of digital recording and digital signal processing, the background hiss, pops and other annoyances of both tape and the record were eliminated entirely. By the 1990s, the CD became the new standard, growing hand-in-hand with automotive and portable players.

By the early 2000s, another medium shift was underway, facilitated by concomitant technological advances in both the storage capacity of digital devices and the compression capabilities of digital algorithms. First, the number of 1s and 0s which could be crammed into the memory of any single digital device shot up dramatically. Indeed, in the 15 years from 2001 to 2016, the storage capacity of a desktop computer multiplied by more than 1,000 – with a correspondingly smaller footprint. Second, scientists developed the MPEG Audio Layer III standard (known more commonly as MP3), which can compress a digital file into about 1/12th of its original size. Together, these two advances triggered a musical metamorphosis – the music which was once 'recorded' on its own tangible media (record, tape, CD) suddenly became ethereal, with an almost other-worldly existence. Music could now be played back seemingly anywhere, at any time and on any device, both dedicated music players and non-traditional devices such as computers and mobile telephones.

The MP3 standard was also propelled forward by a host of other factors, including the penetration of personal computers in the home; the growth of residential, broadband Internet access; the creation of file-sharing sites such as Napster; the inclusion of CD burners on computers; the introduction of the iPod and other portable MP3 players; and the launch of the iTunes store. The result has been a complete re-jiggering of the entire music industry, not to mention mutations of consumer electronics retailing, radio broadcasting and the wider entertainment machine.

New technologies are unquestionably on the horizon – or

probably more accurately, being developed in the computer laboratory – which will cause other dramatic and unforeseen changes in society. But a closer inspection raises doubts about the veracity of this claim – and indeed about the claim regarding the power of previous technologies. The shift from the record to tape certainly brought portability, plus the possibility of curation. The CD improved the aural experience. And the MP3 standard expanded access.

At the core, however, people did not listen to music differently, following each shift in medium. Indeed, they did not change their underlying human behaviours. On the contrary, each shift in medium simply made music more prevalent, and allowed for more portability, more customisation and, well, more music. The cassette, for example, enabled people to listen to music anywhere and at any time – greater prevalence and higher frequency. But this shift in medium did not change the fundamentals of listening to music. That would come with Spotify.

It's the Network, Stupid

Spotify is the online music-streaming service which provides subscribers access to compressed music files which are stored 'in the cloud' on remote servers. The seismic shift which Spotify has engendered is not so much a result of a shift in medium. On the contrary, it is a result of Spotify's ability to recommend new musical groups and new musical genres according to a user's listening behaviours (music preferences) and those of their friends. In other words, Spotify's power resides in social networks.

When subscribers login to Spotify via their social-networking accounts (Facebook and Twitter, for example), the company is able to leverage the 'wisdom of the crowd' by mining their subscribers' networks. Music recommendations are served up based on the music to which their network members are listening. It leads not to music for the masses, but instead to a bespoke musical experience which is derived from people 'just like them'. Spotify's ability to leverage the network of people using digital technology is thus that which makes for a true musical – or rather social – revolution, and not the digital technology in and of itself.

In short, we suggest that many of the recent changes in society have been mis-attributed to the digital revolution. Indeed, we contend that digital technology, when applied to devices – that which might be called first-order digitalisation – does little to change basic human behaviour. Digital telephones, for example, have simply increased the frequency of interpersonal conversations and the number of situations in which such conversations can occur. Ditto digital books – people can read more books, of more genres, in more places.

When digital technology leads to higher-order effects, however, then behavioural change begins to occur. A digital grocery store, for example, does not change the purchasing of groceries. But when the digital grocery store allows shoppers to share recipes or comment on dinner-party menu plans, then new behaviours ensue. That is more than the power of digital technology: that is the power of the network.

We define a network as a complex system of interconnected nodes which share resources, knowledge, information, experiences and so forth. Arguably, there have always been networks of people: sororities and fraternities, for example, bridge clubs, congregations. And digital technology has facilitated, enhanced, even accelerated these networks of people. Digital technology, however, has also created a new network of things – the so-called Internet of things, or IoT, which consists of devices which are connected and which can communicate with each other, with the help of digital technology. The culmination is that which we call the network of people and things.

Viewing the changes which have resulted from digital technology as simply a shift in medium, therefore, is too narrow. Yes, digital technology allows people to do more and to do it far more conveniently. But the tectonic changes are driven by the network of people and things. Indeed, the power of digital technology is situated not in the 1s and 0s, but in the network which these 1s and 0s aid and abet.

By definition, digital technology generates, stores and processes data as a string of 1s and 0s. It relies on the very simple notion of binary states: on or off, plus or minus, 1 or 0. A digital photograph, therefore, is stored not in its original form but as a string of 1s and 0s. And because all digital devices 'speak the same language', they can communicate with each other. That which was once simply a product can now become a 'smart product'. As more and more of these smart products connect with each other, they begin to form product systems, and systems within systems, leading to remarkable, connected experiences.

Consider Google's Nest thermostat, for example, which gets 'smarter' the more time its occupants spend in a room, adjusting the room's temperature according to the occupants' behaviours. Mint.com pulls together disparate financial information, from checking/savings accounts to credit card transactions, from mortgage payments to student loan repayments, in service of people making better financial decisions. The power of digital technology is situated not in the 1s and 0s, but in the network.

Waze and Means

Frank Moss, the former director of the MIT Media Lab, summarised the power of the digital network: "Every time we perform a search, tweet, send an email, post a blog, comment on one, use a cell phone, shop online, update our profile on a social networking site, use a credit card, or even go to the gym, we leave behind a mountain of data, a digital footprint, that provides a treasure trove of information." It is this information – the reams of digital data – which fuels the network of people and things. Indeed, the more we behave in a digital world, the more our behaviours will change. Two examples will serve as illustrations.

Waze

I (John) remember taking long road trips with my family when I was a child. My father would stop by the automobile club before we hit the highway to retrieve that seemingly magical, multifolded map, whose yellow highlighted route would assuredly lead us to our destination. Yet without fail, my father would somehow wander off-path and get us lost. This problem would be somewhat mitigated thanks to Yahoo's MapQuest which allowed us to key-in our starting location and desired destination, and which subsequently created a turn-by-turn, sequential set of instructions which accompanied a highlighted map route. And my father (and everybody else in those days) would print out the MapQuest map and instructions, in the spirit of its multi-folded, paper predecessor. Despite the shift in medium, little changed in terms of navigation – though maybe there were fewer curse words.

Fast-forward some years later and the Global Positioning System (GPS) shifted the medium again. Indeed, there was no need for any paper of any sort – we now had a device in the car which would provide turn-by-turn voice directives in real time, and recalculating capabilities if we found ourselves deviating from the route. This made navigation much easier – but it did not change the basic notion of getting to the destination.

The introduction of Waze, however, triggered a fundamental shift in driving behaviour. Waze is a network-based navigation application whose purpose is to help people outsmart traffic. The mobile application allows its 'community members' to get driving instructions which are based on the experiences of other community members who are travelling the same or similar routes. Indeed, community members inform others if there is a police officer on the road, or if a traffic jam has developed. Waze helps people outsmart traffic (and avoid fines) by leveraging the network of people. The application also gets smarter the more community members use it, offering, for example, recommendations on the time at which someone ought to begin a journey because of road conditions, typical traffic patterns, known police hangouts and so on. Paper maps and GPS certainly made travelling easier, but Waze ultimately changed human behaviour.

Amazon

'In the beginning', markets were physical places in which buyers and sellers came together to exchange their products. Indeed, people brought fruits and vegetables, cattle, grain and the like to the market, in hopes that other people who were looking for these same products would find the offerings compelling. By the mid-1800s, Sears and Roebuck and other mail-order companies began offering products in a 'catalogue market'. Customers no longer needed to visit the market physically to get their products – although they often took weeks to arrive due to slow order processing and delivery times. Of course, these lead times would eventually shorten to a matter of weeks with advances in operations and logistics.

By the early 2000s, however, the Internet allowed for the creation of 'virtual markets' and e-commerce was born. Orders were placed instantaneously and processed in a matter of hours, thereby reducing turnaround times from weeks to days. This shift in medium obviously made shopping (market exchanges) more convenient, but it did not necessarily change the way people engaged within the market.

Amazon changed all that. The e-commerce behemoth that began as an online bookstore has leveraged the behaviours of its shoppers – their searches, their wish lists, their shopping carts, their purchases and so on – to provide individualised shopping experiences. Amazon gets smarter each time a shopper uses it and its recommendations reflect not only his/her history, but also that of people like him/her. Amazon has also ventured out into the 'physical world' in the form of Amazon Echo, Dash and brick-and-mortar retail outlets, furthering its goal to leverage the network of people and things by connecting previously disparate and isolated nodes.

Battle of the Network Stars

The world is now a global village. So predicted Marshall McLuhan in the early 1960s. But it is digital technology – the processing, generation and storage of information in the form of 1s and 0s – that has truly brought humans closer together. Digital technology has enabled disparate nodes of both people and things to connect in networks like never before, which, in turn, have eased, enhanced and even extended human behaviour. In summary, therefore, we challenge you to re-think the notion of a digital world, focusing not on digital technology but instead on the networks which the digital technology facilitates. Therein will be the innovations of the future.

References

Millar, A. (1960) "McLuhan's They of the Global Village." CBC Television Interview, 18 May.

McLuhan, M. (1964) *Understanding Media: The Extensions of Man.* Mentor: New York.

About the Authors

Marcus Collins is a culturally curious thinker with an affinity for understanding the cognitive drivers and environmental factors which impact human behaviour. He is a Golden Apple Award nominated faculty member at the Ross School of Business at the University of Michigan and leads the Social Engagement practice at Doner Advertising. Marcus was recognised as one of *Ad Age*'s 2016 '40 Under 40' bright young minds who are reinventing and reshaping marketing's future. He is a proud Detroit native, loving father and devoted husband. Learn more at www.marctothec. com.

John Branch is Clinical Assistant Professor of Business Administration at the Stephen M. Ross School of Business and Faculty Associate at the Center for Russian, East European and European Studies, both of the University of Michigan. John is also Visiting Fellow at Wolfson College, University of Cambridge in Cambridge, England. John recently finished a second doctoral degree, his dissertation of which focused on international higher education. In his spare time, John enjoys woodworking and restoring antique sports cars. Contact him on email at jdbranch@umich.edu.

Location, Location, Location – The Influence of the Digital Marketing Context

Marcus Collins and John Branch

Toilet Humour

I (Marcus) have a confession to make. I love toilet humour. From Richard Pryor to *South Park*, Sarah Silverman to Sacha Baron Cohen, and anything in between, I am a big fan. The raunchier the better, as far as I am concerned. I suppose that growing up listening to stand-up comedy recordings of Eddie Murphy – at far too young an age, admittedly – had a large effect on my current comedic palette. And from time to time, I feel licensed to infuse friendly dialogue with some off-colour jokes – I know that my friends are also fond of the same kind of humour and that they will appreciate the reference. (N.B. I am no Eddie Murphy, but I can practically recite his show, *Raw*, line by line. Just sayin'.) These 'vulgarities' take place in the everyday – at a football game, walking down the street to Subway or at the photocopier. But I would never stoop to the profane – even with the same people – during a conversation at church, with my child's paediatrician or in the classroom. Why is that?

I certainly do not believe that I am pretending to be someone else at church, that my child's physician is humourless or that the classroom is some sort of sacred space. But the answer is obvious – there are social expectations which dictate which behaviours are acceptable in which contexts, and people consciously (and perhaps even subconsciously) adhere to these expectations by behaving accordingly. That is to say, my proclivity to behave in a certain manner is influenced not only by my personal disposition, but also by the hidden sways of the situation. In short, context matters!

This idea that context matters is not new to marketers. Research in the social sciences has for decades illuminated the influence which other people have on the things which we think, feel and ultimately do. Consequently, marketers invested huge resources to exploit this influence, in service of achieving their marketing objectives.

For example, the Internet has democratised creativity, and in turn birthed a cadre of amateur content creators (YouTube and Instagram stars, for example) who have amassed large populations of followers. In many instances, these creators have attracted and, perhaps more importantly, influenced millions of people. Marketers court these creators with big pay cheques, hoping to benefit from the influence which they have over their followers. The outcome is the new sub-genre of 'influencer marketing', replete with its own conferences, agencies and business models. For marketers, influence is hot.

With all this enthusiasm for and investment in influence, therefore, it is surprising to us that marketers have paid such little heed to the influence of the context. Indeed, channelling our inner Marshall McLuhan (who coined the phrase "The medium is the message" – see Chapter 3 by Collins and Branch) we wonder why more marketers have not considered the influence which the marketing context has on people. The marketing context, like that of a church, physician's office or classroom, undoubtedly has its own communicative powers and hidden forces which guide our cognitions, affects and behaviours. Psychologist and author of *Situations Matter*, Sam Sommers, summed it up well: "Just like the museum visitor pays little heed to the painting's frame, we fail to notice the impact of outside influences on our innermost thoughts and instincts." In turns out that the frame means a lot.

This a-ha creates a great opportunity for marketers not only to engage influencers who deliver messages on behalf of the brand mark, but also engineer the marketing context in ways which influence customer cognitions, affects and behaviours. Consider the inherent wisdom in the old real-estate chestnut of placing fresh-baked cookies in show houses. And what about the effect which clean toilets have on customers' evaluation of restaurant quality?

Life is not constrained to the physical world, however; people also live in a 'digital world'. Indeed, more and more time is spent searching the Internet, pouring over blogs and updating social-media sites. This chapter, therefore, explores the digital marketing context. It begins by discussing defaults – the pre-established factors in a digital space. It then investigates the semiotics (the meanings) of digital 'signs and symbols'. Chapter 4 continues by examining the placement, or spatial arrangement, in a digital space. Finally, it underlines the importance of cultural nuances in the digital marketing context.

Defaults: The Condition Set by Pre-established Factors

You have waited and waited with Monk-like patience, and now it is finally here... the new iPhone with all the latest bells and whistles! After wading through the seemingly endless queue at the Apple Store, you finish the transaction with the sales representative and the phone is now yours. Oh, happy day! You arrive home, unwrap the meticulously designed packaging, walk through the user-friendly activation and turn your new iPhone on for the first time. The device illuminates and you find yourself on the home screen with 22 mobile apps, beautifully laid out, just waiting to be explored. Which apps do you see? Or to put it better, *whose* apps do you see?

Of course, the 22 apps which you see first are all products of Apple, the maker of the iPhone. It is no wonder that Apple would design your first home-screen experience to be made up of Apple apps exclusively. Because the apps to which you are introduced first are the apps which you are more likely to use first and also most often. Sure, iPhone users can go to the App Store (another Apple product) to obtain other (non-Apple) apps, but that takes effort. Like most things, people tend to take the path of least resistance. Thus, the pre-established factors which we experience in a digital space – the defaults – can have a tremendous impact on our behaviour.

Designers have been leveraging the influence of defaults for ages and marketers can stand to benefit from similar thinking. This influence can be seen in both offline and online experiences. Consider the differences between a traditional paper diary and Facebook. On the surface there are plenty of similarities between the two contexts. People commit their feelings, experiences and happenings in a form of syntax which documents their life and the people around them. Obvious medium differences aside, the defaults play a large role in how users behave when engaging with these outlets. In its default condition, the diary is literally kept under lock and key, signalling that its contents are meant to be kept private and only shared with discriminating bias. Surely, a diary is not meant for everyone and, if its owner decides to disclose its secrets, unquestionably this is a special occasion and consequently ought to be treated as such.

Facebook's default, in contrast, has a public setting which signals that its contents are meant for everybody. Of course, this is desirable to Facebook. The more people share, the more compelling the platform becomes. Inactivity makes a 'social' environment less attractive. Who likes a party when no-one is dancing? Same thing here. The more active the platform – that is to say, the more people share – the more attractive Facebook becomes. Facebook's defaults, therefore, are set to encourage this behaviour. While users do have the ability to set their profile to private or to restrict access to their content for selected individuals, the majority of users do not go through the hassle. Defaults prevail.

The inconvenient steps which are necessary to keep Facebook content private create the perfect barrier to doing so, and consequently influence behaviour toward Facebook's desired outcome to share publicly. This is especially critical for marketers because the core function of their discipline is to influence behaviour. Drink this, not that. Buy these shoes, not those shoes. Vote for this candidate, not that candidate. Marketers, therefore, ought to pay more attention to designing defaults, especially because the more complex it is for people to alter the defaults, the more influential those defaults become. Indeed, the more hoops though which people must jump, the more they rely on the status quo – on the defaults.

This notion was illuminated vividly in research by Eric Johnson and Daniel Goldstein (2004) who explored variation in organ donation decisions. The researchers collected data from driver's licence renewal offices in a number of European countries in order to quantify the participation rates of citizens in their national organ donation programs. The results were startling (see Figure 4.1).

The group of countries on the left had very low donation participation. In the case of Denmark, for example, less than 5% of citizens were willing to donate their organs in the event of a deadly accident. Contrast that with the group of countries on the right, which saw organ-donation consent rates approaching 100%. What explains the sharp contrast?

One might hypothesise that this contrast was due to cultural differences. Perhaps the countries on the right are more altruistic than the countries on the left. This hypothesis, however, was immediately challenged when considering the cultural similarities between Germany and Austria, for example, or between Sweden and Denmark.

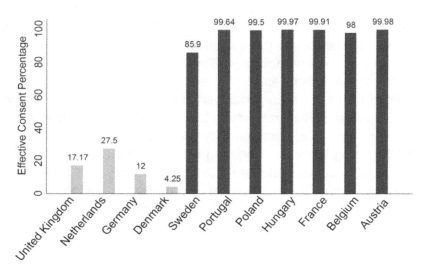

Figure 4.1. Organ Donations
Source: Johnson and Goldstein, 2004

The explanation for the contrast, however, was much simpler. Johnson and Goldstein found that the reason for country differences in proclivity to donate organs had nothing to do with altruism and everything to do with the form at the driver's licence renewal office. Indeed, those countries which had low organ-donation consent rates had renewal forms which required residents to 'opt in'. Citizens did not check the box and so, by default, consent was not given. Those countries which had high organ consent rates, on the contrary, had 'opt-out' renewal forms. Citizens did not check the box and, by default, consent was given. The defaults, it appears, are highly influential!

With an understanding of the influence of defaults, therefore, marketers can design marketing contexts whose defaults influence behaviour toward a desired outcome. One of our favourite examples of this in practice was seen in Panama City, whose city officials needed some 'persuasion' to repair the pervasive and pesky potholes throughout the city. We live in Michigan which, despite its self-proclaimed title of automotive capital of the world, is notorious for its potholes. And like many Michiganders, the residents of Panama City had fallen victim to the ramifications of driving over these structural flaws in the streets: shredded tires, broken wheels and a host of other vehicular and corporal forms of damage. But rather than report the potholes to their city officials in an effort to get the streets repaired, the residents of Panama City took no action – other than complain incessantly to their friends and families.

In stepped a Panamanian advertising agency and a local news show, Telemetro Reporta, which together decided to change the default of driving in Panama City by creating El Hueco Twitero (The Tweeting Pothole). Targeting the busiest streets of Panama City, the agency and Telemetro installed devices inside a number of potholes which tweeted a complaint automatically to the Twitter account of the Department of Public Works whenever a driver traversed the pothole. This new contextual default allowed drivers to continue with their current behaviour, but with a secondary outcome. Not surprisingly, after more and more tweets began to accumulate – and the news show covered the on-going frustration of Panama City drivers – potholes started disappearing.

It demonstrates the power which marketers wield to effectuate behavioural change by manipulating the marketing context – in this case, by resetting the defaults, which in turn reset human agency.

Semiotics: The Condition Set by Implicit Meaning

Signs are everywhere: that 'Do not disturb' announcement on an office door, cloudy skies in the late Spring or police tape surrounding a grassy knoll. According to Ferdinand de Saussure, Charles Sanders Peirce and other semioticians, social meaning is conveyed through signs – linguistic or otherwise. That is to say, the human condition is largely symbolic.

Formally, semiotics is the study of semiosis, the production of meaning through signs. In his seminal 1966 work *Course on General Linguistics*, Swiss linguist de Saussure suggested that any sign is comprised of three inter-linked elements: 1. the 'referent' (the object to which the signifier refers), 2. the 'signifier' (the word, symbol, or other communicative device which refers to the object) and 3. the 'signified' (the conceptual meaning or sense made of the signifier). Consider a red rose, for example. The referent is the rose itself. The signifier is the image of a red rose or the words 'red rose'. The signified is love or passion.

Signs are ubiquitous and people often fail to realise that social meaning is symbolic in nature. Moreover, they rarely – if ever – consider the effortlessness with which these meanings are interpreted. For example, imagine that you passed a person in uniform whose left jacket breast was adorned with a plethora of coloured ribbons and medals. Without thinking, you would presume that the person is from the military, is a decorated hero and is probably someone of high stature who deserves your respect. And as such, you would act accordingly, despite any affiliation with the armed services. It is this meaning-making which is the core of semiotics.

Signs, however, also have a conative effect. Indeed, humans interpret meaning from signs, but they are also triggered to act in response to signs. Imagine that you are in the swankiest part of the city, treating yourself to a night on the town with a visit to the newest dance club which is all the rage. As you approach the club, you can hear the bass of the dance music thumping. There are two bouncers standing at the entrance of the club, granting and denying access, thereby providing the perfect tension of popularity and exclusivity. Two queues have formed, one to the left of the bouncers and another to the right of the bouncers. The two queues look identical, except one queue is corralled by red, velvet ropes which are suspended by shiny, metallic stanchions. Which queue would you join? Our bet is that you would not join the roped-off queue, because the red, velvet ropes communicate exclusivity (unless, of course, you think that those two bouncers will vouch for you as a VIP). Signs have meaning; but they also induce behaviour.

We also see semiotics at play in marketing. Consider the quick service restaurant (QSR) Subway, for example. Before Subway entered the sandwich business, the status quo for most QSR restaurants was for customers to place their orders at the register, then wait for pick-up while cooks prepared the food in the hidden-away 'back stage' area. That the food preparation happened out of sight raised doubt and speculation around the order accuracy, the cleanliness of the prep area and the integrity of the food.

Juxtapose this with Subway, however, in which customers' orders are both placed and prepared in front of their eyes, behind a glass counter. And that glass counter conveys transparency, leaving no doubt about the veracity of the sandwich or its production value – what you see is what you get! The glass counter also gives Subway a 'licence' to boast a healthy alternative to fast food. And thanks to the help of a spokesman's radical weight-loss story, the people came in droves. The semiotics of the Subway environment changed people's expectation of QSR restaurants and have since ignited the rise of other competitors which have emulated a similar physical (and semiotic) design.

Semiotics are not limited to the physical world, of course. *Au contraire*, signs also materialise in digital space. On Facebook, for example, brand marks are constantly serving up (commercial) messages which disrupt the stories and photos from our friends and families. Figure 4.2 shows a recent message which

I (Marcus) received and which you can see was accompanied by the claim "Someone you know and possibly others like this brand." The semiotics of this message connote that my friends like this, so I also ought to like it. But it is not just any friend who likes the brand: it's Damon Williams who, in my mind, is a snazzy dresser. Consequently, I check it out. This sign serves as a stamp of approval. Indeed, when friends like something, it lowers our resistance to it and consequently make us more inclined to adopt it. The signs sway behaviour!

Marketing-engineered signs like this can also have power, even if the signs are communicated by strangers. Recall a recent search for a video on YouTube, the top-two results of which had identical descriptors and thumbnails. The only difference is that one video has 700 views and the other has 8,000,000 views. Which do you click? Of course, you choose to watch the video with 8,000,000 views. Why? Because 8,000,000 people cannot be incorrect. The view count on YouTube acts as a public progress bar, conveying the message that this video is the one which everyone is watching. Again, this is the potential of semiotics in marketing.

Armed with this understanding of semiotics, therefore, marketers can design marketing contexts in order to influence people to take action. One of our favourite examples of semiotics in practice took place at the Oldenplan subway station in Stockholm, Sweden. Like most subway stops, the escalator to exit the station is over-used because for most passengers an escalator is more compelling than the stairs. Remember, people tend to take the path of least resistance. How might a marketer shift the environment using semiotics to encourage people to take the stairs instead? At the time, Volkswagen was in the midst of its 'Fun Theory' campaign which hinges on the notion that if something is fun, people will be inclined to do it. Unbeknownst to Stockholm commuters, Volkswagen outfitted the stairs of the Oldenplan subway station with piano keys which emitted sound when stepped on (think Tom Hanks in the movie *Big*). Each stair tread activated a piano key. Come the next morning, commuters faced a choice – take the boring escalator, as they normally did, or take the newly minted piano stairs. It ought not to be surprising that most people took the stairs – 66% more than usual, in fact. The semiotics of the piano stairs signalled to subway passengers that the stairs were fun, despite – even because of – the effort it took to climb them.

Figure 4.2. Facebook Message

Placement: The Condition Set by Spatial Arrangement

There are no certainties in life, except death and taxes. So goes the old saying. But here in the United States, there is seemingly one other bankable fact – that in a grocery store, the milk will always be at the back of the grocery store. Nope, not in the middle, and certainly not in the front – always in the back. And grocers have made this design choice for one simple reason: milk is among the most frequently purchased items in grocery stores. Grocers, therefore, place milk in the back of the grocery store so that shoppers must wander through aisles of other (often higher profit margin) products in order to collect their dairy staple. And consequently, instead of only buying milk, shoppers often leave with a basket brimming with unplanned purchases. The placement of things in the marketing context has the ability to shape human behaviour – often without the humans being aware.

Consider this other more extreme example. It is 1952 and Carnegie Hall is jam packed. Everyone is waiting with bated breath to see and hear the famed experimental composer John Cage debut his newest piece. People are dressed to the nines and expectations are high. Cage walks on to the stage, sits at the piano and begins to play 4'33". It is his most daring work yet. But as you read this, if you listen very carefully, you can also hear Cage's composition. How so? Because 4'33" is actually 4 minutes and 33 seconds of silence. Total, absolute silence. If you were reading the sheet music to the piece, you would see measure after measure of notational rests.

Perhaps the shocking thing about 4'33" is that people not only dressed up and paid top dollar to hear silence for 4 minutes and 33 seconds, they loved it! Indeed, it became John Cage's most significant work. It has since been performed by a variety of musicians, from guitarist Frank Zappa to the BBC Symphony Orchestra. And 4'33" is now for sale on iTunes as a digital download, with a four out of five stars rating – 4 minutes and 33 seconds of silence!

The key to understanding the example is in its placement. That 4'33" was performed at Carnegie Hall means that it must be art. That it was catalogued and archived on musical notation paper means that it must be real. That it is available on iTunes means that it must be music. The placement of this 'musical' piece influences how people perceive it and, ultimately, how they behave with respect to it.

And as before, placement applies to both the physical and digital worlds – in both offline and online marketing contexts. Consider email, for example. If your name is in the 'To' line, it most definitely means 'this is for you'. And as such, you behave accordingly – by responding to the email, for example. If your name is in the 'Cc' line, however, it means 'heads up or FYI'. After you read the email, you might chime in with a response, or not. Either option is acceptable. But if your name is in the 'Bcc' line, then the message is clear – 'Ooh, watch this! It is gonna be good.' This email is not really for you, but I the sender am letting you know that something is going on. You definitely will not respond to the email, because you would be disclosing a secret. The placement changes everything.

Marketers can exploit this notion of placement, therefore, with purposeful design of the placement of marketing vehicles within the marketing context. Think billboard advertisements, those ubiquitous marketing communications which appear in high-traffic areas of many major cities. For many people, these are irksome and so, more often than not, they are completely ignored – and consequently are ineffective in terms of marketing spend. IBM's recent campaign to make 'smarter cities', however, leveraged the placement of its billboards in order to catch the attention of passers-by, to reduce their negative sentiment and ultimately to reinforce the core marketing message that IBM technology can help make smarter cities. So that which was once a flat billboard on the side of a building can become a shelter from the rain or a seat for the weary (see Figure 4.3). Placement matters.

Figure 4.3. IBM Smarter Cities Billboards

Nuances: The Condition Set by the Cultural Backdrop

In January 1964, Bobby Vinton's rendition of 'There! I've Said It Again' reached Number One on the Billboard 100, remaining at the top spot for four weeks. Vinton's velvety voice captured the sonic silhouette of contemporary American society at the time – at least until four lads from Liverpool disrupted it with their raw energy, cheekiness and, well, hair. Indeed, that February, The Beatles' 'I Want To Hold Your Hand' rocketed to Number One, usurping Vinton and changing society forever.

The shock that was The Beatles, however, was for many, er, shocking. The *Chicago Tribune* quipped that "The Beatles must be a huge joke, a wacky gag, a gigantic put-on." Ditto the *Boston Globe*: "The Beatles are not merely awful; I would consider it sacrilegious to say anything less than that they are god awful." Even Elvis chimed in, lamenting that "The Beatles laid the groundwork for many of the problems we are having with young people today by their filthy unkempt appearances and suggestive music." How could they have missed something which would become so salient in society at that time – and in decades to come? The answer is obvious to us – that predicting societal change requires an intimate understanding of culture. Indeed, the marketing context also serves as a cultural backdrop whose nuances influence behaviour.

'Culture' is one of those words that is often bandied about but seldom understood. This is not surprising, considering both the intangible nature of culture and the word's relatively loose quotidian use in colloquial language. Indeed, people talk about culture all the time, dropping the term alongside media, pop and celebrity. Or consider the way in which recruiters tout their fun or familial office culture – which usually simply means having a foosball table in the kitchen or offering summer Friday gatherings. Despite the prevalence of culture and conversations thereof, there is a broad deficiency in our ability to talk about culture in a sophisticated manner.

More concretely, therefore, anthropologists define culture as the amalgam of four elements of a society: beliefs (values and principles), artefacts (tools, clothing, music, poetry, etc.), behaviours (norms and rituals) and language (lexicon, dialect, vernacular). This makes sense intuitively when you think of culture as it pertains to a nation. But perhaps less intuitively, culture also applies to societal sub-groups – micro-cultures. Consider yoga enthusiasts, for example, who share a common set of beliefs about yoga, yogis and other derivative terms; who have similar artefacts like yoga mats and yoga pants; whose behaviours (dietary routines) overlap; and who use the same language ('namaste' and the 'downward dog').

These four elements have a normative effect on people: they serve as unspoken rules which keep members of a society in lockstep. That is to say, in order to remain as members in good standing in society, people adopt the societal beliefs, don the artefacts, adhere to the behaviours and use the language, the ultimate purpose (and outcome) of which is to be 'normal'.

And of course, these cultural elements and their normalising effects manifest themselves in both the physical and digital worlds – in both offline and online marketing contexts. In Facebook, for example, it is perfectly acceptable for people to post anything and everything under the sun: yesterday's evening snack, the movie which they are currently watching or the horrible rash which suddenly appeared. Any of these posts, however, would be unacceptable in LinkedIn, whose beliefs, artefacts, behaviours and language are 'controlled' by different societal norms. Notably, although in many cases the same people who post on Facebook also 'reside' on LinkedIn, they are able to code switch in order to abide by the cultural norms of the different online societies.

It ought to be obvious, therefore, that understanding a society, and subsequently predicting changes in it, requires a sensitivity to the nuances of these four elements. This sensitivity, however, implies intimacy – something which is natural if you are a member of the society, but which is limited or altogether lacking when you are an outsider, a stranger, an alien. Herein lays the challenge but also the opportunity for marketers – with an understanding of the cultural nuances of a society, marketers can design marketing vehicles in subtle ways which align and resonate with societal norms.

A good example of this in practice centres on the notion of 'first-world problems', the term which is given to things about which people in wealthier countries complain, but which only people of privilege would see as an annoyance or inconvenience. You know, when your phone charger will not reach your bed, for example, or when you ask for no pickles but your hamburger still comes with pickles. Twitter, which is to some degree a measure or mirror of the cultural zeitgeist, is replete with these absurdities, many of which are punctuated with the hashtag #FirstWorldProblems.

As benign as these grumblings might be on the surface, they become increasingly uncomfortable for the privileged people when they are juxtaposed with the disparity of wealth across the globe. The WATERisLIFE organisation, a non-profit entity whose mission is to provide clean drinking water to under-privileged communities, leveraged this cultural nuance in a campaign which enlisted victims of the horrific 2010 Haitian earthquake to recite some of the most ridiculous #FirstWorldProblem tweets. Imagine a young man, for example, standing in front of a dilapidated, tin-roofed shack saying, "I hate it when my house is so big I need two wireless routers". The contrast between the cultural lexicon which is used in the advertisement and the young man's living conditions is so striking that viewers cannot help but question the degree to which they take things for granted. The WATERisLife advertisement was viewed more than eight million times.

Jerome McCarthy

In his classic 1960 book, *Basic Marketing: A Managerial Approach*, Jerome McCarthy introduced the now-famous four 'P's framework: product, price, place and promotion. The idea was simple – that marketers, when going to market, must manage these four elements. Over time, the four 'P's became known as the marketing mix, intimating that marketers, like cooks, have four ingredients to mix together in their commercial (culinary) concoction. Some marketers also use the term 'controllables', referring to the four 'P's as the levers which marketers can pull when going to market. We have come to think of the four 'P's as a company's performance on the (front) stage, which demarcates marketing very clearly from the other functions of the company (accounting, finance and human resources, for example) which occur in the company's backstage, away from the customer's eyes.

The secondary benefit of treating the four 'P's as the performance on the (front) stage, is that it also points to the stage itself as a controllable feature of marketing. That is to say, this theatrical metaphor emphasises that marketers can control both the four 'P's and the marketing context. In this chapter we have argued that this marketing context is comprised of four conditions: 1. defaults – the pre-established factors in a digital space; 2. the semiotics (the meanings) of digital 'signs and symbols'; 3. The placement, or spatial arrangement, in a digital space; and 4. cultural nuances in the digital marketing context. Understanding these conditions enables marketers to design marketing contexts in order to influence people toward desired cognitive, affective and behavioural outcomes.

References

de Saussure, F. (1966) *Course in General Linguistics*. Translated by W. Baskin. New York, USA: McGraw Hill Books.

Johnson, E., and D. Goldstein (2004) "Defaults and Donation Decisions." *Transplantation*, Vol. 78, pp.1,713–16.

About the Authors

Marcus Collins is a culturally curious thinker with an affinity for understanding the cognitive drivers and environmental factors which impact human behaviour. He is a Golden Apple Award nominated faculty member at the Ross School of Business at the University of Michigan and leads the Social Engagement practice at Doner Advertising. Marcus was recognised as one of *Ad Age*'s 2016 '40 Under 40' bright young minds who are reinventing and reshaping marketing's future. He is a proud Detroit native, loving father and devoted husband. Learn more at www.marctothec. com.

John Branch is Clinical Assistant Professor of Business Administration at the Stephen M. Ross School of Business and Faculty Associate at the Center for Russian, East European and European Studies, both of the University of Michigan. John is also Visiting Fellow at Wolfson College, University of Cambridge in Cambridge, England. John recently finished a second doctoral degree, his dissertation of which focused on international higher education. In his spare time, John enjoys woodworking and restoring antique sports cars. Contact him on email at jdbranch@umich.edu.

Chapter 5

Marketing as a Service

Jon Bond

Introduction

People love to buy. They just hate being sold. Having grown up in the advertising business, I often heard about the dreaded huckster image of the classic man in the grey flannel suit, always trying to sell something but with truth and integrity being 'optional'. Every couple of years, studies come out showing advertising as one of the least trusted occupations. It is not a coincidence that advertising and used car and insurance salespeople are often seen in the same light. Management consultants, art gallery owners and even department store salespeople are also in the business of selling, but are not marked by the reputation of distrust. Let us examine the five roots of the problem.

1. The Cold Call

When a seller first reaches a prospective buyer without an invitation, there is a high probability that the buyer will not be in the market for the seller's product at that precise time. Thus, the query is often seen as an annoyance or intrusion. Compare this seller–buyer interaction with the situation when you walk into a store of your own volition and are greeted by a salesperson asking politely to assist you. Obviously, the latter demonstrates a completely different type of buyer–seller relationship.

One of the worst experiences for any prospective buyer is being cold-called at home during dinner. This kind of intrusion has sparked legislative action and is a major reason why the 'Do Not Call' list was created. Now consider advertising. Is having your favourite TV show interrupted by an advertisement for a product in which you have no interest nothing more than an electronic cold call? It is no surprise, therefore, that most people do not like advertising – or its practitioners. Likewise, it is no surprise that advertisements often have little impact on consumers.

2. Trust

Another factor in determining the nature of the seller–buyer dynamic is the perceived trustworthiness of the seller – a notion which is sometimes referred to as 'source credibility'. When people read a neutral party's review or recommendation, they are more likely to believe the message. Sellers who represent a vast range of products are able to take on the role of objective 'consultant', as compared to sellers with only one product. Indeed, it is much easier to play the consultant role, matching products, budgets and a range of other variables to buyers' specific needs. It is more difficult, in contrast, to become the 'trusted advisor' who is perceived to have the buyer's best interests in mind. This is why influencer marketing is an important part of the modern marketing mix – especially for large companies. The ever-growing number of YouTube millionaires is testament to the perceived trustworthiness of these influencers – whose credibility is considered more authentic than the sellers or the companies whom they represent.

3. Repeat Buyers

The holy grail of marketing is sometimes said to be repeat purchases. Indeed, the Pareto principle suggests that 80% of a company's revenue is generated by 20% of its customers. Many start-ups look at customer lifetime value as the most critical factor in their growth formulas. If the relationship is transactional (one-time), as opposed to a long-term relationship, then seller behaviours might become more self-serving, because there is little opportunity for repeat sales. Creating mechanisms and relationships which foster repeat buyers is the heart of marketing communication and seller–buyer dynamics.

4. Shared Risk

Another important element between seller and buyers is alignment of agendas. We all saw the results in 2008 when Wall Street and consumer interests were not aligned. When sellers, however, show that they have 'skin in the game' it fosters trust. People tend to be self-interested, and so buyers appreciate when those interests are aligned with their own. I once did a successful campaign for Neuberger and Berman funds which revealed that the partners had invested their own money in the company's funds, suggesting that they had as much to lose as their buyers.

5. Control

Consumers want to decide what to buy, when to buy, where to buy, how much to spend and when it gets delivered. That is why Internet e-commerce is still growing so quickly: it offers the ultimate in control.

When buyers believe that they are in control, they do not feel like they are being 'sold'. When customers are online, the expectation of control is what makes the practice of retargeting offensive to them. Retargeting allows advertisers to follow a consumer journey through cyberspace with tag-along advertisements. We have all experienced those advertisements which seem to pop up on any website we are visiting.

A great example of the power of control is the airline business. When there is complete pricing transparency online, you inevitably book the least-expensive flight you can find. But after boarding, you have no problem being charged 8 USD for a magazine or a movie because it is your choice whether or not to buy. Had the wine or snack been added to the ticket price, you might not have bought the ticket.

The opposite of control is captive marketing, whereby people have no choice but to be exposed to your messaging. That is the basic idea behind many practices in traditional marketing, and it still dominates the mindset among many marketers today. But the number of captive marketing occasions is declining quickly and exposure to marketing messages is becoming a voluntary act, not a given.

The age of marketing as a service is upon us. The best companies are already embracing the concept that marketing can and ought to have intrinsic value beyond its role of overt selling. Or, as my wife puts it, "You must give to get." Consider AEP, a power company in the mid-western United States. AEP delivers to all its customers a customised dashboard which tracks the energy efficiency of their respective households and provides suggestions for how to optimise consumption. AEP delivers these additional services which can help customers solve 'problems'. It is about being helpful, not overtly selling – and it is the best way to sell because buyers do not feel annoyed or infringed upon.

The Origins of the Mass-marketing Mindset

The rise of mass marketing as we know it coalesced as a perfect storm of events after WWII: mass demand for goods and services, mass production, mass distribution through our new national highway system and, the ultimate mass medium, television. Mass advertising in this environment was so effective that P&G called its marketing department the advertising department – but it might as well have called it the television department. The Mad Men series captured this era of marketing well because it highlights that, with only three television channels, there was not much in the way of sophisticated targeting.

In the decades when families gathered around the television set, almost everyone saw every campaign, whether or not they were part of the target audience. This created some very iconic brands, not to mention slogans which virtually everyone knew by heart. Advertising was excellent at generating large-scale awareness and that was all it took in those days when category growth was a given.

Consumers understood the deal which they had made with the television channels. They received free programming and all that was required in return was to suffer through a slew of nightly advertisements for products, some of which they had no interest in buying. Eventually, some of the advertising agencies developed advertisements which were at least entertaining and made the brands a bit more 'likeable'. But the problem of how exactly to create deep brand relevance and loyalty continued on until at least the 1980s, when cable television emerged.

Cable television really meant choice for consumers. Indeed, channels began catering to specific audiences by creating specialised content targeted at them. Consequently, one would think that the lowest-common-denominator approach to advertising would transform into highly targeted messaging. But instead of viewing this as an opportunity, most advertisers described it as a problem, dubbing it 'media fragmentation'. And subsequently, advertising reach became the name of the game. Two things followed:

1. The idea of multiple segments for a single brand emerged, and

2. Costs increased as advertisers created multiple advertisements for different audiences.

Agencies made a fortune in those days, however, running a single advertisement repeatedly whilst collecting the full 15% commission with each spot.

By the 2000s, however, media fragmentation morphed into an opportunity, as more and more advertisers begin to view these narrower audiences in terms of effectiveness rather than efficiency. Technology made micro-segmentation more feasible, the inevitable goal of which is 'segments of one'. And this extreme personalisation has reframed marketing in the eyes of the consumer from an unwanted intrusion to a valued service which allows customised offerings – what people want, when they want it, where they want and so on.

Perhaps more importantly, with this new version of marketing, consumers might start to identify it not as an annoyance but as helpful, because it does not waste their time or infringe on their attention with messaging which they have no interest in seeing. I predict that some forms of marketing will be considered so valuable that consumers will actually pay for it. It might be argued that this is already happening because people are 'paying' with their attention for the many email newsletters and push notifications which they opt into and accept.

We all know Amazon's recommendation engine, which makes recommendations based on your behaviours and the behaviours of other buyers. Of course, this is marketing, although it appears as friendly advice – the kind of service which a store clerk at a local bookstore might have made in years gone by. Amazon derives these insights from cold hard data based on consumer actions. The recommendation engine does not come from qualitative attitudes or responses to inane survey questions, but actual behaviours which mirror buyers' interests.

The more a customer interacts with Amazon, the more data it acquires and the more accurate its predictions become. This is how its marketing acts more and more like a valued service, and why many people are not bothered by the recommendations and, more importantly, why they have become so integral to the Amazon shopping experience. The sophisticated customer profiles take years to construct and consequently make imitation very difficult for other online retailers.

To me, there is one more secret to the success of Amazon's recommendation engine – transparency. Amazon not only makes recommendations, but it also states very clearly why it makes the recommendations. This is one of the ultimate trust-builders because its users are shown what is behind the wizard's curtain. And as users experience the recommendation engine more and more, they will accept that it will not always be perfect. Consequently, if you were buying a book for your twelve-year-old niece and Amazon began recommending all kinds of Nancy Drew books, you might forgive it for the poor assumption because it 'told' you why it made the recommendation.

Additionally, these kinds of recommendations do not look like marketing, so your anti-marketing radar does not automatically screen them out. Many users probably even swear by the Amazon experience due to the five seller–buyer dynamics which it counteracts. This is the long-term relationship from which both Amazon and the buyer benefit. The transparency of the suggestions is perceived and accepted as objective – and voilà, Amazon is now a trusted advisor and marketing is seen as a helpful service.

Amazon does not develop these recommendations by accident. It is highly committed to testing the recommendation engine, running thousands of experiments every year in order to identify what works. It is interesting to me that its recommendation engine seems to mirror the role of the traditional bookstore clerk, who interacted with customers, thereby building an understanding of their likes and dislikes.

Amazon uses the great data-based insights from its users' website visits along with a type of artificial intelligence, which, at some point, will rival that of humans. And the majority of the public will not be able to distinguish between machine-based marketing and human-originated marketing. This era is in its infancy and there are already many companies harnessing AI to 'design' more efficient marketing campaigns, perhaps rendering high-priced advertising account executives jobless.

The Era of Awareness Has Been Replaced by the Era of 'Brandom'

Like seemingly everything in life, marketing continues to evolve. The era of Mad Men and brand awareness was about carving out a swath of 30 million people and then trying to understand what this mass had in common. In marketing parlance, this was called an 'insight' and it led marketers to create messages which would appeal to all 30 million people. This evolved into a new problem, however – trying to know if consumers liked or loved a brand. Recall those few years when Facebook was growing exponentially. Every user was chasing 'likes', assuming that each new like somehow added value to your Facebook page.

The problem with like (as opposed to love) is promiscuity. Indeed, 'likers' will move from one brand to another, often with nothing more than a few cents discount as the incentive. This led to companies such as Groupon which present multiple offers of savings, thereby giving consumers the feeling that they are more in control of the buyer–seller dynamics. Groupon was able to also show a shared risk to buyers because, if the deal did not meet certain sales levels, it was retracted. Simultaneously, objectivity was shown via social proof – star ratings and the number of offers purchased are visible as you scroll through the multitude of deals.

Today marketers must forget awareness and focus instead on the bottom of the funnel – those people who truly love the brand, who love it enough to continue buying for the next five-to-ten years, and who love it enough that they recommend it to their friends – who are likely to buy it many times over. In this sense, modern marketing is more like a cult. Marketers are no longer focusing on the Pareto rule of 80:20. It is more like a 95:5 rule because social media creates a network effect in which a brand advocate can also be an influencer reaching a number of other prospects efficiently. Influencers are three-to-five times more effective than advertising, plus this influence has the double benefit of being free (versus paid media) and more convincing.

Today, there is a war brewing among companies to seduce these powerful brand influencers. Even influencers with small followings are treated like royalty with all kinds of perks, special access to events and so on. And the public perceives this influence as authentic and objective. Talk about a complete flip from marketing as an intrusion on a favourite TV show!

With influencer marketing, the followers celebrate marketing. "Hooray, it's more information from BMW!" I believe, however, that the practice of buying these influencers will decline, in favour of a more authentic strategy which relies on true brand advocates. They will then be armed with inside brand knowledge which they can impart to their fans and followers. This is more similar to how companies, especially those in technological industries, invite journalists to open days and tour them around the company offices and factories. While the visits are scripted to show the best things about the company to the journalists, it appears authentic and objective because the journalists can write what they deem to be the story at the end of trip. The risk here is that the journalists might write a bad story about the company – or no story at all.

For decades, marketers have worked under the assumption that the purchase funnel moves in only one direction – top down. But the truth might be that the more powerful direction is from the bottom up, whereby the brand advocates recruit prospects and turn them into customers via the age-old dynamic of word of mouth. Today, when you say 'word of mouth', everyone instantly thinks of social media, the electronic form. But 95% of conversations about brands still take place offline. Media have always been social. But Internet-based social media have made word of mouth more obvious, more visible and most importantly, more measurable.

The issue is that most companies still start at the top of the purchase funnel, pushing messages to people who know and care little about the brand. Those people will not become interested in the brand until someone they know and trust tells them they ought to become interested. This is a reason that focus groups do not work very well. They are usually comprised of followers, rarely the influencers or early adopters. Twelve housewives, for example, cannot tell you if they will buy your new vodka; the stylish crowd ordering at a bar share that message without saying a word. This is why visual media like Instagram and Facebook can lead people down the buying funnel through slick images and short videos.

Influencers are a fickle lot, however. Recruiting these apostles requires work. It often means offering them services which they value more than cash. I call this the non-monetary value exchange, because it involves a trade between the brand (which has several brand assets that can be of value to an influencer) and the influencer. Influencers are in the business of serving their own audience and are sensitive to being seen as shills for brands. It is best to provide them with non-commercial assets which charm and delight their own audiences.

One of my favourite stories showcasing this non-commercial approach involved a tweet from a blogger who was boarding a plane in Miami for Newark. As a joke, he tweeted that he wished there would be a Morton's steak waiting for him when he landed. Morton's astute social-media team picked up the tweet and quickly arranged to have a man in full tuxedo attire waiting at the gate with a steak. The incident generated millions of impressions for Morton's at the cost of a cab ride and a steak. The most impressive part for me is that Morton's had a team monitoring social media which had the latitude to improvise, in real time, in order to capture a fleeting opportunity.

The One Day When Everyone Loves Advertising

There is one day during the year when the television ratings actually spike when the advertisements appear, when people choose to go to the restroom when the program, rather than the advertisements, is running. That day is Super Bowl Sunday. It is the day when companies launch exciting new products, and turn their agencies loose to develop short little 'epic films' which are meant to entertain groups of people at Super Bowl parties across America. People often discuss and critique the advertisements much more than the actual game itself. The digital run-up to the event can often be the key to success for a specific advertisement. Indeed, a smart digital strategy will treat the advertisement like a blockbuster movie and stagger its 'release' in the same manner as a Hollywood studio.

If your advertisement can target a community which is passionate and digitally savvy, you have a high probability of generating a great deal of earned media from your expensive Super Bowl buy. A great example from a few years back occurred when VW used a Star Wars theme to launch a new model of vehicle. The strategy played to the Star Wars community the way the actual movie franchise does, using teasers and intrigue before the actual showing. The result was the most earned media views of any advertisement in history.

Strategies such as this are becoming the norm and not just for Super Bowl advertisements. Indeed, the foundation of a good advertisement is not just the creative idea, visually engaging content or a good story. More critically, it is the personalisation of the advertising campaign which turns marketing into a service.

Social media thought leader Jay Baer captures it well – "Sell something, and you make a customer. Help someone, and you make a customer for life." The difference is based on being able to identify the pain points of your audience and not only state the benefits of a product, but also underscore how your product is the solution. This is often completed through testimonials and case studies. People have moved beyond the blind acceptance of "four out of five dentists recommend…". They want to see the story of the person who used and benefitted directly from the product. Two stories about the same person might illustrate how personalisation is transforming marketing by helping, not selling.

In the first story, a wine aficionado is strolling the streets of San Francisco. On his smartphone, he looks at a wine site and receives an endless stream of advertisements about wines which he would not even drink for free. In the second story, a wine aficionado is strolling the streets of San Francisco. She receives an alert on her smartphone, informing her that her favourite wine which is produced in limited quantities has just arrived at the wine shop three blocks from her current location.

In the second story, the message is not viewed as marketing, but as a service – one for which she might even be willing to pay. This is because the marketer was able to create a strong profile of her interests and preferences, and subsequently deliver exactly what she wanted to see at the right time and right place. And the technology exists today to create these sorts of experiences for consumers. Marketers need simply to pull it all together to deliver:

- A centralised data source in which to store profiles and which allows marketers to ensure that the person who visited a website is indeed the same person who is now strolling past the wine store on her smartphone;

- A team of data analysts who have the skills to leverage the data which the company collects; and

- Coordination of the media buying, targeting data and creative concepts, so that consumers receive a targeted and seamless (but not endless) stream of messages which are appropriate to their changing circumstances, moods and locations.

Despite the challenges of personalisation, it is proving to be extremely effective. Data giant Merkle recently released a study showing that personalisation delivers the highest ROI of any form of targeting. eMarketer released in April 2017 its forecast estimating that nearly four of every five US digital display dollars will transact programmatically in 2017, totalling 32.56 billion USD. By the end of the forecast period, that share will rise to 84.0%, leaving little doubt that buyers and sellers are continuing to invest in automated advertisement.

Where personalisation becomes a bit more difficult is in the creative unit. Machines today can create an almost infinite variety of versions of a creative execution, but they cannot create concepts. The human cost to create concepts is still relatively high and it takes time.

Even with the increasing efficiency and technological advances, however, after nearly three decades there has still never been a famous banner campaign. Online video promises to be the creative saviour for digital. If not, there is always the hope that VR/AR becomes mainstream, which might lead to some memorable work that could cure us long-term sufferers of banner blindness.

Marketing Might Be Most Effective When It Does Not Look Like Marketing

The ability for marketing to become a service, rather than an intrusion, is becoming more evident. And we are gaining the tools to make this a reality. Consider 'native advertising', for example, a modern version of the 'advertorial' which describes a newspaper or magazine advertisement that gives information about a product in the style of an editorial or objective journalistic article. A whole industry has developed around companies which can generate clicks from eye-catching headlines. Taboola, Outbrain and even Buzzfeed are raking in money by placing sponsored content at the bottom of actual articles.

Native advertising, however, has become controversial. Consumers might not know that the sponsored content is an advertisement. Regulatory bodies have consequently decided that all such advertising must identify itself as advertising, in order to protect the consumer from being deceived.

The idea that advertising ought not to look or feel 'addy' has been around since the creative revolution of the 1960s. Mad Men of that era were not trying to fool anyone into thinking that they were not seeing an advertisement; they were trying to create messages which consumers wanted to look at because it was interesting. Today's more savvy and time-constrained readers can see when campaigns are full of 'addy' clichés. Within seconds, readers can decide that the clichés are not interesting and then ignore them. When marketers make interesting advertisements, they are simply giving consumers a little bit of entertainment value and maybe even teaching them something new. Is that not another version of advertising as a service? Bloggers seem to navigate this grey area between church and state perfectly well, knowing that if they turn into shills for products, their integrity and audience will begin to wane.

What Is Marketing Today?

With the evolution of marketing and our ability to reach consumers – be it through superior recommendation engines, influencers or programmatic media – there are a few other realities which must be integrated in order to help create the end goal of marketing as a service.

The Importance of the CEO

Some of the best 'marketing' does not come from the marketing department. It is admirable if your hiring policies include transgender people, your CEO is a woman and you actively recruit minorities. But today, it is also good marketing. Ben and Jerry's committed itself to social good from the day it launched its eponymous ice-cream brand. It is who Ben and Jerry claim to be as people. This is also what makes it good marketing, even if was unintentional. Amazingly enough, these policies have remained intact a decade after Unilever acquired Ben and Jerry's, clearly demonstrating that the company understands brand equity.

Unbeknownst to many, having an engaging and charismatic leader (CEO) is becoming a key way to stand out and/or connect with consumers. We know and accept that you cannot have everyone love you. And it is not necessary in order to have great success. Brands such as GoPro and DuckCommander (of Duck Dynasty fame) show how a personable CEO need not have the traditional business background, or a commercial personality, in order to build a successful empire. And because today's marketing requires the involvement of the CEO to be effective, it does not appear that any one method of CEO involvement is superior to another. More top leaders are taking to social media and other forms of communication, for example, in order to help spread the gospel about the company's product. The new CEO is comfortable showing who he/she is as a person.

Perhaps the prototype marketing CEO was Steve Jobs. Only he could have held up production of the new iPhone to install expensive, scratch-resistant Gorilla glass. Some still argue whether this was a product necessity or a savvy, strategic marketing move. Companies ought to look for more CEOs to take on this visible role, especially in light of the growing number of successful CEOs such as Jack Ma and AirBnB's founders.

Customer Service

With the modern CEO it is evident that these leaders understand implicitly that customer service ought to be a part of marketing. Bad news travels faster and further than good news. If you need proof, search 'UNITED BREAKS GUITARS' to see the song which an irate customer wrote about his experience with United Airlines, and which reportedly cost the airline 180 million USD – instead of the 1,200 USD it would have cost to replace the broken guitar. If it had handled the issue correctly, the customer might have written a song about how great United was.

It turns out that how you handle negative experiences is more important than the error. If you do a great job admitting the error and make up for it with some kind of reward, customer satisfaction can actually be higher after the error than it was before the error. You do not need to be perfect, just human. In 2011 Brian Chesky, AirBnB's CEO, did not respond in a timely (or appropriate) manner to the company's first viral PR storm. But the honest letter which he sent days later helped, because people saw him as a person who was admitting his error in handling the crisis. Loyalty remained high and the community stayed.

Community – Belonging Is the Ultimate Service

AirBnB is a customer service example which reflects perfectly that companies today would be clever to develop brand communities which are anchored by passionate brand advocates. It is not by chance that AirBnB settled on "belong anywhere" as the original slogan powering the company and its marketing to the community.

If you are lucky enough, like BMW, to have a product that engenders passion in people then it is relatively easy to cultivate community. If, on the other hand, you make t-shirts or mundane products like laundry detergent, it is more difficult – but that is where symbolism comes into play. Marlon Brando all but invented the t-shirt as an icon by tying it into a biker lifestyle in his 1950s film, *The Wild Ones*. Harley Davidson took the image one step further and created a nationwide cult which kept the brand relevant through trying times, even when its product was not very good. You could buy a better motorcycle, but where else could you buy a community which would accept you and give even accountants from New Jersey an instant anti-hero identity?

No-one Loves Goliath

Today, identity is hyper-critical and branding is ever-more important; because of people's shrinking attention span, you must be able to make a mark at the top of the funnel. With the smaller targeted audiences, marketers need to engage successfully. Every brand ought to be thinking of itself as a series of small niche passion brands. This requires the creation of micro-segmenting strategies, sharing aspects of the brand or product which appeal to specific groups. This way, one brand can become hyper-relevant to a broad range of consumers and avoid the 'lowest common denominator' trap, which is a path to mediocrity. Success is now being won when brands build for distinct communities around each line rather than one large faceless entity. No-one loves Goliath.

To be effective, large brands strive to appear small, cultish and above all personal. Bacardi, the number one spirits brand, has a whole campaign around how the family had to overcome obstacles after being kicked out of Cuba. Nike has always operated with a chip on its shoulder. Apple feels in many ways like it could still be run out of Steve Job's garage. It helps to have a purpose bigger than just making money. Regardless of who you are as a company, you cannot conceive of marketing as a service unless you first believe that the brand itself is delivering an important service to the world.

A great example is the way in which BMW uses its Build Your Own car configurator. More than 120 million cars are possible, allowing the consumer to create and own a car which few people have – all from a company which sells hundreds of thousands of automobiles each year. Note the aspects of control and shared risk here, facilitated with an engine which does not create recommendations, but instead indirectly builds them with you.

The configurator experience is now the number one indicator of vehicle purchase from BMW. Digital companies like Amazon, Spotify and Netflix appear to have always appreciated the long tail, but few offline brands have realised how powerful the long tail can be. Stores or car dealerships can only keep so much inventory in stock. But if you can develop a smart 'matching engine' to help people find their passions, you can have thousands and sometimes even millions of SKUs available online. Not only does a matching engine end-up selling a lot of product, but it is viewed by consumers as a fun experience – a perfect example of marketing turned into a service.

Production Becomes Strategic: Do Not Say something, Do Something

Back in the good old days, advertisers made million-dollar television spots which shot in LA; they stayed at Shutters on the beach and they ordered expensive bottles of wine at the end of a long day hanging out with supermodels. What was there to complain about? Nothing.

Today, you need much more content. It is best if you can segment the audience as much as possible and create advertisements for each segment. It is also a good idea to be able to produce timely spots when a real-time opportunity presents itself. A great example of this is Oreo's Super Bowl moment of Dunk in the Dark. But there are numerous other cases in which companies connect with real-time moments.

The myth of large advertising and awareness means that many

people – both marketers and the public – believe that you must produce expensive films. However, more and more advertisers are becoming nimble by having production vertically integrated. Indeed, when advertisers are able to make content cheaply and fast enough to execute the strategy of hyper-relevance, they start to approach marketing as a service.

Since 2015, YouTube has published a 'Playbook' which highlights a Hero, Hub, Hygiene model. The expensive Awareness films are the Hero content. Yet, when companies regardless of size are able to create content which makes their YouTube channel or Facebook posts function as a Hub, they excel. When consumers return to a Hub regularly, you have developed true marketing as a service – giving an audience content value. This content is often mixed with Hygiene content, the more regular or even daily content such as how-to videos, analysis/opinions on trends, recipes, workshops and so forth. Hygiene content is what people search for and thus you have now created a mechanism to build more awareness via search engines.

That is why marketing as a service will be defined more by what a company does for consumers than what it says to them. Marketing in the past was dominated by messaging which agonised over a single word. Now, it is the actions that a company takes which truly demonstrate what they are about. A great case study is Small Business Saturday from American Express, which rewards consumers who shop at small businesses the Saturday following Thanksgiving with a 25 USD discount. American Express could have done an advertisement reminding consumers not to forget their local proprietors during the holiday season, but instead it created a tangible event that even the President of the United States supported with personal tweets.

Let's Get Personal

In conclusion, marketing as a service needs to encompass the variety of elements which were discussed, so that it can truly build trust with consumers and move past the negative sales/huckster image. Over the past few decades, marketing has been evolving away from a mass approach, speaking to millions at a time with lowest-common-denominator messages, to a dizzying array of options which are empower by highly segmented/ targeted methods. Eventually, this evolution will reach its final conclusion, the marketing singularity of segments of one. Put another way, there will be 360-degree personalisation. Any brand which reaches this point sooner will have a huge advantage over its competitors.

About the Author

Jon Bond is one of the advertising and marketing industry's most recognised thought leaders and entrepreneurs. He was co-founder and CEO of Kirshenbaum Bond and Partners (KBP), arguably the original 'word of mouth' agency, which was launched well before social media appeared on the scene. Jon went on to be CEO of Big Fuel (now part of Publicis), one of the world's largest social-media agencies. Currently, Jon is Founder and Chief Tomorroist at TOMORRO\\\. Established in 2012, TOMORRO\\\ is a value accelerator using marketing, innovation and strategic business development to help visionary companies achieve their ambitions. Learn more at www.TOMORROLLC.com.

Chapter 6
Digital Marketing in Emerging Markets

Thamer Ahmad Baazeem

Introduction

Mature markets have become flooded by many goods and services, and consequently companies are increasingly trying to find more sources of income in emerging markets. The estimated growth rate in international trade for 2016 is 50% higher than that for the gross world product, according to the UN (see Chapter 16 by Rocchi and Watson). According to the WTO, emerging markets consume nearly half of the world's energy and hold around 70% of the world's foreign exchange reserves. When we consider the markets' sizes, multiplying average income by their populations will give emerging markets a larger potential for the future than mature markets. Euro-Monitor International claims that the average age of the emerging markets which account for 90% of the global population is under 30. 51% of the Saudi population is less than 39 years old, for example. International companies are trying to utilise the increasing number of young populations in emerging markets. Other advantages in emerging markets, like the low competitive intensity and less strict regulations, have also caught the eyes of big international companies.

Digital marketing, like other forms of marketing, is often considered the province of mature markets. However, the size and potential of emerging markets necessitate that companies must also consider them when developing digital marketing strategies. Many of the marketing strategies in emerging markets normally involve the development of relationships with local partners to create customised solutions for the market, plus the development of local capabilities. Digital marketing strategies can help to ease the entry of the large international companies into emerging markets. For example, we saw recently Amazon's decision to buy the Middle Eastern online shopping platform Souq.com for one billion USD. Digital marketing, however, cannot be applied to emerging markets in the same ways as in mature markets.

Consumers in this era are no longer hostage to the inflated prices of local retailers, because they can buy whatever they want from the producer's website or from any electronic retailer around the world. Nevertheless, there are countries which lack protection for intellectual property, have political instabilities and suffer from government interference and bureaucracy; and these are factors which can lead to consumers possibly losing the product in the mail or in customs, or getting their credit cards hacked. This means emerging markets might have special characteristics which make digital marketing more or less effective. Therefore, discussing issues facing the various aspects of digital marketing in emerging markets will help to enlighten both the different contexts in which these situations arise and how to address them. This kind of discussion will provide some significant insight into improving the applications of digital marketing in emerging markets.

Many agree that the digital revolution influences marketing and consumption in both mature and emerging markets. However, there are many obstacles to successful marketing posed by this phenomenon, and these barriers are larger in emerging markets. Barriers of culture and religion need significant attention from digital marketers. Moreover, because trust is still an issue for digital trading in mature markets, it has by default a bigger effect in the emerging ones. The ways of using information technology in emerging markets have their own uniqueness, so extra effort is required when it comes to the creation and the implementation of digital marketing in such markets. Therefore, the barriers of culture, religion and trust-building, and the way of using information technology, will be illustrated in this chapter. Real-world examples can help clarify the importance of these barriers.

Culture

In traditional marketing strategies, marketers consider cultural variables such as language, values, lifestyles, moral standards and tastes. Digital marketing strategies ought to follow the same path. However, cultural issues can be more sensitive in digital spaces because any error can easily go viral, which often leads to significant problems with brand image and can affect the company's influence within that particular culture. This means that marketers must be more careful when determining which kind of content they provide in their digital marketing tools.

Content in digital marketing always faces problems with language when it is provided in the native tongue of the emerging market, especially when it comes to the usage of nuance and idioms. Even when the content is provided in a global language such as English, digital marketers ought to understand how the content is translated in a particular country.

Another issue facing digital marketers is the use and interpretation of signs and emojis in different cultures. This problem might appear to digital marketers in two manifestations. The first is when they are creating content to be distributed digitally in different parts of the world. The second is when they analyse consumers' reactions towards the content which they created. This means that digital marketers must have a full understanding of how different cultures interpret the same emoji. Additionally, they must consider this matter when they use mainstream Western analytics to understand reactions.

One of the most important cultural values which must be carefully considered when creating digital content for emerging markets is ethnocentrism. Any Western company ought to avoid flaunting its Western roots when developing a digital marketing strategy. This might happen when Western companies decide to use Western imagery in their digital content when targeting emerging markets, for example. This strategy might create a backlash against the company due to a potential misunder-standing that it is trying to impose its Western influence on consumers.

Religion

Religion is one of the key elements of culture (Sood and Nasu, 1995). When thinking about religion in the context of marketing and consumer behaviour, the perception might be that religious norms affect only purchasing decisions and choices that relate to products prohibited for religious reasons. For example, Hinduism prohibits the consumption of beef products, while in Islam, religious norms prohibit gambling. However, the influence of religion on marketing and consumer decision making is an issue far more complex than one which is simply limited to product prohibition or services that are contentious to the religious norms of individuals or communities (Vitell, 2009).

The first online sex shop in a Middle Eastern Islamic society was launched recently. As the business was designed to target Middle Eastern consumers, the owner (an Arab-American entre-preneur) sought approval from Islamic religious leaders (*Daily Mail*, 2013). The business owner was granted authorisation from religious leaders with the condition that no prohibited promotional activities such as images of lingerie-clad models would be allowed. The business owner had to follow certain processes to be permitted in that country, seeking permission from leaders and customising the appearance of the website to follow the religious restrictions. Such processes are unusual in developed countries and members of the target market still held many concerns. Some of these concerns were of a religious nature. Islamic culture views sex as an intimacy reserved for the sanctity of marriage and it is reasonable to deduce that some Muslim consumers were not only uncomfortable with the introduction of an online sex shop within their community, but that they also foresaw some risks.

Firstly, depending on the degree to which individuals commit to Islamic norms, it is probable that the introduction of the online sex shop into a majority Muslim community could cause community members to be concerned about the prohibition of buying sexual products or using such a website. Secondly, potential consumers would be worried that their support for the business might reflect poorly on their reputation or condone such behaviour for other members of the community. The question, therefore, is whether or not international companies must follow the same pattern when developing digital marketing strategies in such a country. To answer the question, deeper research is needed. However, the above story suggests that any digital marketing strategy which is religiously delicate will carry levels of perceived risk for consumers in emerging markets (Garner, 1986; Taylor, 1974). These feelings might then affect consumer decision making and the adoption of products.

Trust Building

A group of investors led by the popular UAE businessman Mohamed Alabbar and Saudi Arabia's Public Investment Fund launched the largest e-commerce platform in the Arab world in November 2016. Named noon.com, the e-commerce platform raised questions in the media and public about how noon.com could build strong trust with consumers, and how it will prove that it is a safe platform for them to order international products.

One of the vital concepts of marketing is maximising relationships with stakeholders in order to sustain equity and grow revenue and profit. Investing in systematic trust-building helps marketers to create and maintain relationships with all kinds of legitimate stakeholders, especially consumers. In the past, international companies focused on listening to the complaints and comments from developed nations, which resulted from legal sources and which were supported by the ease of communications. At the same time, consumers in emerging nations were left for local agents to deal with. Individual consumers in emerging markets previously had no options if they were facing a problem in buying or using a product which had been produced by an international company; they could either not buy the product or complain to unequipped local agents. Nowadays, however, consumers everywhere around the world can speak up and share their experience of any kind of product with nearly everyone in the world. This means that there is a wider number of consumers who are more conscious and empowered, and that they can vote effectively for or against a particular brand. A single consumer in the middle of Africa can create an international digital rally against a company. Therefore, digital marketing must build trust between the company and its customers around the world. But the question is, how?

Although the size of e-commerce in the MENA area exceeded 3.5 billion USD in 2016, Hanaa Alzuhair, the general secretary of the Prince Sultan Fund for Women Development in Saudi Arabia, announced that the fund would sponsor several workshops and campaigns to improve the trust between people and companies on the Internet, and to teach people how to respond to commercial activities on the Internet. Many marketers think about traffic when building digital marketing strategies in emerging markets, following the saying, "where there is traffic, there is hope". However, as argued by Schaefer (2015), traffic will not help a website or a social-media page to predict the success of a company in a particular country. Traffic means customers pass by – and that is it. Instead of focusing on increasing traffic, therefore, marketers can use specific strategies to create trust.

First, companies ought to generate customised content – sort of. It is a bit tricky because companies often choose to follow a global approach, using the same content universally (see Chapter 16 by Rocchi and Watson). The other extreme is for companies to create all-new customised content for emerging markets, in deference to cultural differences. However, the correct path is probably a combination: maintaining a global approach will help consumers see that they are a part of the bigger picture; and having a local touch will give consumers the sense that they are respected, which will in turn make them feel closer to the company. Content must serve as an extension of people's self-identity and ought to make them believe that the company is speaking to them.

Second, it is well known among marketers that education and information-sharing build credibility, visibility and marketability. Building trust through digital marketing, therefore, is key in emerging markets. This means providing valued information far beyond the direct product offering (see Chapter 5 by Bond). International companies can offer value and boost marketing impact by simply sharing educational materials and tips behind their own digital marketing tools. This strategy can be linked to the first strategy, by using local educators who can share their experiences.

Information Systems

For marketers in international companies to apply their global/ customised digital strategies in emerging markets, they need to understand how digital information systems are used in these markets. They must leverage personal contacts and interests to use them for developing strategies. However, the ways of getting this kind of data online differ from country to country. While Facebook is the most popular digital platform for information about people in many Western countries, WeChat is more popular in China. WeChat is a messenger but it is becoming a full social platform, including features which might not be available from other messaging apps: e-payments, taxi hailing, WeShop, plane tickets, bill payments and schedule planning. The availability of different consumer information, therefore, requires different protocols. Also, these different kinds of messaging apps in different countries require international companies to cooperate with them, explaining why international companies have begun to build apps which can be used directly within the messaging app. WeChat users, for example, can create full Microsoft Office documents and share them with their contacts without leaving WeChat.

Conclusion

This chapter argued that marketers must consider some matters differently when they decide to plan and apply digital marketing in emerging markets. The ways of building trust to maximise relationships with customers in emerging markets are, in most cases, unlike those in the West. Focusing on providing customised content and educating consumers with valuable information will help to build solid trust with international companies. Another consideration is that marketers must be more cautious when establishing which kind of content they provide in their digital marketing campaigns when serving emerging markets. They must ensure that there is no conflict with any sort of local cultural elements, especially religion. Likewise, marketers must consider how digital information is used and shared in emerging markets. A popular platform in the West might not be used, or might be banned altogether, in some emerging markets.

References

Daily Mail (2013) "First-Ever Palestinian Sex Shop Opens Online to Spice Up Marriages After Being Given the Go-Ahead by Sheikhs." *Daily Mail*, 7 December. Retrieved from: http://www.dailymail.co.uk/news/article-2519787/First-Palestinian-sex-shop-opens-online-spice-marriages-given-ahead-sheikhs.html

Fletcher, R., and H. Crawford (2014) *International Marketing: An Asia-Pacific Perspective*. Sydney, Australia: Pearson Higher Education.

Garner, S. (1986) "Perceived Risk and Information Sources in Services Purchasing." *Mid-Atlantic Journal of Business*, Vol. 24, Iss. 2, pp.49–58.

Schaefer, M. (2015) *The Content Code: Six Essential Strategies to Ignite Your Content, Your Marketing, and Your Business*. New York, USA: Schaefer Marketing Solutions.

Solomon, M. (2014) *Consumer Behavior: Buying, Having, and Being*. Engelwood Cliffs, USA: Prentice Hall.

Sood, J., and Y. Nasu (1995) "Religiosity and Nationality: An Exploratory Study of Their Effect on Consumer Behavior in Japan and the United States." *Journal of Business Research*, Vol. 34, pp.1–9.

Taylor, J. (1974) "The Role of Risk in Consumer Behavior." *Journal of Marketing*, Vol. 38, pp.54–60.

Vitell, S. (2009) "The Role of Religiosity in Business and Consumer Ethics: A Review of the Literature." *Journal of Business Ethics*, Vol. 90, pp.155–67.

About the Author

Thamer Ahmad Baazeem is Vice Dean of Research and Consulting Institute and Assistant Professor of Marketing at King Abdulaziz University in Jeddah, Saudi Arabia. Thamer also works as a Visitor at the School of Advertising, Marketing and PR in the Queensland University of Technology in Brisbane, Australia. He is also an Executive Consultant at a firm called Um Al-Qura Real-Estate Development in Mecca, Saudi Arabia. Thamer loves academia, but he does not want to stay away from business. Consequently, he presses himself by working on too much research and too many business projects. He has won awards for academic performance and community involvement, the most cherished being recognition as the Volunteer of the Year at Queensland University of Technology in 2015. Thamer is very active on social media. Follow him on Instagram and Snapchat at @tbaazeem, and on Twitter at @drtbaazeem. Contact him on email at tbaazeem@kau.edu.sa.

Chapter 7

The Seven Stages of the Digital Marketing Cycle

Tom van Laer and Ian Lurie

Introduction

Imagine you are shopping for lettuce. You see a sign which reads "Leafy green vegetables" and you enter a large and quite striking farmers' market. You can enter this market through many doorways and inside, several stalls clamour for attention with their bright, perfect fruits and vegetables. Next to each stall are lists of the awards which this market has won for design and layout.

You cannot find lettuce, however. Neither can anyone else. The market has cabbage and kale, but no lettuce. You walk around with other people, trying to find what you want, but to no avail. Worse for the stall owners, people outside are trying to enter the market to buy cabbage and kale, but they cannot, because the lettuce seekers have filled the market. You leave exasperated.

As you leave, you see another sign which reads "Lettuce". You enter a different, less-glamorous market. The products look edible, but they are not shiny and perfect. But you find lettuce, big and small. You find what you want, buy it and leave the market satisfied.

The first market was gleaming and perfect, but you did not buy anything. Instead, you bought from the functional but less-glamorous market. The former market was practising what might be called outbound marketing – accumulating traffic in the hopes of getting lucky with a customer. The latter market, on the contrary, identified you as a potential customer and understood your wants.

Outbound marketing is common but ineffective. Good digital marketing, however, can repair it. This chapter introduces you to a digital marketing cycle (see Figure 7.1) which is used to select an audience and make the most of its attention. The cycle scales well and works for many organisations. Indeed, during the past 20 years, we have seen this cycle generate a return for banks, creative agencies, fast-moving consumer goods companies, railway services, start-ups, telcos and universities (Tom); plus bulletproof-vest manufacturers, dress designers, labour unions, law firms and mom-and-pop businesses (Ian); and consultancies (both Tom and Ian). After reading this chapter, you will:

1. Understand the Internet as a two-way marketing medium to get attention, attract customers and do business;

2. Know what is necessary for a virtuous digital marketing cycle; and

3. Understand the seven stages of the cycle.

Digital Marketing Defined

Digital marketing seems stuck in 'hey-want-a-cheap-watch?' mode – Companies try to get customers to their site, then worry about whether they really want to be there or whether they will buy, or inquire, or vote or anything else. This outbound, accu-mulation-type marketing is not always obvious. It takes other, more subtle forms, such as campaigns which overgeneralise or which are ego-driven. Outbound marketing is not based on selection of potential customers. It is relatively indiscriminate, leaving businesses and customers frustrated. It grows out of broad assumptions about audience and strategy which are both inaccurate and unsubstantiated. As a result, outbound marketing can accumulate high traffic numbers – but fail to generate any useful business.

Typical outbound marketing revolves around a drive to get more traffic, no matter what. Banner ads, email marketing (not spam),

spam, pay-per-click marketing, search marketing, viral marketing – name the method and the majority of marketers uses them as blunt instruments in a get-all-the-traffic-and-hope-for-the-best kind of way. Never mind whether or not the traffic represents qualified potential customers. Never mind the cost of driving useless traffic. Just keep them coming. Everyone – marketing practitioners and scholars alike – is to blame for this. We have all said 'More traffic!' at least once in our careers. In traditional media – print, television, etc. – it made sense to start off with this approach. Yet digital marketing is different, and much more powerful. It is a polite, empirically measurable, two-way conversation in an effort to exchange something. This means that companies can converse with their customers and select traffic rather than accumulate it. The digital marketing cycle is our attempt to demonstrate how companies take advantage of the two-way street and start a real conversation with potential Internet customers.

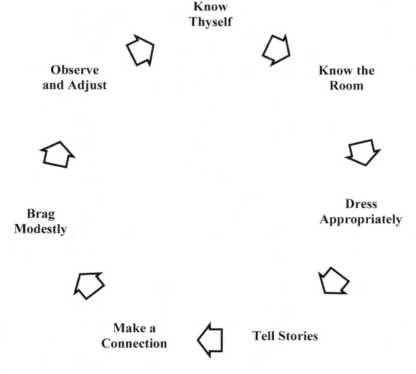

Figure 7.1. The Digital Marketing Cycle

The Digital Marketing Cycle in a Nutshell

The Internet is the only two-way medium outside of a face-to-face meeting, a telephone call or a video conference. That uniqueness makes digital marketing more efficient and profitable, and much, much more complex (Hoffman and Novak, 1996). We have grappled with this idea for twenty years. One of the most common errors which marketers make when marketing on the Internet is to treat it like any other medium. Our digital marketing cycle is a way to address this error because it is a cycle which builds on the view that the Internet allows a dialogue between a company and its audience. Our digital marketing cycle is able to meet age-old marketing challenges on the Internet. It is a methodology which makes use of the changes which are brought about by new, faster, more interactive media, without discarding the basic, sound principles of good communications. It also ties together creative (copy)writing, web design and aspects of web analytics in a way which not only makes sense but provides a blueprint for long-term Internet strategies. It is where the Internet's communications and technical strengths come together that our digital marketing cycle really takes root. Companies which have used our cycle to good effect generally 1. have a story to tell, 2. are ready to commit for the long term and 3. know their limitations.

A conversation is, at a minimum, a two-way exchange of information – someone talks, someone else listens and responds. The first person hears the response and answers accordingly, the second person does the same and so on, until the conversation concludes. Marketing in traditional media is not a conversation. Information is delivered, but there is no observe-and-respond cycle. Companies cannot quickly adjust to their audience's needs, wants or approval/disapproval of their initial message. Considering digital marketing, marketers deliver a message to their audience via a website, advertisement on another website, or email marketing piece. Customers see the message and companies know that they see it because marketers can measure 'views'. Customers click on the advertisement, a link in the email, or click deeper into the company's site, and companies know that, because marketers can also measure it. Then customers do or do not take the action which companies want them to take (buy, join, rent, sign up, etc.) and companies also know that, because marketers can measure it. Marketers can do all of this anonymously, at a fraction of the cost of traditional marketing. Most importantly, marketers can do all of this in real time, so companies can modify the advertisement, landing page or entire website after days, hours or even minutes of beginning a campaign. Marketers deliver a message. The audience responds. Marketers observe and adjust their message accordingly. A conversation occurs. The Internet is the first mass-marketing medium where this level of two-way conversation can occur in a polite, empirically measurable way.

Stage-by-Stage Guide

The digital marketing cycle consists of seven stages, whose narrative entreats marketers 1. to know themselves, 2. to know their audiences, 3. to target these audiences appropriately with 4. engaging stories, 5. to retarget, 6. to brag (modestly) and 7. to observe their audience's responses and adjust accordingly. The following sections outline the digital marketing cycle stage by stage, overviewing specific tools for implementing the cycle.

Know Thyself

To begin, marketers must know what their company is trying to accomplish. Aaker and Smith (2010) suggest five principles for creating goals which help to drive social change. They use the metaphor of a dragonfly, whose four wings work in sync to allow the insect to fly in any direction. The five principles can be remembered by the mnemonic HATCH (Humanistic, Actionable, Testable, Clarity, Happiness).

To create goals which are humanistic, marketers must focus on understanding their audience rather than making assumptions about quick solutions. Companies including General Electric and Procter and Gamble have replaced the segmentation, targeting and positioning model with a more effective, human-centred approach to goal setting which places more emphasis on understanding consumers as individuals (Cayla and Arnould, 2013).

To create goals which are actionable, marketers must use short-term tactical micro goals to achieve long-term macro goals. A macro goal is a long-term goal which identifies the problem – the 'gap' which marketers intend to close (Aaker and Smith, 2010). A micro goal is actionable, small and measurable (Fogg, 2009). Whereas a *know thyself* stage of only macro goals quickly becomes overwhelming (Bandura and Cervone, 1983; Thaler and Sunstein, 2009), a *know thyself* stage which breaks down macro goals into tactical micro goals is encouraging (Liberman and Trope, 1998; Seijts and Latham, 2001).

To create goals which are testable, marketers must identify metrics which help evaluate their progress and inform their actions. They must establish deadlines (Ariely and Wertenbroch, 2002) and celebrate small wins along the way (Bandura and Cervone, 1983). Testable goals combine the *know thyself* stage with the *observe and adjust* stage, which leads to a virtuous digital marketing cycle.

To create goals which are clear, marketers must increase their odds of success and generate momentum. They must not overtax their prefrontal cortex (Muraven, Collins and Neinhaus, 2002). To create goals which ensure happiness, both marketers and their audience must find them meaningful. Goals which are based on personal interests and values are achieved more often because they continually energise people and help them stay more focused (Koestner et al., 2002).

Marketers' goals change while they plan and even after they launch their digital marketing cycle. However, the cycle is flexible and is meant to be adapted after marketers get started. They must meet some basic criteria for a virtuous cycle. To make sure that those criteria are reasonable, marketers need all HATCH components to focus on the cycle (Aaker and Smith, 2010). If one or more is missing or deficient, their task is that much more difficult and they might not achieve a virtuous digital marketing cycle.

Know the Room

When people arrive at an event, the next thing they do is look around to see if they know anyone. To *know the room*, by trying to learn the nature of the audience with whom the company converses, is also a good idea on the Internet (Van Laer et al., 2013). Marketers' audiences are the groups with which they are trying to communicate and which they are trying to persuade. Awareness of audience requires awareness of:

1. Personas (the attributes which define an audience)

2. Workflow (the way the audience is most likely to move through the site) and

3. Calls to action (the places in that workflow where marketers want the audience to take some specific action, such as download a white paper, sign up, or purchase).

First, marketers must understand who is using their site. If the goal is to create a product which satisfies a broad audience, logic tells us to make it as broad in its functionality as possible to accommodate the most people. As Bond argues in Chapter 5, however, this logic is incorrect in digital marketing. Digital marketers have more success by designing for singular people. To do that, they create definitions of the different typical consumers. These definitions are called personas. Cooper (2004) was the first to coin the notion of personas in a digital context.

To define a persona, marketers can use many different resources which are beyond the scope of this chapter. But after marketers have collected data about customers, they can build the personas. They ought to expect to have two or three different personas on a particular project. Few organisations have only one and, if they find more than three, they need to re-examine the goals of their cycle – in twenty years we have never seen a website cater to more than three distinct groups successfully.

Although satisfying the customer is marketing's objective, the term 'customer' causes trouble. Its imprecision makes it unusable. 'Customer' reads as 'elastic customer'. The elastic customer must bend and stretch and adapt to the needs of the moment. However, marketers' objective is to design a cycle which bends and stretches and adapts to the customer's needs. Designing for the elastic customer gives marketers licence to do as they please while paying lip service to the 'customer'. Real customers, however, are not elastic. A virtuous digital marketing cycle does not refer to the 'customer'. Instead, it refers to a specific individual... a specific, hypothetical, precise persona.

The more specific marketers make their personas, the more effective they are as marketing tools. For example, marketers ought to give a persona a name, a face and a job. Thus, identifiability is the property which a persona must satisfy, such that marketers understand the experience of the persona by knowing and feeling the world in the same way (Escalas and Stern, 2003). The central focus of persona creation is on believability and not on diversity (Bal, Butterman and Bakker, 2011).

Many scholars and practitioners alike, with a reverence for the empirical, confuse real customers with hypothetical, archetypical (more valuable) personas. One real customer might be (in)capable of controlling the software, whereas the majority of other customers can(not). A persona, therefore, ought to be representative.

As a digital marketing tool, it is more important that a persona be precise than accurate. In the interest of being precise in the definition of personas, averages must be ruled out. A customer might on average have 2.3 children, but not a single customer actually has 2.3 children.

Marketers need not *know the room* perfectly right away. It is a digital marketing cycle, so marketers can learn more about their audience later and act on what they have learned.

Second, marketers must determine a model for how each persona might use the site. They can do that using workflows. A workflow is a simple, common-sense map which describes how a persona moves through a website – it might include a single visit, but typically spans several, and ends with some desired conclusion.

A workflow might be a simple list, a flowchart or a mind map. Typically, marketers use flowcharts (also known as swimming-lane diagrams) which they can later combine to show all personas together. The workflow is not necessarily web-centric – many actions might not take place on the website. It need not end with a purchase. Upgrades and accessories keep the digital marketing cycle going.

Third, now that marketers know who is using their site and have sketched out how these people use it, the final step in knowing the room is understanding where opportunities exist in this process to help potential consumers move forward in their decision making, even if they are just trying to persuade them to sign up for a newsletter or to download a document. The possibilities of what marketers are trying to persuade consumers to do are endless. 'Buy this' is only one, narrow message. 'Elect me', 'sign up for our newsletter', 'have another look', 'download our white paper' and 'take a test drive' are also valid calls. Marketers ought to consider their call to action carefully.

Typically, marketers have several different calls to action. If, for example, they sell something, the ideal call to action is 'make a purchase'. However, their audience can take other actions which lead to a good outcome. Consumers could sign up for their newsletter, order a free sample or tell a friend about their product. A virtuous digital marketing cycle does not depend on consumers to take the best possible action the first time they visit the site. Instead, it gives them options which escalate to that best action.

To identify their calls to action, marketers might think about what they would do upon first visiting their site. They might make an ordered list or a flowchart of the actions which a consumer takes, up to the best possible action. This can be the most difficult part of knowing the room. A call to action is legitimate if:

1. The call to action addresses a need of one or more personas

2. The call to action presents an opportunity to measure audience response or

3. Answering that call to action means a persona does something which marketers seek.

Dress Appropriately

If people know their audience, they can wear the right clothes to an event. People do not wear a ripped T-shirt to a black-tie dinner or a tuxedo to a football game. Marketers must also make sure they *dress appropriately*. 'Dress', in this case, means the appearance of their website. 'Appropriately' means catering to and delivering an experience which is designed expressly for the audience. 'Appropriately' does not necessarily mean cool. Digital marketing is a communications contest, not a design competition.

This stage is as much about what not to do as it is about what marketers ought to do. Design is an exercise in avoiding pitfalls just as it is a creative act. This section is not an attempt to set broad boundaries for what constitutes good or bad web design. It is written to make marketers educated judges of good versus bad design in the context of the digital marketing cycle – good being a design which connects with an intended audience quickly and which ushers them into a virtuous cycle; and bad being a design which either fails to make that connection or actually breaks it. Practising audience-focused design leads to a virtuous digital marketing cycle. Real-life conversations are painful when one person ignores the other's (dis)likes and the digital marketing cycle is no different.

By this time in the digital marketing cycle, marketers have (hopefully) put a lot of time into knowing the room. They have pondered their audiences, considered calls to action, mapped out workflows and generally tied themselves up in knots trying to anticipate the who, how and why of their digital marketing cycle. But now they can put that to work by creating a look which appeals to the personas which were created in the *know the room* stage, thereby making it easy for them to use the website. By doing so, marketers ensure that the digital marketing cycle is virtuous. A website's look and feel is not about what marketers like. The objective of this stage is to get consumers to stay just long enough to start reading or viewing the message – no more, no less. What they see first, therefore, must evoke the correct response.

In any conversation, first impressions matter – at an event and in digital marketing. At an event, people are more likely to talk to people whom they expect to be good conversationalists. Within the first ten seconds after consumers arrive at a website, they make a near-instant decision as to whether it has what they need

(Nielsen and Budiu, 2013). Most consumers process elements of the site's design in this order: 1. colours, 2. textures and effects, 3. typefaces, 4. complexity and 5. layout and positioning.

First, people react in certain ways to certain colours. Nothing starts or stops a conversation faster than a bright green shirt. The same goes for a website. These are all value judgments – different cultures interpret colours in different ways (Gage, 2000). When consumers arrive at a website, colour typically is the first to evoke a response. Whether they see a splash of red in a photograph or the background colour used in the overall layout, that first bit of colour drives their experience. So marketers must select colours carefully. Note usability: 8% of the male (versus 0.5% of the female) population has a form of shade blindness which makes it difficult for them to see, for example, blue text on a red background. Many sites have this colour scheme.

Second, texturing and effects have their place even if many designers and marketers turn their noses up at the idea of a drop shadow (Savage and Hartmann, 2011). Some examples of effects are: bevelling, shine, drop shadow, gradient fills and rounded corners. Used correctly, texturing and effects can help emphasise a point, isolate a message or make a website more usable. But marketers ought to have a good reason to use any kind of effect in a website. Textures and effects must make sense. Used in combination with different colours, effects can elicit subtle or strong responses. Effects ought to help consumers get the point, but not be the point. If a button or effect is not helping to keep the digital marketing cycle going, marketers ought to get rid of it.

Third, type and typesetting are a critical part of dressing appropriately. Consumers who have now arrived at the site have, in the first seconds, processed the colours and textures which the marketers used. Now they will see if there is anything worth reading. They are not reading it yet, but their eyes are tracking the page, looking for cues and calls to action. Choosing fonts is like deciding whether to speak loudly or softly, quickly or slowly, with small or big words. This choice is fundamental to the digital marketing cycle. Fonts are not just for reading. They are shapes and lines which can generate as strong a response as splotches of colour. Their application to a page can have similar implications for a site.

In any conversation, the way people present their words is important. In digital marketing it is crucial because it sets the tone for the entire digital marketing cycle. Using the incorrect font or overusing a text effect is like showing up at a beach party in a suit. Typefaces are an art form, however. Offering a complete primer on typesetting is beyond the scope of this chapter, but Zeldman (2016) sets out the typographical principles.

Fourth, complex information is carefully considered if three conditions are satisfied:

1. High levels of ability and competence – that consumers ought to be able to weigh the information carefully (Noordman, Vonk and Kempff, 1992);

2. High levels of motivation – that consumers ought to be motivated to weigh the information carefully (Chaiken, 1987; Chaiken, Liberman and Eagly, 1989); and

3. Ample opportunity – that consumers ought to be in a position to weigh the information carefully (Novemsky et al., 2007).

The number of columns, shapes, text blocks, images and other widgets which marketers include on a page pertains to complexity. So does any use of motion graphics, such as Flash. If an audience is less experienced in using the Internet, marketers need to keep matters simple. The same holds true if an audience is looking for convenience – if it is looking to digital marketing to make something easier. If, on the other hand, an audience is made up of experienced Internet users who are looking for lots of information or who are generally tech-savvy, marketers can create a more complex layout and let the audience explore.

Fifth, eye-tracking and mouse-tracking studies show that the occidental eye takes in a page of information in an F-shape or Z-shape, respectively (Nielsen and Norman, 2006). Items at the corners of the page are emphasised. Items at the top and bottom left are the first and last items consumers see when they first scan the page. The top-left corner is the most-viewed, most-studied part of any page. Whereas the most important items do not need to be at the top and bottom left, marketers need to consider what they put there. If they put a bright graphic, boldface type or something which is otherwise an attention grabber in either of those locations, it dominates the page – which is like standing on a podium with a microphone, in conversational terms.

In summary, how a website looks is important. In those crucial first seconds after consumers arrive at the homepage, they want to see something which appeals to them. After marketers have generated that appeal and dressed appropriately, however, they must *tell stories*.

Tell Stories

When you have a conversation with someone who holds your attention, you probably keep listening because:

1. He or she speaks clearly
    (You can understand what he or she is saying. For the digital marketing cycle, this means good architecture and good code.)

2. If he or she spills a drink on you, he or she apologises
    (When these inevitabilities happen, people apologise, fix the problem and move on. For the digital marketing cycle, that is a scantly researched discipline known as 'contingency design'.)

3. He or she has an engaging story to tell.
    (You want to hear what he or she is saying. For the digital marketing cycle, this means good content.)

First, conversations have a certain flow. That flow is not necessarily linear. Although people say hello, talk a bit and then eventually say goodbye, in between, a discussion can meander down many different paths. People tend to jump from one subject to the next, but they often have a goal in mind. A website must treat content in that way. It might all be 'static' information on a page, but consumers move from the homepage to their goal (which might change) in many different ways. Great websites include great information architecture, which is the practice of providing clean, useful, practical routes between pieces of information, with routes anticipating common lines of inquiry.

We assume three basic types of users. *Browsers* want to click through a site, finding what they need by using buttons and doing little typing. *Searchers* want to get to a site, type in a phrase and go directly to the page which they need (or start on a search engine, such as Google and do the same). *Navigators* want to see a site map or other high-level view of a site, find the area which is relevant and go there. A site needs to cater to all three audiences without playing favourites. Structuring content so that an audience gets to pick its own route through it, while at the same time subtly steering it so that the right parts of a message receive emphasis, is the other side of good information architecture.

In digital marketing, good code is also part of how marketers build a virtuous digital marketing cycle. Imagine hearing someone speak who has great ideas but just cannot convey them clearly. Listeners can almost feel the brilliance, but they cannot get at it because of background noise, which is frustrating. If a marketer's site is not coded properly, it may not look right and the cycle will be viciously frustrating. Whether using Google Chrome, Microsoft Edge, Mozilla Firefox or Apple Safari, visiting any website, right-clicking then selecting 'View (Page) Source' on the drop-down menu will reveal the HyperText Markup Language (henceforth HTML) code which makes the page look the way it does. HTML is a language of structure. It lets a webpage designer organise content into paragraphs, tables and so on. It also includes several ways to control how content looks – marketers can control the font, colour and size of text, place images on a page and so forth. People have been trying to improve HTML since the advent of the World Wide Web. It is an imperfect language, particularly when marketers are trying to make an attractive, usable website. For example, HTML forces designers to use tables – originally meant for the presentation of tabular information – as a layout tool. It also often forces designers to use pictures of text, rather than real text. It is easy, then, to build a webpage which looks acceptable in many web browsers, but has a terrible foundation of noncompliant code. Few websites are built on good code. Many print-design or web-design professionals who build websites often cut corners by using a content management system or a visual layout tool (Adobe Dreamweaver or Microsoft Expression Web, for example). After all, consumers do not see the code, so they do not care as long as the webpage looks acceptable.

Marketers ought to care, however. Bad code creates many

problems which can turn a digital marketing cycle into a vicious cycle (Zeldman and Marcotte, 2010). This is largely because marketers have feigned knowledge on a topic. They can probably get away with it for a while, but eventually someone who knows the subject finds them out. It is tough to recover from that kind of gaffe. The same is true if someone visits a website and it appears broken – worse, if a search engine visits the homepage but finds what appears to be an attempt to 'cheat' by tricking the search engine into awarding a higher ranking (see the *brag modestly* stage). It might be an honest coding error, but many engines ban sites attempting to game the system. Good code provides a solid foundation. If marketers use it, everything which they build afterward will be easier. No-one notices good code, just like no-one notices if someone speaks clearly. Good code is a hygiene factor (Herzberg, 1966) and, as a result, a virtuous digital marketing cycle needs it.

Second, a technique called 'contingency design' is essential if marketers want a virtuous digital marketing cycle. If consumers have a miserable customer experience, but walk away smiling, a company most likely will respond with "We are sorry and here is how we experienced it." The company expressed concern and told consumers the story from the company's perspective (Van Laer and de Ruyter, 2010). Marketers can do the same thing on their website, through contingency design – the art of admitting that things go incorrectly, and of figuring out how to apologise, in advance (Linderman and Fried, 2004). Because no web interaction can be perfect, it is up to marketers to help their audiences walk away smiling.

Third and equally important as architecture, code and contingency design, is what people actually see – content (see Chapter 14 by Goldring). It must be crafted to tell an engaging story. Since the Lascaux Caves dwellers first drew on their walls, stories have been universal and ubiquitous. All human cultures have (had) master storytellers at their centre: the Native American shaman, the European troubadour, the West-African griot, the Hindu pundit and the Celtic bard. Stories, such as fairy tales, are also the way consumers make sense of the world from a young age (Bettelheim, 1976). They are sufficiently powerful to serve as vehicles for rendering consumer lives intelligible (Gergen and Gergen, 1988). As Schank (1995, p.115) comments, if marketers want to be truly memorable, they "need to tell someone else a story that describes our experiences because the process of creating the story also creates the memory structure that will contain the gist of the story". The mind is narrative. Stories are the essential building blocks of all human thought. For example, the morning after reading the novel *Pompeii*, participants in a neuroscientific study showed heightened brain connectivity, almost like a muscle memory (Berns et al., 2013). Not surprisingly, stories take centre stage in online content delivery (de Ruyter and van Laer, 2014). Stories are highly engaging and effective content for a virtuous digital marketing cycle if they provide identifiable characters, an imaginable plot and verisimilitude (Van Laer et al., 2014).

A virtuous digital marketing cycle requires good architecture, good code, contingency design and good content. They keep the cycle going, keep it entertaining and steer consumers back on track if their attention wanders.

Make a Connection

Many marketers invest resources to build a website which grabs the attention of consumers. Then they invest more resources to get consumers to their site, in pay-per-click advertisements, search-engine optimisation and so forth. Then they do the online equivalent of walking away. Many consumers who want to learn more need to be reminded of a company's existence and important news. Retargeting comes in there. It is great to meet everyone at an event, but many people also want to talk to each other later on. At an event, people exchange business cards or phone numbers. On the web, the most common way to *make a connection* is email. It is ubiquitous, everyone knows how to use it and it does not depend on consumers coming to find a company. However, retargeting advertisements are also worth mentioning.

First, permission-based email marketing draws subscribers to an email newsletter and actually makes them feel good when marketers send them something (Cheng et al., 2009; Waring and Martinez, 2002). Arguably, though, the first word which pops into people's heads when they hear 'email marketing' is 'spam'. However, not all email marketing is spam. Marketers can use email as a marketing tool and not get tagged as a spammer, if they keep in mind both interpretations of spam: the legal interpretation, with which it is pretty easy to comply, and the emotional interpretation. It is the emotional interpretation for which marketers must take care – consumers are quick to call any email which they feel is either unsolicited or inappropriate 'spam'. It is easy to be perceived as emotional spam, so marketers ought to follow Schiff's (2016) fundamentals for delivering successful permission-based email marketing campaigns. If the email which marketers are planning to send would annoy them or feels like someone on a sidewalk is pushing flyers in people's faces, marketers ought to reconsider. Chances are that they do not engage in a conversation with someone or hand them a business card unless it's for a reason. Making a connection through email ought to follow the same heuristic.

Second, retargeting, also known as remarketing, is a cookie-based technology which uses a JavaScript code to anonymously 'follow' an audience over the web (ReTargeter, 2016). Marketers can place a small, unobtrusive piece of code, sometimes referrered to as a pixel, on their website. The code, or pixel, is unnoticeable to their consumers and does not affect their site's performance. Every time a new consumer comes to their site, the code drops an anonymous browser cookie. Later, when their *cookied* consumers browse the web, the cookie lets their retargeting provider (Facebook, for example) know when to serve advertisements, ensuring that their advertisements are served only to people who have previously visited their site. Retargeting is effective because it focuses marketers' advertising spend on people who are already familiar with the brand and who have recently demonstrated interest.

Whichever way marketers decide to keep the conversation going – email, retargeting ads or something else – they ought to ensure that they live up to expectations. They ought to send subscribers an email when they have important news; update their retargeting ads regularly; record some new audio and post it; and so on. And remember, these people said "Yes, please talk to me!" If marketers do that, the chances are greater that they can stay top of mind and turn consumers into customers. They can also draw people to their website if they *brag modestly*.

Brag Modestly

At an event, a great boost to someone's reputation is having the host introduce him or her as "The person I told you about. You *have* to talk to [him or her]." The host bragged for him or her – that is modest, but still a great boast (Scopelliti et al., 2015). The same technique works well on the Internet. The event is typically a search engine and marketers *brag modestly* by achieving a high natural ranking or by creating a well-composed pay-per-click advertisement. They can start many conversations through search engines. Blogger sponsorship, social media and press releases are, of course, other ways to get people to visit a website. However, most Internet users visit a search engine to find what they want online. Search engines are at the centre of bragging modestly, if marketers are trying to grow their business using the Internet. A digital marketing cycle which works balances paid advertising and natural rankings.

First, search engines typically deliver two sets of results: 1. free, or natural, results and 2. sponsored, pay-pay-click (hereafter PPC) or product listing advertisements (hereafter PLA) results. Consumers type in a keyword or phrase, resulting in a list of results which are ranked by relevance. They click on a result, leading to a website. On Google, for example, the natural search results are displayed in the large column to the left. The PPC and PLA results are at the top and in the small column on the right. The difference is that search engines determine natural results by applying algorithms which they develop – payments or sponsorship cannot influence the results. Advertisers pay for PPC and PLA results. They bid for the highest ranking on a keyword-by-keyword basis. The advertiser with the combination of the highest bid, the best click-through performance and the greatest keyword relevance of the advertisement gets the number one spot (Marshall, Rhodes and Todd, 2014). Natural search results are where the long-term virtue of the digital marketing cycle lays

(Aders, 2013). Fifty-two per cent of Google users click on one of the top-ten natural results. However, the click-through rate of the tenth position in the search engine results page is 1.04% – and getting a high natural ranking takes time and effort. PPC and PLA results attract a smaller audience, but marketers can get a top rank with less time and effort – it is more about how much they want to bid.

Keywords are the crux of a search-engine campaign – if marketers pick the correct keywords, they can set up PLA and PPC advertisements and pursue natural rankings which select and deliver useful traffic. If they pick the incorrect keywords, they end up accumulating costs instead – a number-one rank might not generate useful results for them. In other words, keywords ensure marketers enter into the correct conversations, with the correct people. Marketers ought to put careful thought into the phrases which they pick. They can use a search engine's keyword suggestion tools to find the best phrases. Tools such as Wordtracker can also help, as can marketers' knowledge of the room. Marketers ought not to compete for ranking across a broad subject area. It is inefficient and can lead to a poor return on investment. Instead, keywords for more specific or less popular products or searches create a 'tail effect'. These keywords are less costly and provide higher click-through rates. The tail presents interesting opportunities and is particularly attractive for e-commerce sites which do not have to stock all their products (Amazon, for example). Marketers ought to try to match the tail precisely. A balanced campaign, therefore, combines smart PPC and PLA with a long-term focus on natural results. The PLA and PPC advertisements quickly generate returns. The natural rankings might do more, if marketers can achieve a high enough position.

Second, companies can also make themselves available to everyday consumers – especially those who have blogs. Marketers can reach out to them, giving them personal access to the company, essentially trying to influence the influencers in the blogosphere. In exchange for perks, such as free products or trips, access to important people and, sometimes, financial compensation, bloggers are encouraged (or contractually bound) to write about a company. The benefits go both ways. Through bloggers, companies reach an audience which has become wary of advertisement campaigns.

Third, using social media is a form of *bragging modestly*, which represents a great cultural shift for digital marketing. New communities come together and disperse quickly, and often different people at different moments for differing reasons lead them. The main reasons why individuals use social media are to keep in touch with current friends and to reconnect with old friends and work colleagues (McGrath, 2016). Not surprisingly, clicking on advertising, receiving promotional information or purchasing a product does not motivate consumers to use social media. The aim is to build social brand equity, a brand's social capital, which is found in the relations among individuals (Coleman, 1988). Those organisations which innovate early, often and incrementally, in particular, gain social capital (Kane et al., 2009). According to Meeker (2016), consumers favour Facebook the most, followed by Instagram, Twitter, LinkedIn, Pinterest, Snapchat, tumblr and Vine.

Fourth, sending out a press release using one of the web-based wire services can generate great buzz and get marketers some additional search benefits. Marketers can supplement any campaign using these methods. They ought to remember, however, that any effective digital marketing cycle must take into account the search engines. Regardless of how marketers *brag modestly*, they must understand that this is not an option, but a requirement. If marketers can take a moderate tone and pick the correct audience, they will stand out.

Observe and Adjust

A conversation is really millions of near-instant observations and adjustments. If someone is talking to someone else and the other person looks at the first person as if he or she just turned bright yellow, the first person might change the subject or ask if the other person is OK. If the other person had laughed, the first person might have told another joke. Marketers can function similarly on a website. By tracking, they can gather information about their audience's response to their campaign and adjust accordingly. This allows them to provide a more relevant digital marketing cycle which feels as if it is directed at the audience. Nothing keeps people in a conversation like knowing it is just for them.

If marketers are hosting their website with a web-hosting company or if they have an IT department at their disposal, they ought to have access to a traffic-tracking tool, such as Google Analytics. After marketers have access to their web traffic report, there are four metrics on which to focus:

1. Page views – one browser downloading one page, one time

2. Visits – one browser visiting a site, one time

3. Visitors – one browser coming to a site any number of times in a given time period, and

4. Conversions – one visitor answering a call to action.

These metrics demonstrate customer engagement (page views divided by visitors, for example), acquisition (the absolute difference between visits in time period t and visits in time period t+1, for example), retention (the absolute difference between visits and visitors, divided by visitors, for example), volume (visitors, for example) and return. Typically, a conversion means someone completes some kind of form, downloads a file or takes some other action, and then lands on a page on a website which they would not otherwise see (a checkout page, for example).

Beyond these bottom-line metrics, marketers also need a visual timeline to demonstrate sustainability – it helps them understand how seasonality affects traffic and returns. Dashboards and network analyses can also demonstrate sustainability in traffic from different channels (see Chapter 13 by Watts and Shmargad, for example) and identify keywords and referrals which are most vital to a site. They ought to show sufficient detail to encourage further investigation without surfacing too much. Five-to-ten keywords and referrals offer enough consistency to show important trends and enough variance to warrant deeper investigation (Wiegand, 2012). Finally, discovering how good (or bad) landing pages are can be beneficial. Excluding the homepage, it gives marketers a better sense of how consumers find the digital marketing cycle, and how sticky the site's core pages are after they arrive.

Over time, marketers will learn the patterns and flow of traffic on their site and be able to recognise a good from a bad effect. Then they can adjust accordingly and keep the digital marketing cycle going.

Conclusion

In conclusion, there is no conclusion, of course. Through this chapter, we have moved from the old, outbound marketing style to leaner, more efficient digital marketing. But this process is not finished. Virtuous digital marketing is a cycle, not a straight line. Marketers must move through the seven stages: 1. know thyself, 2. know the room, 3. dress appropriately, 4. tell stories, 5. make a connection, 6 brag modestly and 7. observe and adjust. Marketers ought to use what they observe to refine their picture of the room, then start again at the know thyself stage. They must remember that it is a cycle, which never stops. It pauses sometimes, but if marketers *make a connection*, and if what they have to say is of value, then new participants will come. The digital marketing cycle works.

For example, many management consulting firms come to us feeling that their site is not generating any real business. We suggest restructuring their site around their intellectual assets and placing on the home page an offer to download a free white paper from the site – after registration. Traffic falls steeply, but they begin getting a steady stream of qualified leads to their site. With a measurable conversion goal – the white-paper download – in place, they are able to track how efficiently they are selecting traffic.

If most digital marketers do it poorly, a few do it well. The success stories, such as Amazon and Google, have one thing in common: they understand their audience, market effectively and deliver with sensible, functional design. Then they listen to their customers, in order to improve their sites and digital marketing cycle. They make it work by understanding the Internet's unique position in the media world as a two-way, mass-communication environment. They study their audience and design a site which looks good. They fill it with great content, then observe how people respond. Then they fine-tune and adapt accordingly. After reading this chapter, you might not be ready for a career as a digital marketer, but you are definitely ready to talk to one. Digital marketing can be confusing and sometimes frustrating, but it can also work brilliantly. Hopefully this chapter has moved you closer to brilliance and helped you cut through the confusion of digital marketing.

References

Aaker, J., and A. Smith (2010) *The Dragonfly Effect: Quick, Effective, and Powerful Ways to Use Social Media to Drive Social Change.* San Francisco, USA: Jossey-Bass.

Aders, A. (2013) *A Tale of Two Studies: Establishing Google and Bing Click-Through Rates.* Indianapolis, USA: Digital Relevance.

Ariely, D., and K. Wertenbroch (2002) "Procrastination, Deadline, and Performance: Self-Control by Precommitment." *Psychological Science*, Vol. 13, Iss. 3, 2002, p.219.

Bal, P., O. Butterman and A. Bakker (2011) "The Influence of Fictional Narrative Experience on Work Outcomes: A Conceptual Analysis and Research Model." *Review of General Psychology*, Vol. 15, Iss. 4, pp.361–70.

Bandura, A., and D. Cervone (1983) "Self-Evaluative and Self-Efficacy Mechanisms Governing the Motivational Effects of Goal Systems." *Journal of Personality and Social Psychology*, Vol. 45, Iss. 5, pp.1,017–28.

Berns, G., K. Blaine, M. Prietula and B. Pye (2013) "Short- and Long-Term Effects of a Novel on Connectivity in the Brain." *Brain Connectivity*, Vol. 3, Iss. 6, pp.590–600.

Bettelheim, B. (1976) *The Uses of Enchantment: The Meaning and Importance of Fairy Tales.* New York, USA: Random.

Cayla, J., and E. Arnould (2013) "Ethnographic Stories for Market Learning." *Journal of Marketing*, Vol. 77, Iss. 4, pp.1–16.

Chaiken, S. (1987) "The Heuristic Model of Persuasion." In M. Zanna, J. Olson and C. Herman (eds) *Social Influence: The Ontario Symposium.* Hillsdale, USA: Lawrence Erlbaum, pp.3–39.

Chaiken, S., A. Liberman and A. Eagly (1989) "Heuristic and Systematic Information Processing Within and Beyond the Persuasion Context." In J. Uleman and J. Bargh (eds) *Unintended Thought.* New York, USA: Guilford, pp.212–52.

Cheng, J., C. Blankson, E. Wang and L. Chen (2009) "Consumer Attitudes and Interactive Digital Advertising." *International Journal of Advertising*, Vol. 28, Iss. 3, pp.501–25.

Coleman, J. (1988) "Social Capital in the Creation of Human Capital." *American Journal of Sociology*, Vol. 94, pp.S95–S120.

Cooper, A. (2004) *The Inmates are Running the Asylum: Why High-Tech Products Drive Us Crazy and How to Restore the Sanity.* 2nd edition. Indianapolis, USA: Sams.

de Ruyter, K., and T. van Laer (2014) "It's the Social, Stupid! Leveraging the 4C Markers of Social in Online Service Delivery." In R. Rust and M. Huang (eds) *Handbook of Service Marketing Research.* Cheltenham, England: Edward Elgar, pp.413–36.

Escalas, J., and B. Stern (2003) "Sympathy and Empathy: Emotional Responses to Advertising Dramas." *Journal of Consumer Research*, Vol. 29, Iss. 4, pp.566–78.

Fogg, B. (2009) "Creating Persuasive Technologies: An Eight-Step Design Process." *Persuasive Technology Conference.* Claremont, U.S.A, 26–29 April.

Gage, J. (2000) *Color and Meaning: Art, Science, and Symbolism.* Berkeley and Los Angeles, USA: Thames and Hudson.

Gergen, K., and M. Gergen (1988) "Narrative and the Self as Relationship." In L. Berkowitz (ed.) *Advances in Experimental Social Psychology.* New York, USA: Academic Press, pp.17–56.

Herzberg, F. (1966) *Work and the Nature of Man.* New York, USA: World.

Hoffman, D., and T. Novak (1996) "Marketing in Hypermedia Computer-Mediated Environments: Conceptual Foundations." *Journal of Marketing*, Vol. 60, Iss. 3, pp.50–68.

Kane, G., R. Fichman, J. Gallaugher and J. Glaser (2009) "Community Relations 2.0." *Harvard Business Review*, Vol. 87, Iss. 11, pp.45–50.

Koestner, R., N. Lekes, T. Powers and E. Chicoine (2002) "Attaining Personal Goals: Self-Concordance Plus Implementation Intentions Equals Success." *Journal of Personality and Social Psychology*, Vol. 83, Iss.1, pp.231–44.

Liberman, N., and Y. Trope (1998) "The Role of Feasibility and Desirability Considerations in Near and Distant Future Decisions: A Test of Temporal Construal Theory." *Journal of Personality and Social Psychology*, Vol. 75, Iss. 1, pp.5–18.

Linderman, M., and J. Fried (2004) *Defensive Design for the Web: How to Improve Error Messages, Help, Forms, and Other Crisis Points*. Indianapolis, USA: New Riders.

Marshall, P., M. Rhodes and B. Todd (2014) *Ultimate Guide to Google AdWords: How to Access 1 Billion People in 10 Minutes*. 4th edition. Irvine, USA: Entrepreneur.

McGrath, R. (2016) *Social and Media Networks, United Kingdom, May 2016*. London, England: Mintel.

Meeker, M. (2016) *Internet Trends 2016 Code Conference*. Menlo Park, USA: KPCB.

Muraven, M., R. Collins and K. Neinhaus (2002) "Self-Control and Alcohol Restraint: An Initial Application of the Self-Control Strength Model." *Psychology of Addictive Behaviors*, Vol. 16, Iss. 2, pp.113–20.

Nielsen, J., and R. Budiu (2013) *Mobile Usability*. Berkeley, USA: New Riders.

Nielsen, J., and D. Norman (2006) *How People Read on the Web: The EyeTracking Evidence*. Fremont, USA: Nielsen Norman Group.

Noordman, L., W. Vonk and H. Kempff (1992) "Causal Inferences During the Reading of Expository Texts." *Journal of Memory and Language*, Vol. 31, Iss. 5, pp.573–90.

Novemsky, N., R. Dhar, N. Schwarz and I. Simonson (2007) "Preference Fluency in Choice." *Journal of Marketing Research*, Vol. 44, Iss. 3, pp.347–56.

ReTargeter (2016) "What is Retargeting and How Does it Work?" Retrieved from: https://retargeter.com/what-is-retargeting-and-how-does-it-work

Savage, J., and S. Hartmann (2011) "The Whys and the Hows of Texture in Web Design." *Smashing Magazine*, 3 October.

Schank, R. (1995) *Tell me a story: Narrative and Intelligence*. Evanston, USA: Northwestern University.

Schiff, J. (2016) "15 ways to Improve Your Email Marketing Campaigns." Retrieved from: http://www.cio.com/article/3057992/email/15-ways-to-improve-your-email-marketing-campaigns.html

Scopelliti, I., G. Loewenstein and J. Vosgerau (2015) "You Call It 'Self-Exuberance'; I Call It 'Bragging': Miscalibrated Predictions of Emotional Responses to Self-Promotion." *Psychological Science*, Vol. 26, Iss. 6, pp.903–14.

Seijts, G., and G. Latham (2001) "The Effect of Distal Learning, Outcome, and Proximal Goals on a Moderately Complex Task." *Journal of Organizational Behavior*, Vol. 22, Iss. 3, pp.291–307.

Thaler, R., and C. Sunstein (2009) *Nudge: Improving Decisions About Health, Wealth, and Happiness*. New York, USA: Penguin.

Van Laer, T., and K. de Ruyter (2010) "In Stories We Trust: How Narrative Apologies Provide Cover for Competitive Vulnerability After Integrity-Violating Blog Posts." *International Journal of Research in Marketing*, Vol. 27, Iss. 2, pp.164–74.

Van Laer, T., K. de Ruyter and D. Cox (2013) "A Walk in Customers' Shoes: How Attentional Bias Modification Affects Ownership of Integrity-Violating Social Media Posts." *Journal of Interactive Marketing*, Vol. 27, Iss. 1, pp.14–27.

Van Laer, T., K. de Ruyter, L. Visconti and M. Wetzels (2014) "The Extended Transportation-Imagery Model: A Meta-Analysis of the Antecedents and Consequences of Consumers' Narrative Transportation." *Journal of Consumer Research*, Vol. 40, Iss. 5, pp.797–817.

Waring, T., and A. Martinez (2002) "Ethical Customer Relationships: A Comparative Analysis of US and French Organisations Using Permission-Based E-Mail Marketing." *Journal of Database Marketing*, Vol. 10, Iss. 1, pp.53–69.

Wiegand, M. (2012) "The Perfect Google Analytics Dashboard." Retrieved from: https://www.portent.com/blog/analytics/perfect-google-analytics-dashboard.htm

Zeldman, J., and E. Marcotte (2010) *Designing with Web Standards*. 3rd edition. Berkeley, USA: New Riders.

Zeldman, L. (no date) *A List Apart*. Retrieved from: http://alistapart.com/

About the Authors

Tom van Laer is Senior Lecturer in Marketing at Cass Business School at the University of London in London, England. His research is published in leading academic journals, including the *Journal of Consumer Research*, the *Journal of Management Information Systems*, the *International Journal of Research in Marketing*, the *Journal of Business Ethics* and the *Journal of Interactive Marketing*. His work has been covered by the BBC, *Newsweek*, the *Daily Mail*, the *Telegraph* and other news outlets. He studies narratology, storytelling and digital marketing. Although Tom has won awards for his academic research, teaching and media exposure, he still counts winning his high school's story-reading competition in 1995 as his most impressive accomplishment. Find him on LinkedIn at tvanlaer. Follow him on Twitter at @tvanlaer. Contact him on email at tvanlaer@city.ac.uk.

Ian Lurie is CEO and founder of Portent, Inc. He has been published on AllThingsD, Forbes.com and TechCrunch. Ian speaks at conferences around the world, including ad:tech, MozCon, SearchLove and Seattle Interactive Conference. He helps companies with digital strategy, online copywriting, organic search engine optimisation, PPC advertising, social media and analytics. Ian occasionally geeks out by building fun, new tools. Find him on LinkedIn at ianlurie. Follow him on Twitter at @portentint. Contact him on email at ian@portent.com.

Chapter 8

Building Communities of Influence

Andrew Zarick

Introduction

Building communities of influence is essential to the success of brands and organisations. Before now, it has been incredibly costly to build a valuable community, because large media and entertainment companies have served as gatekeepers to highly sought-after audiences. However, the democratisation and digitalisation of media have allowed start-ups, brands and everyday people to cultivate significant communities of influence affordably.

This chapter introduces a framework for building communities of influence online and in-person. It begins by exploring the deterioration of social capital in real-life communities due to the rise of television. It then traces the evolution of the media landscape. Chapter 8 continues by highlighting how social platforms now have larger audiences than major media networks. Finally, it discusses how to exploit this new media dynamic.

The Decline of Communities (in Real Life)

Leading minds like political scientist Robert Putnam have written extensively about how, starting in the 1950s, American society began disengaging with the 'third place'. This refers to the idea that the home is one place, your workplace is another and your regular hang-out spot or social club is the third. Instead, more people began staying at home in the evenings due to the increasing popularity of television and, later, the rise of sitcoms in the 1960s and 1970s. As families engaged with media celebrities at home, participation in community activities steadily declined, with an over 25% drop in all types of group membership. These factors and more began to cause an over 30% net loss in social capital within communities of the time period, giving rise to individualism – a trend never more prevalent than in today's media landscape of social-media influencers and the emergence of new types of communities of influence (Putnam, 2000).

Evolution of Media Distribution and Publishing

In order to understand the forces which allow new types of communities of influence to exist, we must look more closely at how media have evolved from millions of televisions, to millions of computers, and now millions of smartphones in homes and pockets all over the world.

Since the late 1930s and early 1940s when televisions first started entering our homes, transmission, screen display quality and programming have improved dramatically. The way in which we consume broadcast media from our televisions, however, has remained largely unchanged (see Chapter 3 by Collins and Branch). As theorised by Lazarsfeld, Berelson and Gaudet (1944) in their study *The People's Choice*, this dynamic between traditional televisions and consumers created a two-step flow of information. Information would first reach the opinion leaders who were paying close attention to mass media and its messages, who in turn layered on their personal interpretations of the messages. As a result, the opinion leaders influenced the viewpoints of their direct network of contacts, sometimes in ways which differed from the original mass-media message.

Although the two-step flow of information model enabled by traditional media has existed for the past 70 years, the previous two decades have given rise to a new and dynamic media environment which is enabled by the Internet. While television is limited to being a social experience in the living room, the Internet is a social experience at near global scale.

The one-way model of Internet communication was first highlighted by technologies like Usenet and Bulletin Board Systems (BBS). Usenets allowed users to post articles to newsgroups, features which have since been popularised by services like Google Groups and Yahoo! Groups.

The one-way model, however, only began to go mainstream with the release of online services like CompuServe and then America Online (AoI) which allowed everyday people to connect easily to the Internet. These services and their chat applications were responsible for ushering in Internet culture like avatars, profiles and early slang, forming the foundation for the early social-networking experiences created by companies including Friendster, BlackPlanet and MySpace.

These social networks pioneered features like connecting with friends, friends-of-friends and professional contacts, and further allowed expressing individualism through profile customisation and blogging. Social networks like Flickr, Photobucket and then YouTube in 2005 added a new layer of features which blended photo and video distribution with the social features which were invented by many of the original social networks. This combination of features became the precursor to the real-time status updates and tweets which we now see on platforms like Facebook and Twitter. Adding to the technological advances which made social networking possible, companies like Livejournal, Blogger and Wordpress made the publishing and sharing of content accessible to anyone, not just those with web-development skills.

These advances led to the original Internet memes and first viral video stars. As showcased in VH1's 40 Greatest Internet Superstars, Lonelygirl15 was the YouTube username of a 16-yr-old girl, Bree, who ended up being a fictional character in a complex story universe which was manufactured by an actual production company. Similarly, Tila Tequila was an unsigned musician and MySpace user who garnered over 31 million hits to her page, thereby leading to a cell-phone endorsement and photo shoots with *Maxim* and *Stuff* magazines. Blogger Mario Armando Lavandeira Jr. rose to fame after he quit his day job working as a writer for gay magazines and started writing under the pseudonym Perez Hilton. He quickly gained a large following by being the first to post pictures of Angelina Jolie, Brad Pitt and their then newly born son Maddox on the Internet.

Each of these early Internet stars took advantage of push-button publishing features that allowed them to push content to people in a two-way flow of information system (Dash, 2009). This created a major shift away from the domination of content production by a limited number of entities (largely print, radio and television companies) to the world that we have now, in which millions of content producers race to share information with millions of people in a many-to-many system. Due to this shift, a new one-way model of information has emerged, as described by Bennett and Manheim (2006). In this new model, information is now delivered directly to individuals and the opinion leaders of old no longer influence opinions before the message's arrival, but rather, give latent analysis. This new system not only democratises the issue of who can create and publish content, but also provides recipients of content the opportunity to easily share media with their networks, in turn furthering the content's reach and rewarding good content producers and curators of information with audience growth.

Rise of Global Scale Communities

The unfathomable growth of Internet usage over the past two decades has allowed digital platforms to grow into global scale communities. As a result, this is the first time in history in which individuals and brands on these platforms have been able to gain audiences which far surpass those of both old media and first-generation social networks. To put this into perspective, if we look at MySpace, the world's most popular social network in 2008, the platform had 75 million users in a world with 1.5 billion Internet users. In 2016 there are over 3 billion Internet users and the world's most popular social network, Facebook, has over 1.65 billion users (Internet Live Stats, 2016). To understand how this compares to traditional media platforms, over 114 million people watched the Super Bowl in 2016, but this represents less than 10% of Facebook's total audience.

The emergence of global scale communities on social platforms has allowed individuals on these platforms to gain audiences that rival the viewership of the most popular TV shows. As an example, NBA star Russell Westbrook of the Oklahoma City Thunder generates over 400 million content views per year across his social-media channels, whereas a local telecast of an Oklahoma City Thunder game reaches fewer than 200,000 people.

However, like media networks before them, digital influencers need access to capital in order to be able to produce content and to sustain audience growth. As audiences have gone digital, so too have advertising dollars. By 2017, total digital advertising spending is expected to surpass TV ad spending for the first time in history. This shift has led to completely new types of companies and job titles which never before existed. We now have digital agencies dedicated to social-media channels, talent agencies that represent digital influencers, and content studios that specialise in producing branded content.

Brands themselves have also become influential voices as they have been pulled into the social-media ecosystem by their consumers. This has created a world in which Burger King has developed the brand voice of a late-teenage music-loving stoner on Twitter. The brand has leveraged that voice to gain over 1.43 million followers. Likewise, personalities like hip-hop producer and entrepreneur DJ Khaled have used smart social-media marketing to take their once-limited brand reach into the mainstream. DJ Khaled, through a constant stream of Snaps, has grown a massive SnapChat audience. As of December 2015, DJ Khaled averaged just under two million impressions per Snap as reported by Heath (2015). This means that on any given day, he could easily generate over 12 million impressions per Snap-Chat story via his account. This tremendous following, now over six million people, has led to sponsorship deals with brands like T-Mobile, not only because he's famous, but because he has an audience which is larger than any single television channel on an average day.

Although Burger King and DJ Khaled were somewhat well known before they gained influential followings on social media, there are countless other digital influencers who have come to fame purely on social media itself. Lele Pons is a Vine user who became the first user of the application to hit a billion video views. Most of her videos are of practical jokes which Pons plays on friends, family, classmates and others. She now has over 8.4 billion plays across her videos and 11.1 million followers. Pons has used her influence to collaborate with brands like Ritz Crackers, HP and Kotex, and is represented by a talent agency which is called Grapestory. There are many more influencers like Lele Pons across all platforms and in many different verticals, from fashion and beauty to sports, food and travel.

A Framework for Building Communities of Influence

Digital influencers are not the only people who have built large audiences through social platforms. These same platforms have set the foundation for organisations to be able to spark socio-political movements around the world. The movements which are sparked on these platforms signify a subtle difference between social influencers who have large audiences and organisations which have built communities of influence. Typically, people within a community of influence share in the belief set of the organisa-tion and have a shared connection not just to the organisation but to each other (see Chapter 13 by Shmargad and Watts). Most importantly, the shared connections within these communities transcend the digital space and extend to the real world.

In 2014, Johnetta Elzie and DeRay McKesson live-tweeted the racial protests in Ferguson, Missouri, helping shape the #Black-LivesMatter movement. In doing, so they have since gained a combined following of over 400,000 on the platform. With this audience, they have been able to give a voice to a movement which previously had no official leader (*Time* Staff, 2016).

Likewise, the hacktivist group Anonymous was formed in 2003 in an online forum which was originally called 4chan. The group was established as a decentralised online group, a global brain, acting in a coordinated manner. The group's first mission was pranking, protesting and hacking the Church of Scientology. With the mainstream success of its first effort, the group moved on to more serious hacktivism efforts against governments and corporations around the world. The group has proven to be a force in standing up for issues like liberty, privacy and equal rights, all coordinated online.

In 2010, Google executive and Egyptian Wael Ghonim became an accidental activist when he came across an image of a bloodied face. The face was of Khaled Mohamed Sai who had been beaten by Egyptian police. Ghonim, tapping into the frustration of young Egyptians who had been long oppressed in their homeland, created the Facebook page 'Kullena Khaled Said' (We Are All Khaled Said). Within three months, the page had over 250,000 members. What started as an online movement culminated with a historic rally in Tahrir Square and ended with the resignation of President Hosni Mubarak (Vargas, 2012).

These movements are a testament to the fact that social media is not always about the funniest videos on Vine or the beautiful pictures of food on Instagram. While social media can be used for entertainment, the technologies which lay behind these platforms have drastically evolved media and communication, creating a new type of third space which blends online and in-person engagement – a space which is socially inclined, opinionated, entertaining, funny, civically engaged, capitalistic and digital.

What is understated, however, is that more often than not the individuals who, and the brands and organisations which, are most successful in building communities of influence have a very intentional strategy for doing so. It is also important to note that building a community of influence is not only about having a large community: it is also about the online and in-person influence of the individuals who make up the community (see Chapter 13 by Shmargad and Watts). If you agree with this perspective, then it has implications for strategies in digital marketing. For example, in my own work, I have adopted a five-phase framework for building a community of influence. The phases are community research, conversion, engagement, amplification and measurement. In the following sections, I outline each phase in greater detail.

Community Research

The community research phase begins with identifying which influencers match the values, interests and demographics of the community that you would like to build. The goal of the first phase of influencer research is not to define the entire community but rather to find influential persons who can serve as nodes for your community. There are many ways to go about conducting research to identify relevant influencers, but here are a few critical starting points:

1. Competitive analysis
   (By analysing competitor's social followings, it is possible both to identify commonalities across the competitor's followers and to pinpoint the key nodes of influence with the follower set.)

2. Social listening
   (Through the utilisation of tools which can examine large publicly available data across social platforms like Facebook and Twitter, it is possible to identify quickly those influencers who are discussing relevant topics.)

3. Social-media interest mining
   (By exploring relevant hashtag mentions, pages and associations to places, businesses, interests and searches on platforms like Facebook, Twitter and YouTube, it is possible to identify relevant influencers.)

4. Platform data mining
   (By mining publicly available databases and niche online communities, it is possible to identify influencers by name, title, company, and more.)

5. One-degree connections.
   (Perhaps the easiest and most logical starting point for identifying influencers is starting with one-degree connections – influential connections which are only one-degree of separation from the community which is being built.)

Conversion

Before the implementation of the engagement strategy (which I shall discuss next), it is important to map out which channels you will use to convert influencers into engaged members of the community. It is also important to lay the proper foundation for tracking success. Consider the following:

1. Channel development
   (The mix of channels that are used to communicate your message often include a mix of owned and external platforms. Examples of owned platforms include your website, email list, mobile apps and in-person events. External platforms include your Facebook Page, Twitter and Instagram accounts, and LinkedIn profile.)

2. Conversion events
   (Setting up various points of conversion across your channels is essential to converting actions that are driven by your engagement strategy into relationships. Examples of conversion events include an email list opt-in, membership sign-up and new followers. A conversion event signals the beginning of a relationship which then needs to be nurtured. Without channels and conversion events, there are no on-ramps in place for new individuals to join the community.)

3. Customer relationship management (CRM)
   (As conversion events begin to occur, it is recommended that a platform be in place to manage the relationships and the captured data. The type of data which is managed here might include name, email address, job title and company. Usually, a CRM platform also houses a log of contacts which have been made and also, in some cases, conversation notes. Likewise, some marketers simply use their email platform of choice as a CRM.)

4. Conversion tracking.
   (Typically, savvy marketers use a web analytics platform like Google Analytics to track conversion events. Each time a conversion action like a form submission, click or transaction occurs, the web analytics platform reports the conversion event to a marketing dashboard for review. Web analytics platforms usually make use of JavaScript placed on websites or in mobile

applications to track conversion events. This data is then reviewed on a regular basis as described in the measurement phase.)

Engagement

After the initial influencers are identified through community research, it is necessary to develop an engagement strategy which entices influencers to engage with the community. The engagement strategy is then activated through the community's owned platforms and marketing channels. The following three activities are key:

1. Campaign ideation

    (A content strategy and overarching marketing message will be developed based on the interests, values, shared beliefs and unwritten rules of the community, and on the influencers whom the campaign hopes to target (see Chapter 4 by Collins and Branch). The ideation process will also help inform which media and media types ought to be leveraged.)

2. Content creation

    (After the overarching campaign concept is developed, a team will work on creating content to support the campaign (see Chapter 12 by Pedersen). Content might be written, and visual imagery or videos and even audio might be included. The content will be created with the strategy and chosen marketing channels in mind – six-second videos for Vine, for example, long-form videos for YouTube or a set of images for Instagram.)

3. Channel activation.

    (Based on the engagement strategy, channels are then activated with the release of content. Often this approach is orchestrated with a content schedule and, at times, cross-promotion across channels. Many campaigns will make use of social platforms, email marketing, web and mobile platforms, and, occasionally, experiential events. As an example, a campaign might start with an Instagram post, be followed by an email marketing campaign and culminate with the release of a video which contains a teaser to attend an event in the real world.)

Amplification

Many campaigns get organic traction from owned channels early on, but require further amplification to expand their reach and to capitalise further on their initial success. Through media channels like paid search, display advertising and paid social posts, combined with earned media through content marketing, PR and other sources, the initial organic reach of a campaign can be taken to a whole new level. For example:

1. Paid search

    (By targeting advertisements to users on search engines like Google, as potential influencers search for interests which might align with the interests of your community, it is possible to communicate a solution to them at the time in which they are showing clear intent. For example, if a large automobile company were launching a smarter cities accelerator program, it might run advertisements which target individuals who are searching with 'smarter cities incubator program' or other relevant keywords.)

2. Display/retargeting

    (To reach those people who might not be searching actively for interests which are relevant to your community, it is possible to reach them by targeting websites and mobile applications which they might visit frequently. Using the same example above, the automobile company might run an advertising campaign on Fast Company or WIRED in an effort to reach entrepreneurs who may be a fit for the accelerator program. After potential community members then show interest by visiting the program's website or mobile application, and then leave, marketing messages can be retargeted to them, as they spend time elsewhere on the web, in an effort to bring them back into the community.)

3. Paid social posts

    (As social-media channels are activated in the engagement phase, many posts might not immediately reach the entire intended community, without additional activity. By paying for greater reach, the message is guaranteed to reach the entirety of the community. Additionally, paid posts can also be targeted to individuals with interests that are shared by the community, based on their profile data. In this way, paid social fills a void when paid search and display fall short.)

4. Public relations such as content marketing, influencer marketing and the press.
   (These days, there is much debate about where digital marketing ends and public relations (PR) begins. For the sake of this framework, I shall use PR to describe the method of securing earned and paid media through content marketing, influencer marketing and press mentions. Content marketing might involve a content strategy on your website, guest writing for relevant publications or sponsored content published on targeted media properties. Influencer marketing, on the contrary, involves engaging individuals who are deemed worthy advocates of your brand, in service of furthering your marketing message to their networks. Finally, obtaining press mentions involves the process of soliciting journalistic coverage from relevant publications. In tandem, these three tactics can create a groundswell of positive momentum for your campaign and build an influential community.)

Measurement

By utilising data captured through many of the techniques that were outlined in the conversion phase, community-builders can quickly gain insight into what is working and what is not. To do so, marketers track, analyse and optimise, based on campaign performance. This is typically done by looking at key performance indicators in a web analytics dashboard. Consider:

1. Key performance indicators (KPIs)
   (At the onset of any community-building effort, indicators of campaign success ought to be defined. KPIs are typically a combination of critical conversion events like signing up for a membership and the associated cost per sign-up and minor engagement metrics like the number of webpages visited.)

2. Measuring results

(Analytics reports are generated from the KPIs, often on a daily, weekly and monthly basis. These reports are more than just raw dashboard data, but instead also include actionable insights which are based on campaign performance.)

3. Optimising campaigns.

(Based on these actionable insights, adjustments can be made across all facets of the campaign. Optimisations are often made to messaging, website structure and colours, paid media targeting criteria and other areas of the campaign.)

Conclusion

Pulling the levers in this framework alone is not a fool-proof method of building a community of influence. Doing so successfully also requires an understanding of context (see Chapter 4 by Collins and Branch). When content meets context, however, and when influence meets networks, the resulting union can spark movements, sell products, and lead to a loyal and engaged community.

References

Bennett, W., and J. Manheim (2006) "The One-Step Flow of Communication." *The Annals of the American Academy of Political and Social Science*, Vol. 608, Iss. 1, pp.213–32.

Dash, A. (2009) "The Pushbutton Web: Realtime Becomes Real." Retrieved from: http://anildash.com/2009/07/the-pushbutton-web-realtime-becomes-real.html

eMarketer (2016) "Digital Ad Spending to Surpass TV Next Year." Retrieved from: http://www.emarketer.com/Article/Digital-Ad-Spending-Surpass-TV-Next-Year/1013671

Heath, A. (2015) "We Talked to DJ Khaled About His Amazing Snapchat Account." Retrieved from: https://www.juniperresearch.com/researchstore/iot-m2m/smart-cities/strategies-forecasts-in-energy-transport-lighting

Internet Live Stats (2016) "Internet Users." Retrieved from: http://www.internetlivestats.com/internet-users/

Lazarsfeld, P., B. Berelson and H. Gaudet (1944) *The People's Choice*. New York, USA: Columbia University Press.

Olken, A. (2009) "Do Television and Radio Destroy Social Capital? Evidence from Indonesian Villages." Retrieved from: http://economics.mit.edu/files/4120

Putnam R. (2000) *Bowling Alone: The Collapse and Revival of American Community*. New York, USA: Simon and Schuster.

Time Staff (2016) "30 Most Influential People on the Internet 2016." Retrieved from: http://time.com/4258291/30-most-influential-people-on-the-internet-2016/

Vargas, J. (2012) "Spring Awakening: How an Egyptian Revolution Began on Facebook." Retrieved from: http://www.nytimes.com/2012/02/19/books/review/how-an-egyptian-revolution-began-on-facebook.html?_r=0

Wikipedia (no date) "Lele Pons." Retrieved from: https://en.wikipedia.org/wiki/List_of_social_networking_websites

Wikipedia (no date) "List of Social Networking Websites." Retrieved from: https://en.wikipedia.org/wiki/List_of_social_networking_websites

About the Author

Andrew Zarick is the CEO and Founder of Digital DUMBO, a community of, and an event series for, digital and creative influencers in New York and London. He also consults with companies which want to build communities of influence to drive marketing and innovation goals. Prior to founding Digital DUMBO, Zarick was a digital marketer for brands like MTV, Time Inc, Univision and Michael Kors. In his free time, he spends far too much time looking for new restaurants to try, listening to new music and traveling to any country which touches the Mediterranean. Learn more at www.andrewzarick.com. Follow him on Twitter at @A2Z. Contact him on email at andrew@digitaldumbo.com.

Chapter 9

Dimensions of Voice in Social Media

Stephanie Leishman, Frédéric Brunel and Barbara Bickart

Introduction

"The human voice is the most beautiful instrument of all, but it is the most difficult to play."

Richard Strauss

Social-media marketing includes a process of identifying and managing the voice of an organisation. But what does it mean to say 'social-media voice'? Is there only one voice or many voices? And does it refer to the voice of the company, the brand, the employees, current customers or even the public?

In literature, 'voice' is considered a technical term, defined in various ways. Cavarero (2004), for example, considers voice to be the unique style of a writer. Others describe voice by its sonic qualities, even in textual form, which can be applied in ways that convey meaning.

What explains the variation in the definition of voice? It is possible that the variation occurs because voice is a multi-layered concept and different people differ differently across layers. The goal of this chapter, therefore, is to explore voice in all its layers and the relationship between these layers. We provide a conceptualisation of voice in social-media marketing, which draws on work in the humanities, the arts and social sciences, and which identifies three layers to social media voice which together comprise the 'vocal stack'. We then describe how individual vocal stacks contribute to collective voice. Finally, we examine implications of this model of vocal stack for managing a company's social-media voice.

The Layers of Voice

In social-media marketing, voice described merely as style is an oversimplification. Voice can be defined across several dimensions, which make up layers. These layers – vocal quality, meaning and identity – make up what we call the 'vocal stack' (see Figure 9.1). The vocal stack is built from the bottom upward, with the lower layers providing a foundation for the higher layers.

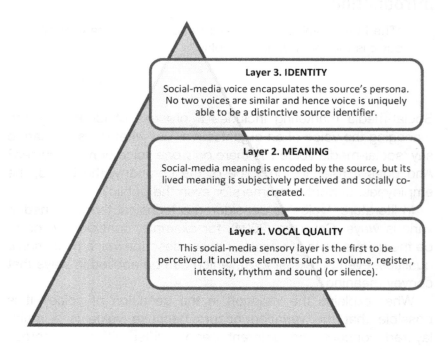

Figure 9.1. The Social-media Vocal Stack

At its core, voice is sonic. Those who define voice as style are focused on attributes at this layer, such as pitch and intensity. Sound makes up words – or the absence of words, such as pauses – which create the second, semantic layer to voice. Meaning is voiced with purpose. This third layer is what makes voice a unique mark of an individual, an identifier of one's personhood.

There is another dimension to voice, which creates a shared layer to the vocal stack: voice is social. A thought is usually voiced because it needs to be communicated to another person. The sonic, semantic and individualistic layers of voice are made communal or social in the transfer of meaning through sound between individuals. Social communication is put into voice form in its transfer from one person to another and within networks.

An understanding of the essential characteristics of voice can help companies and individuals leverage social media in productive ways. First is the importance of knowing how to develop a voice which resonates with others in ways which support business goals. Second is the importance of engaging with the world at the social layer by leveraging what you know about the other layers which make up and define voice.

Layer 1. Vocal Quality

At its most basic level, voice is sensory. The primary attribute of voice is sensory, described physically as vibration, which includes vocal qualities such as volume and register. Vibration represents a unique attribute of voice which delivers other vocal qualities through data over a period time. Walter J. Ong explains that:

> The very condition of sound is vibration. Voices move. They move in time, according to rhythm and tempo. They move, rhythmically and speedily, in the body. They shift pitch and volume and timbre, and there is a rhythm to these shifts as well. Speech, like sound, 'exists only when it is passing out of existence'. Although confounded with the very breath of life, speech dies on the lips that give it form.

(Ong, 1967, p.69)

Content at the sensory level is best described as being conveyed through vibration. This movement over time matters in all communication and therefore also in social-media contexts. A slower rhythm and a low volume might convey a more relaxed tone or perhaps a sombre mood. Words which are spoken quickly at a higher register can convey urgency or happiness. The sonic layer encapsulates all the physical attributes of voice. Social-media managers can make deliberate changes to content at this layer in order to prepare the layer to be encoded with intended meaning.

Vocal quality is sensory and is both the most basic level of communication and the easiest attribute to apply to social-media content. Sonic qualities denote a relation to sound waves, the understanding of which expands as there is an expanded understanding of how these waves affect not only the ears, but the entire body. Silence, or the absence of sound, is sensed physically, as is a whisper. Colour, expressed in light waves, hits the body with similar vibration.

Social-media content can be sonic (not to be conflated with sound, which is only one type of sonic expression). Content can be expressed either as audio – such as music or spoken words – or with sonic qualities, such as intensity and rhythm, in a form which is not necessarily auditory. Consider poetry, for example.

In social media, voice is able to express sonic quality in a form that is sonant, surd (whisper, for example) or even silent (the absence of sound). How does voice happen? Mazzei answers, suggesting that:

> Voice clearly happens in spoken utterances 'voiced' by our participants, but does it not also happen when they/ we fail to audibly voice an opinion with words and instead voice displeasure, discomfort, or disagreement with silence? Does it not also happen through other nonverbal forms such as art, or dance, or music? Are there not other unthought ways in which our participants voice their thoughts, resistances, and desires?

(Mazzei, 2008, p.45)

Just as our eyes pick up colour but also distinguish when there is no light, our sonic senses, which extend beyond what the ears can do, pick up many types of sound and also the absence of it. In a *PR Week* article, Bradley (2016) asked the question, "How long should brands stay silent on social media after a deadly crisis?" She interviewed public-relations experts to find the answer. One expert, Aaron Gordon, a partner at Schwartz Media Strategies, argued that silence sends as loud a message as does publishing content. He said, "Running for cover when times get tough sends a message that there's no communications strategy in effect and that the company is in damage control." Bradley also asked the question of Jeff Eller, founder of Jeff Eller Group, who answered, "Social media silence in the face of a crisis is a sign of a company that is not in control of its organizational response or communications efforts."

There are others who argue for silence. Indeed, in a recent post on Likeable.com, the author noted that "there are times when the correct strategy is to remain silent in order to avoid snowballing a negative conversation," also explaining that "[y]our Facebook communities are filled with fans that are passionate brand loyalists. When they see that you as a brand are being questioned or attacked, they will jump into the conversation in your defense" (Barton, 2013).

While both sides disagree on whether or not to go silent, both sides do agree that people notice the silence – that silence says *something*. In the case which was presented by Likeable.com, silence can give space for other voices to enter the conversation.

Textual voice has been described in sonic terms. Even when written, it is as if it were heard, like dialogue that occurs in fiction which plays a movie reel in our minds when we read it. Cavarero speaks of written text, "[b]rought back to life by its first love, the voice, the text therefore sings: it becomes musical, enchanting, just like epic song. It is made more for the ears than for the eyes" (2004, p.143). Hollander (1956) explains that the 'music of poetry' includes non-semantic properties, its sound read aloud, and even its syntax and imagery.

The vibrational layer includes the medium in visual form. The artist Wassily Kandinsky is known for his explanations of colour as sound, and although most of us are not synaesethetes like Kandinsky, colour affects the senses in sonic terms. "People are concerned with the possibility of constructing a system of counterpoint for painting also in terms of these many-sided similarities (e.g., the physical vibrations of air and light)" (Lindsay and Vergo, 1994, p.159).

The social-media manager must acknowledge that this first layer of the vocal stack, the sensory layer, is the first to be received. It will be the layer upon which meaning and identity are formed. Therefore, the sensory qualities such as sound, light and colour matter to the composition of social-media content.

Layer 2. Meaning

Whether or not it is your intention, your content is imbued with meaning. Beyond the sonic qualities of voice – whether written or heard – is the layer of meaning. For voice, this semantic layer includes language, lexical choices and syntactical structure. These choices help to convey meaning.

The receiver of social-media content can take meaning from that content. The transfer of meaning is two-sided. If content does not have voice, or the creator's 'presence' as Romano (2004) would say, then it is content which is void of encoded meaning. This does not mean that the receiver will not take any meaning from it; that meaning, however, will be impressionistic, created by the receiver as he/she receives it.

Voice is not meaning; it only carries meaning. But to carry – or to be encoded with – meaning, social-media meaning must be encoded deliberately by the creator. Social-media voice is purposeful. The sender encodes his/her message, but the receiver must decode the message. When encoding the message (and voicing it) for another person or group, the meaning will always be slightly different from what the sender intended. What is the context in which the message will be received? Does the receiver share the same cultural lexicon as the sender? Which unintended audiences will receive the message and how might they interpret it?

Many social-media managers intend for people to receive the message of the content – instead of just the sonic layer. Although managers lack control over all interpretations, they neverthe-less ought to think about how their audience will interpret the message. At any moment, a sarcastic comment could be taken literally or a literal comment could be interpreted as sarcastic. A tweet could seem jovial to some and serious to others. At this layer of the vocal stack – the layer where meaning is encoded and decoded – social-media managers experience the most fear. Juntae DeLane (2017), founder of the Digital Branding Institute, describes this as a "fear that saying the wrong thing on social media will have an unintended backlash that can plummet sales and destroy your brand images."

If we all understood and interpreted content in the same way, these managers would feel safe. However, there are some unstable and shifting boundaries of meaning despite a shared lexicon. Carlile explained that:

> When common lexicon sufficiently specifies the differ-ences and dependencies of consequence at the boundary, the boundary proves 'unproblematic'; the primary concern is one of 'processing' or transferring knowledge across it. What is not always acknowledged from such a perspective are the stable conditions that allowed a common lexicon to be created and to adequately function as a common knowledge. This failure often leads to underestimating the effort required when those stable conditions change.

> (Carlile, 2004, p.558)

Social-media content acts as a medium between two players and meaning is conveyed through that medium. Misinterpretation is a by-product of this conveyance. According to Carl Jung, artistic creation is presented on two levels: the psychological and the visionary. These levels affect the type of interpretation which is necessary. The psychological is intelligible, within "the realm of clearly understandable psychology" (Jung, 1978, p.90). Content conveyed at the visionary level surpasses consciousness and is not so easily explained. The semantic dimension of voice encom-passes these two levels of creation – at both the psychological and visionary levels – at which a person can encode and decode messages.

Meaning does not exist in a vacuum; meaning exists in the transference of a message via a medium. The attributes which are selected at the other layers of voice carry through to manifestation and influence at a deeper layer. As mentioned above, voice can be manifested in silence, because silence is an attribute of the sensory dimension. This silence is noticeable through higher dimensions of voice and can affect meaning. Ginsburg explained that:

> understanding radio requires attention not only to the sonic – the sound of the human voice, language, music, and even static – but also to the ways that radio is embedded in and sometimes constitutive of "inaudible" social practices such as kinship, religion, technology, personhood, and social movements.
>
> (Ginsburg, 2012, p.269)

Often the sensory qualities of voice determine the semantic qualities. For example, the words, sound or tones which are chosen at the most basic level of content creation can change meaning at the higher level. Meaning cannot be applied first without considering the sonic elements which will lead up to the next step of meaning.

Companies with little knowhow do what they can to take advantage of meaning which they think is mere graphic and text selection within a cultural context. Meaning is not so simple, however, and their posts can be misconstrued, which is damaging to the brand because they are vapid copies. At the sonic level, for example, they might copy other online content by choosing the graphic from a meme, or similar text from a popular Instagram post. They might then add on a hashtag to attempt to attract a collective. All of these attempts at content creation silo the several attributes of the sonic and semantic dimensions, as if these attributes have no relationship to each other. Companies would do well to start at the core and work outward, creating content which can manifest true voice.

Layer 3. Identity

As mentioned before, Romano posits that "voice is the writer's presence in a piece of writing." (2004, p.20) Voice is connected with the person who creates it. *Presence* is a word which connotes humanity.

In many fields, voice is one dimension of personhood or of the self. Often, a sound is considered a voice when that sound comes from a human being. In normal circumstances, an alarm clock's chime is not considered its voice; but when it is personified in a Pixar movie, the chime acts as its voice. But a corporation is not a person – so can it have a voice?

Some consumers perceive companies as 'intentional agents' (Kervyn et al., 2012) that fall on a spectrum of well-intentioned or ill-intentioned, and on a spectrum of unable or capable. Consumers even relate to brands as they do to other people, forming relationships with these brands (Fournier, 1998).

There are many attributes of identity which scholars believe to be distinguishable through voice. For example, voice can be gendered. In *On Gendering Texts: Female and Male Voices in the Hebrew Bible*, Brenner and van Dijk-Hemmes (1993) presented a new concept of authorship. They no longer searched for historical authors, but rather for gender-specific voices which might be heard on the textual level – that is to say, "voices within a text" (Bail, 2014, p.182). Of all the attributes of identity, what really defines identity in social media?

Key elements of identity are choice and self-control. Beyond its sonic qualities, voice must be voluntary – it must be the speaker's choice to speak. The opposite to voice, then, would be an automated response or an instinctual reflex. Would an auto-DM on Twitter count as the tweeter's voice?

Involuntary sound cannot be defined as voice. Romano's (2004) use of the word 'presence' puts the burden of proof for voice on whether or not it was created voluntarily. In the field of anthropology, Tomlinson discusses the earliest voices of mankind: "this early hominim voice was not merely an innate one, elicited by external stimuli in preprogrammed ways and involving little voluntary control, like a wolf's howl or a cat's hiss. Instead, it has already begun to shift along the biosocial spectrum toward modest voluntary control and social complexity" (Tomlinson, 2015, p.89).

Artificial intelligence raises the question to a new level. Is cognitive computing able to have a voice if it is learned from other human beings? Are the chatbots used for online customer service able to convey true voice?

A defining characteristic of human identity is that no two people are the same. The word 'identity' comes from the Latin *idem* meaning same. Same, not to be confused with similar, is self-referential – it means there is no other. Same means self. Indeed, the concept is revealed through the word selfsame which became popular in the 1800s. The concept is most evident in other languages like Spanish, in which self and same are the same word – *mismo*.

What makes the self so unique is its peculiarity. The etymology of 'peculiar' derives from the Latin *peculium*, which means property, and *peculiaris*, or private property. A peculiar style, therefore, is one's own style. It cannot be claimed by another. This is also why the contemporary reading of the word 'peculiar' is strange – the more unique it is, the more it is defined as an outlier from the average.

It is perhaps worth pointing out here that, in the language of literary criticism, 'voice' today is a technical term which indicates the peculiarity of the style of a poet or, more generally, of an author. This use is interesting above all for the way in which it recalls a vocal uniqueness which is implicitly understood to be removed from the acoustic sphere. So, "the fact that there are no two human voices that are absolutely identical makes it so that in literature 'voice' becomes the general equivalent of expressive difference, losing all reference to orality" (Cavarero, 2004, p.89).

In social-media marketing, the more peculiar the style, the more unique it seems. Take, for example, the tweets of Southwest Airlines. In response to a tweet about the record amount of baggage fees which American passengers paid, @SouthwestAir replied, " ☺☺☺ #bagsflyfree." (Southwest Airlines does not charge baggage fees). The Twitter style is unique – outside the average for tones which corporations use on Twitter. This lends to a strong brand identity for the airline.

One reason we use our voice – whether in art, writing or speech – is to present the self to others. This need to present the self and define one's voice through that presentation is one reason why content in social media 'goes viral'. Berger and Milkman (2012) argue that social-media content sharing is not just driven by valence (positive or negative), but that "consumers often share content for self-presentation purposes... or to communicate identity".

One's identity can be represented only by one's own voice. Voice, therefore, is not transferable. An attribute of identity as a vocal dimension does not just involve choice; it includes self-representation. If you are speaking for someone else, you are still using your own voice. This principle is best described by the word 'agency': a person acts for herself and represents herself when she speaks.

The act of translation is one example of one speaking for another. Although the translator might be translating text which another has written, the voice changes. The same can be seen in narration, where one person provides the voice for words which have been written by another. In an article on narratology and translation, O'Sullivan writes about the presence of the translator and narrator in the translated/narrated text, noting that "the narrator is the one who tells the story, hers/his is the voice audible when a story is being told" (2003, p.203).

When the speaker's voice does not match the voice of the author, people can tell – it is very difficult to fake it. In fact, there are blog posts and Facebook thread discussions arguing vehemently that the best audiobooks are read by their authors. In a *New York Times Magazine* article, for example, Mason (2016) insists that actors ought not to read authors' works, arguing that "in prose, the author's voice is even more essential to making the text not only intelligible but also meaningful".

Narration is essentially applying another person's voice to an author's text. The listener receives content through the narrator's understanding of the text. If a person can speak in more than one voice (to speak as herself and to speak as the company), but voice cannot be transferred to another person, this must mean that company voice, once created by one person, will only remain the same if continued to be managed by that same person. Once transferred, the voice changes.

Can Institutions Have One Voice?

Institutional social-media communications are perceived by some consumers as an amalgamation of the voices which contributed to the social-media campaign, for example, or the voice of the social-media manager. Other consumers view companies as people.

The Man-Behind-the-Curtain Model

"Pay no attention to that man behind the curtain."

The Wizard of Oz

When companies have mishaps on social media, some people tend to blame the company's social-media manager, not the company. Indeed, they attribute the voice to a single person – the man behind the curtain. For example, the 49ers' Twitter account tweeted the following text with an image which read 'Christian Ponder':

> #49ers sign QB @cponder7 to a one-year deal; place Thad Lewis on IR: 49ers.co/4Oo7xn

Mike Tunison @xmasape quoted the tweet, adding:

> This is was a weird way to announce this @49ers

Creeper VanDude @Blazefire84 replied:

> @xmasape @celebrityhottub @49ers Their social media manager is a 60 year old man who took one online course. "Mixing Popular Memes".

This is one example of how people attribute corporate communications via social media to the individual who is responsible for those communications. Negative comments about corporate social-media content not only mention the social-media manager, but often create an individual identity to attribute to that social-media manager. In this example, the tweeter perceives the social-media manager to be of a certain gender and age with a low level of cultural understanding.

Another example of attribution of voice to the man behind the curtain appeared when @bryisms tweeted about the 'penguins account' (the basketball team, as explained in the emoji of a basketball that followed). @bryisms wrote:

> @troonooyawker I find them highly annoying. I'm convinced their social media account manager is a 12 year old teeny bopper.

Similarly, the independent news organisation Mother Jones received this reply to one of its tweets from @Danieldcclark:

> @MotherJones this is the weirdest and probably most effective means of social media marketing. Kudos to the intern or social media manager.

Users increasingly see social media which are published by companies, but believe that there is likely one person behind the corporate name. People recognise that the company is not a person, but consider the social-media voice to be that of a person. Consequently, a company cannot have a voice, especially because that voice will change with each new social-media manager. The voice must be unique, human and voluntary in its sonics.

Comcast was quick to acknowledge that corporate voice was killing its brand on social media, when it had social-media customer service representatives set up their own Twitter profiles with names like @ComcastLarry and @ComcastMelissa. Comcast has since then turned away from that method and instead has all its customer service representatives on Twitter append replies with initials. For example, @comcastcares replies to @DrBrianCook:

> @DrBrianCook I would be more than happy to assist you with your appointment. Can you please DM me your information so that I may help? -IB

The tweet is not only signed with the initials of the representative, but it is also written in the first person. Although Comcast has unified its Twitter customer service back to one Twitter handle, it has remained transparent to customers about the identity of the service representative. People already know that the company is not a person, but an organisation of people, and personifying the company does not make it more personal or personable.

The Wizard Model

So, it seems that it is impossible for a company to be perceived as having its own voice – but maybe not. The wizard model, unlike the man-behind-the-curtain model, occurs when a brand is presented as a person. Like the Wizard of Oz does with the curtain and the projection screen, the brand downplays the people who write the copy and publish the Facebook posts, and instead expresses itself as a persona with its own human-like voice.

Some consumers, therefore, accept the personification of companies and address them in the second person. Indeed, consumers often form relationships with brands and the brands become "animated, humanized, or somehow personalized" (Fournier, 1998, p.344). Consider these examples:

> I love you @Vogue, but I [sic] Birkenstocks are absolutely NOT back. No. Way.

> Dear @EsteeLauder You broke my heart when you discontinued More Than Mascara Black/Brown, my day mascara since the beginning of time 😔💔

Collective Voice

While voice can be individual, there is a powerful dimension of voice beyond the individual: the collective voice. If, as we do, you live in a big city like Boston, hearing many voices at once is commonplace. Of course, this cacophony might be the norm on the street. But in social-media marketing, many individual voices resonating with one another can create a harmony or even a unified mass melody (see Figure 9.2). In music, this might be described as sympathetic resonance. One instrument initiates the sound, but if there are other objects in the room, they resonate with it.

> The principle of sympathetic resonance in the scientific endeavor is best introduced with an analogy. If one plucks a string on a cello on one side of a room, a string of a cello on the opposite side will begin to vibrate, too. Striking a tuning fork will vibrate another tuning fork some distance away. ... The principle of sympathetic resonance introduces resonance as a validation procedure for the researcher's particular intuitive insights and syntheses.

> (Anderson, 2000, p.33)

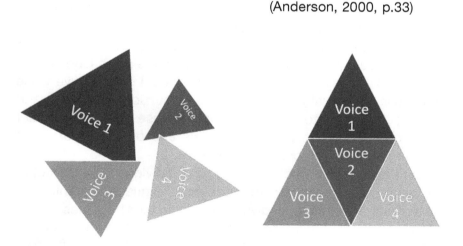

Figure 9.2. The Challenge of Social Media Multi-vocality – From Dissonant Voices to Collective Harmonious Voices

And in social media? Although there might be many voices joining a conversation in a group effort to 'voice' a message, all those voices still retain their unique identity. The collective voice, therefore, is not a voice, but exists when two or more vocal stacks contribute to one vocal space or collective message, whether cacophonous, harmonious or melodic. Vocal quality, meaning and personal identity remain a part of an individual's vocal stack, but the stack gains the social level when contributing to shared communication. This can be expressed in shared hashtags, one comment thread on a social-media post or through the use of social votes, such as Facebook reactions.

In the case of hashtags, for example, the collective appears to have a single voice because a hashtag presents a unified semantic direction through a large volume of individuals. Lopez alluded to this phenomenon when discussing the power of the hashtags #HowIMetYourRacism and #NotYourAsianSidekick – "While media imagery plays a part in contributing to this loss of voice and identity as Americans, this broader idea of cultural citizenship more strongly characterises the sentiment of the collective participating in using this hashtag" (2016, p.190). Lopez added that a collective voice gives consumers power which they would otherwise not have individually to "control their own voice and representation" (2016, p.199).

Some companies 'start' hashtags, hoping that the hashtag will be used by several people, yet still remain focused on the brand. Hashtags, however, become a symbol of collective voice and their use usually grows organically outside of direct brand control. Some brands can earn superfan use of a hashtag, but more often hashtags are about beliefs and purpose more than they are about products and companies.

On Facebook, a reaction to a post is individual. But the act of expressing this reaction with a common language is manifested as a social vote. Indeed, individual meaning thus becomes collective meaning. No longer does a post simply receive 13 likes or 42 likes; your post receives a collective response which is defined as 50% love and 50% sad.

Coca Cola, for example, posted on Facebook "What... ? You don't throw a party every time you have a burger and a Coke?", accompanied by a video. The post received 529 like, 31 love and 8 haha. The reaction was relatively simple with only three reactions used (of six available). Pepsi, on the other hand, posted on Facebook "It's time to get to know Alessia Cara our newest artist on #TheSoundDrop! The sounddrop.com/alessiacara" accompanied by a video. This post received 10k like, 1.1k love, 44 haha, 19 wow, 8 angry and 5 sad. The response was highly positive, but with the entire spectrum of emotion. At the other extreme, a post by Ocean Spray about #NationalCoopMonth received 503 like and 34 love, which is perhaps simply translated as a general positive response, with a few folks more passionate than the rest.

How should a company decode meaning from collective reactions like these, some simple and others with mixed emotions? While all companies publish content, who is listening and what do they uncover about the collective voice which is responding to their content? How can such a complicated message be decoded into something more than 'impressions' and 'engagement'?

Concluding Thoughts

The vocal stack comprises three levels: vocal quality (sensory), meaning (semantic) and personal identity (self). The framework explains the vocal dimensions of people and suggests that these three levels are attributable to individual voice, and that many voices can come together to share in the collective voice. Can this framework be applied to corporations? Does Southwest Airlines have a voice because of its uniqueness of style and purposeful messaging, or should it be understood as an internal collective voice of a finite group of individuals who employ their intrinsic vocal dimensions to fabricate a 'voice' for the company? And is that company voice really a 'voice'?

References

Anderson, R. (2000) "Intuitive Inquiry: Interpreting Objective and Subjective Data." *ReVision*, Vol. 22, Iss. 4, Spring, pp.31–42.

Bail, U. (2014) "On Gendering Laments: A Gender-Oriented Reading of the Old Testament Psalms of Lament." In C. Maier and N.

Calduch-Benages (eds). *The Writings and Later Wisdom Books*. Atlanta, USA: Society of Biblical Literature, pp.179–96.

Barton, A. (2013) "Don't Be Afraid To Go Silent on Social Media." Retrieved from: http://www.likeable.com/blog/2013/04/dont-be-afraid-to-go-silent-on-social-media

Berger, J., and K. Milkman (2012) "What Makes Online Content Viral?" *Journal of Marketing Research*, Vol. 49, No. 2, April, pp.192–205.

Bradley, D. (2016) "How Long Should Brands Stay Silent on Social Media After a Deadly Crisis?" Retrieved from: http://www.prweek.com/article/1384777/long-brands-stay-silent-social-media-deadly-crisis

Brenner, A., and F. van Dijk-Hemmes (1993) *On Gendering Texts: Female and Male Voices in the Hebrew Bible*. Leiden: Brill.

Carlile, P. (2004) "Transferring, Translating, and Transforming: An Integrative Framework for Managing Knowledge Across Boundaries." *Organization Science*, Vol. 5, Iss. 5, pp.555–68.

Cavarero, A. (2004) *For More Than One Voice: Toward a Philosophy of Vocal Expression*. Palo Alto, USA: Stanford University Press.

DeLane, J. (2017) "Are You Suffering from Social Media Anxiety?" Retrieved from: http://digitalbrandinginstitute.com/are-you-suffering-from-social-media-anxiety/

Fournier, S. (1998) "Consumers and Their Brands: Developing Relationship Theory in Consumer Research." *Journal of Consumer Research*, Vol. 24, No. 4, March, pp.343–53.

Ginsburg, F. (2012) "Radio Fields: An Afterword." In L. Bessire and D. Fisher (eds). *Radio Fields: Anthropology and Wireless Sound in the 21st Century*. New York, USA: NYU Press, pp.268–78.

Hollander, J. (1956) "The Music of Poetry." *Journal of Aesthetics and Art Criticism*, Vol. 15, No. 2, December, pp.232–44.

Jung, C. (1978) *The Spirit in Man, Art, and Literature*. New Jersey, USA: Princeton University Press.

Kervyn, N., S. Fiske and C. Malone (2012) "Brands as Intentional Agents Framework: How Perceived Intentions and Ability Can Map Brand Perception." *Journal of Consumer Psychology*, Vol. 22, pp.166–76.

Lindsay, K., and P. Vergo (eds) (1994) *Kandinsky, Complete Writings on Art*. New York, USA: Perseus Books Group.

Lopez, L. (2016) *Fighting for Cultural Citizenship*. New York, USA: NYU Press.

Mason, W. (2016) "Letter of Recommendation: Audiobooks Read by the Author." Retrieved from: https://www.nytimes.com/2016/07/17/magazine/letter-of-recommendation-audiobooks-read-by-the-author.html

Mazzei, L. (2008) "An Impossibly Full Voice." In *Voice in Qualitative Inquiry: Challenging Conventional, Interpretive, and Critical Conceptions in Qualitative Research*. Routledge, p.45.

Ong, W. (1967) *In the Human Grain: Further Explorations of Contemporary Culture*. New York, USA: MacMillan.

O'Sullivan, E. (2003) "Narratology Meets Translation Studies, or, The Voice of the Translator in Children's Literature." *Meta*, Vol. 48, Its. 1–2, pp.197–207.

Romano, T. (2004) "The Power of Voice." *Educational Leadership*, Vol. 62, Iss. 2, pp.20–3.

Tomlinson, G. (2015) *A Million Years of Music*. Cambridge, USA: MIT Press.

About the Authors

Stephanie Leishman is founder and owner of Apiarity, a company which helps organisations develop and execute exceptional social-media marketing strategy; her clients include international corporations, universities, start-ups, non-profits and musicians. Prior to founding Apiarity, Stephanie was the first social-media strategist for the Massachusetts Institute of Technology (MIT), where she directed the university's social-media strategy and advised its many schools and departments. Stephanie has been a guest lecturer at several universities and an invited speaker at conferences on social media, marketing, analytics, platform economics and entrepreneurship; she has designed and authored content for Social Media Marketing, an edX course which has more than 21,000 students enrolled; and she is a co-founder and co-host of Positive Feedback Loop (www.pflpodcast.com), a podcast which is focused on culture and technology. Stephanie earned an MBA and a Master of Science in Information Systems from Boston University and a Bachelor of Arts from Harvard.

Learn more at www.steph.me and www.apiarity.com. Follow her on Twitter at @hatchsteph and at @apiarity.

Barbara Bickart is Associate Professor of Marketing and Department Chair at the Questrom School of Business at Boston University. Her research examines how the context of communication influences consumers' inference and judgment processes. Current projects explore how consumers create connections in the context of both consumer-to-consumer and business-to-consumer communication, and how such connections influence the interpretation, perceived value and persuasive impact of a message. Her work has appeared in a number of journals including *Journal of Marketing Research*, *Journal of Consumer Research*, *Journal of Consumer Psychology*, *Journal of Interactive Marketing* and *Journal of Advertising*. Contact her on email at bickart@bu.edu.

Frédéric Brunel is a consumer researcher who is dedicated to informing two main domains: consumer relationships and product design. His research strives for theoretical and substantive contributions, and focuses on concepts which are of direct relevance to academia and practice. These include, for example: consumption communities on and off-line, word-of-mouth dynamics, customer relationship management, and aesthetic response styles and skillsets. In order to inform these domains, Brunel is committed to developing a deep and contextualised understanding of the social-psychological and cultural factors which can guide and moderate consumers' responses in these marketing applications. Consequently, his scholarly work resides at the intersection of social-psychology and cultural studies, and focuses comprehensively on culture, group/community and personality/gender levels of analyses. Contact him on email at brunel@bu.edu.

Chapter 10
The Shared Brand

David Fossas

Introduction

The brand is one of a company's most valuable assets. It serves as a proxy for the quality of the product which the company offers, as a memory aid for customers, as a basis for differentiation compared to the competition, as a driver of customer loyalty and even as a source of credibility for bringing new products to market.

Most executives and marketers, however, cannot define what a brand is, let alone quantify its value. While consultants and marketing agencies might sell their own brand definitions and 'secret sauce' approach to brand valuation, there exist no generally accepted brand valuation principles, comparable to accounting's generally accepted accounting principles (GAAP), to align executives and marketers in how to build and measure brands.

Furthermore, in our modern digital world, the brand is no longer 'owned' solely by the company. Indeed, social media has given a voice and influence to the company's stakeholders (consumers, employees, investors, partners, etc.) such that the perception of a company's brand is shared by the company *and* its stakeholders. As stakeholders create content and share information and perspectives about the organisation, the broader perception of that company shifts to reflect that of its stakeholders.

The purpose of this chapter, therefore, is to present a framework for marketers to harness the full value of their company's brand. It begins by providing historical context and a lexicon for discussing brands. It then proposes a new definition of brand in the context of our modern digital world in which social media give a voice and influence to a company's stakeholders. Finally, it introduces the Shared Brand Framework to guide marketers in evolving their marketing practices and teams to succeed in this new environment, in which control and influence over the perception of a brand are shared by the company and its stakeholders. The key lesson from the chapter is that marketers must align their stakeholders through shared purpose, experiences and culture in order to capitalise the full potential value of the brand. After reading this chapter you will:

1. Understand how digital has evolved the nature of a brand;

2. Appreciate the business value of a strong shared brand; and

3. Possess a framework for creating a shared brand in our modern digital world.

Brand: History, Evolution and Lexicon

What is a brand? The word itself is ambiguous. Often, it is used interchangeably with the word 'company'. Other times, it is used more specifically to refer to the iconography or logo which represents the company. Indeed, the term 'brand' evolved over the years to have both tangible and intangible qualities, as you can see from the following definitions. Famed ad man, David Ogilvy (1985), described a brand as "the intangible sum of a product's attributes: its name, packaging, and price, its history, its reputation, and the way it's advertised". Renowned marketer and writer, Seth Godin (2010), characterised a brand as "the set of expectations, memories, stories and relationships that, taken together, account for a consumer's decision to choose one product or service over another". And the American Marketing Association (2016) defines a brand as a "Name, term, design, symbol, or any other feature that identifies one seller's good or service as distinct from those of other sellers".

These definitions give us only a rough orientation of what a brand might be and leave us wanting for a more actionable understanding about how, as marketers, to develop a valuable brand. Thus, before I dive fully into this chapter, I shall spend some time reviewing the history and evolution of brand, and establishing the lexicon which I shall use throughout this chapter to discuss brand.

History and Evolution

The word 'brand' comes from Old English and Germanic roots. It originally meant burning, as in a piece of burning or smouldering wood. Later, the verb sense of the word – to mark permanently with a hot iron – arose in the Middle English period. Eventually, the noun sense of the word – a mark of ownership made by branding – arose in the mid-seventeenth century. And in fact, brand is translated into the word 'mark' in many other languages: marke (German), marca (Spanish), marka (Croatian), marque (French), markë (Albanian), марка (Byelorussian). When companies began using the word for other commercial activities, brand came to represent the collective name, typography and logo which differentiated the company and its products from others. But things became interesting when marketers began to realise that they could influence the *perception* of the brand and its attributes in the minds of customers through the brand's positioning.

Positioning is an articulation of the unique space which a company wishes to capture in the hearts and minds of its customers, supported by the rational, emotional and social benefits which the company (and its products) provide to customers. In their writings, advertising visionaries Al Ries and Jack Trout (1972) described positioning as follows:

> Positioning starts with a product. A piece of merchandise,
> a service, a company, an institution, or even a person...
> But positioning is not what you do to a product. Positioning is what you do to the mind of the prospect.

In 'the old days' (before digital media) brands were centralised and, thus, companies had an imbalance of power, or control, over their brands. This is to say, a company could frame its brand in the minds of its customers through its market positioning, then simply project that positioning out into the world through one-way advertising and public relations channels, such as TV, radio, print and outdoor, thereby influencing customers' *perception* of the brand and, ultimately, their purchase behaviour.

The problem for the company's stakeholders – particularly its customers and employees – is that the positioning and brand which a company projected did not necessarily reflect the actual values, culture and business practices which played out every day inside the company with leaders, managers, employees and partners. And the brand did not necessarily reflect the actual experiences which customers had with the company's products and services. But there was little to no ability for customers and employees to hold companies accountable for not living up to the brands which they were communicating. Media channels were one-directional, centralised and few in number. These media companies were influenced by the advertising dollars which brands paid them or by the brands' public relations spin doctors who fed stories to their journalists. Outside of investigative journalism, perhaps, company's stakeholders had no voice.

Digital media has disrupted this imbalance radically by decentralising media channels and by democratising information. Indeed, Web 2.0 made it easy for a company's stakeholders to react to content and information which a company releases, and enabled stakeholders to create and publish their own content about the company. The term Web 2.0 describes the second generation of the World Wide Web in which technologies focus on enabling both the publishing of user-generated content (on message boards and forums like Digg and Reddit, blog platforms like Blogger and WordPress, photo platforms like Flickr and Instagram, and video platforms like YouTube and Vimeo) and social networking (on Facebook, Twitter and LinkedIn, for example). Web 2.0 laid the foundation for the rise of social media – an environment in which publishing and social networking converge.

By extension, digital media also disrupted the power structure of the brand. Indeed, power has tipped in the stakeholder's direction, so that control and influence over the perception of today's brands is shared between the company and its stakeholders. Likewise, the company's business practices are influenced by its stakeholders. And the C-suite has taken notice. Indeed, according to a 2013 IBM study, CEOs believe that customers wield more power over the company than the board of directors – second only to the C-suite which manages the company. Consider the following example.

In 2012, fifteen-year-old Sarah Kavanagh and her brother came in from playing outdoors and reached for their Gatorades in the refrigerator. Before opening hers, Sarah looked at the nutrition label and noticed the ingredient brominated vegetable oil (BVO). Sarah googled the ingredient and found that it contains bromine – an element found in flame retardants which has been linked to neurological impairment, reduced fertility, changes in thyroid hormones and puberty at an earlier age.

Sarah threw away the Gatorade and launched a petition on Change.org to have Gatorade (which is owned by PepsiCo) remove the ingredient from its recipe. Change.org is an online platform which enables anyone to create a campaign around a cause, thereby mobilising people around that cause to influence change. Sarah's petition caught fire, achieving over 200,000 supporters and creating a media flurry. While Gatorade and PepsiCo deflected the issue initially, public pressure mounted. In January 2013, fearful that the public perception might cause lasting impact to the reputation of the brand – more pointedly, that it might have long-term negative impact on the business – Gatorade agreed to replace BVO with a different ingredient. And in 2014, PepsiCo and its largest competitor, the Coca-Cola Company, began to replace BVO in all of their drinks.

This is just one example of how, through digital media, companies are being held to a higher level of transparency and accountability for the total experience which they deliver to their stakeholders – across products, business practices and employment. Indeed, stakeholders now have channels through which to voice their opinions about companies. These stakeholder opinions influence the perception of the brand with other stakeholders as much as, if not more than, the communications which come directly from the brand. And if the company feels enough public pressure from these stakeholders – that the company's perception in society is affecting the brand and business results negatively – then the company's leaders are likely to act to mollify its stakeholders. As Sawyer discusses in Chapter 2, leaders must look at the world through an ecosystemic point of view.

Lexicon

Given this context, the chapter will use the following lexicon to discuss brands:

- Brand mark (noun) is a name, term, symbol or design which is intended to identify the product of one company and to differentiate it from those of competitors;

- Brand identity (noun) is the meaning which the brand mark is intended to convey;

- Brand equity (noun) is the value which the brand contributes to the valuation of the company; and

- Brand (verb), as in 'to brand', is the process of developing the brand mark, brand identity and positioning.

With this lexicon established, I propose a new definition of the noun version of 'brand' which reflects the relationship between the company and its stakeholders in a modern digital world:

- Brand (noun), as in 'the brand' is the shared purpose, experiences and culture which align a company and its stakeholders to create mutual value.

The Shared Brand

The key idea in this proposed definition of 'brand' is that brand is now shared. In this section, therefore, I shall unpack this definition, using examples of companies which illustrate the individual elements of the shared brand: purpose, experiences and culture.

Shared Purpose

Purpose is what the company is passionate about. It is the contribution which the organisation aims to make in the world beyond any particular product. It is the lofty problem which the company sets out to solve. As Simon Sinek (2009) suggested, it is the *why* behind the company, arguing that "people don't buy *what* you do; they buy *why* you do it". Purpose, therefore, is what the company's stakeholders buy into.

Purpose drives business value. Indeed, in a study by Jim Stengel (2011), Procter and Gamble's former Global Marketing Officer, analysis of ten years of growth across 50,000 companies around the world demonstrated that companies with the purpose (or 'ideal') of improving people's lives outperformed the SandP 500 by 400% between January 2000 and January 2011. The top fifty companies grew three times faster than their competitors. Notably, each of these companies had a purpose rooted in one of five fundamental human values: 1. eliciting joy, 2. enabling connection, 3. inspiring exploration, 4. evoking pride and 5. impacting society.

TOMS is one company which comes to mind immediately as a company which has created exceptional brands. Each has purpose instilled in its business and that purpose has rallied customers to adopt their products at phenomenal rates. TOMS, for example, believes in "using business to improve lives" (*Harvard Business Review*, 2016). It uses a 'one-for-one' business model, which means that for every shoe which TOMS sells, TOMS also gives a pair to a kid in need. In a *Harvard Business Review* article (2016), TOMS Founder, Blake Mycoskie described getting his first retail account, American Rag, to offer his shoes: "I knew my shoes couldn't compete on quality or price alone, so I told the buyer why I wanted to sell them and give them away. The store became our first retail account".

You see, Mr. Mycoskie told the buyer *why* he wanted to sell and give away shoes. On a trip to Argentina, Mr. Mycoskie met a pair of brothers, aged ten and twelve, who shared one pair of adult shoes between the two of them. The local school required footwear, so the brothers took turns wearing the shoes and going to school. Because the brothers only had one pair of shoes between the two of them, they could not attend school full-time. This experience inspired Mr. Mycoskie to start TOMS (which stands for Tomorrow's Shoes) and this story – this *purpose* – inspired the American Rag shoe buyer to be the first to sign on to offer TOMS shoes to its customers. TOMS' purpose gained word-of-mouth quickly and ignited a movement among like-minded consumers who believed in TOMS' purpose. TOMS has since then expanded its one-for-one business model into a wide range of shoe styles, and into eyewear, coffee and bags. TOMS was founded in 2006 and, in 2014, the company was valued by Reuters at 625 million USD.

Purpose also has the ability to turn around stagnant businesses. Consider Pampers. As Stengel (2011) discussed, in the late 1990s Pampers was the poorest performing brand in P&G's portfolio from a profitability and market-share growth perspective. Pampers had launched in 1961 as the first mass-market disposable diaper and quickly became P&G's fastest-growing business. But by 1997, the business had stalled. At 3.4 billion USD in annual sales, Pampers had the largest market share globally, but competitor Kimberly Clark's Huggies had replaced Pampers as the top brand in North America. Furthermore, Huggies was innovating more effectively.

When Pampers first launched, dryness was the most important benefit to consumers because, before Pampers, consumers were using cloth diapers. But dryness became a commonplace benefit amongst diaper brands (err, a hygiene factor) and, over thirty years after launching, Pampers was still using dryness as the single most important measure of innovation and success. As Stengel described it, Pampers had prioritised dryness "first, last and always." Meanwhile, Huggies had launched its potty-training diapers, Pull-Ups, to enormous success. Achieving higher prices and consequently higher margins, Huggies Pull-Ups had taken 90% market share of the potty-training segment. It took Pampers five years to release a training diaper and it was received so poorly that Pampers took the diaper off the market just two years later. Pampers had become irrelevant with the new generation of moms. Indeed, in focus groups "moms described Pampers as the brand their mothers-in-law told them to use while their friends were using something else" (Stengel, 2011).

When Stengel came in as Pampers' head of brand, he helped the company rediscover its purpose and soon the business began to turn around. Pampers' purpose is now "to help mothers care for their babies' and toddlers' healthy, happy development" (Stengel, 2011). Defining and aligning the company and brand around this purpose shifted the business. Employees discovered an exciting reason to come to work every day. They had a lens through which to evaluate every business activity and decision, and they had a 'north star' to guide all marketing communications. And Stengel held the organisation accountable to its purpose. If an idea was not aligned with Pampers' purpose of helping mothers care for their babies' and toddlers' healthy, happy development, then Pampers did not pursue the idea. Employees understood the purpose and knew that leaders would back that purpose up with action – a key factor in creating the brand experiences and culture which I describe later in this chapter. Aligned around its purpose, the Pampers business turned around and accelerated. Between 1997 and 2007, Pampers grew from 3.4 billion USD to a whopping 8 billion USD in annual sales.

Purpose is the foundation on which successful companies are built. Google's purpose, for example, is "to organize the world's information and make it universally accessible and useful" (Google, 2016). Facebook's purpose is "to make the world more open and connected" (2016). Airbnb's purpose is to enable people to "belong anywhere" (2014). These are all relatively young companies which have grown tremendously in their short lives. But companies with a longer heritage have thrived over generations through their driving purpose.

Apple's purpose, for example, is to "empower creative exploration and self-expression" (Stengel, 2013). Over the last twenty years, Apple has become the most valuable company in the world with steady innovation and by launching new products, from re-envisioned computers to the iPod, from the iPhone to the Apple Watch. Apple is not just a consumer electronics company: it is a company for rebels and artists. It believes in challenging the status quo. How does Apple do that? By designing beautiful, simple-to-use products. And consumers who also believe in challenging the status quo love Apple (and their products) for that. When Apple consumers use their products, they feel like they are part of a community of artists and rebels.

The Coca-Cola Company's purpose is to "inspire moments of happiness" (Stengel, 2013). This purpose has enabled the Coca-Cola Company to maintain a healthy business, expanding into new product lines and growing in market capitalisation, even as its core business of sodas has sustained pressure from the public's increasing concerns around sugar and another ingredient – the low-calorie sweetener, aspartame. The Coca-Cola Company is not just a beverage company: it is a happiness company. How does the Coca-Cola Company inspire moments of happiness? By offering beverages which cause you to pause and appreciate the little moments in life. As Coke's new brand campaign prompts us, you ought to pause and "Taste the Feeling".

As you can see, these companies have purposes that go beyond any particular product which they offer. Instead, their purposes serve as rallying calls into which their stakeholders can buy – beliefs or ideals that their stakeholders share. And this creates not only alignment between the company and its stakeholders, but also a north star for marketers, by informing the messages, stories and experiences that marketers create for those stakeholders. As summarised by Unilever's CMO, Keith Weed, and colleagues, "In addition to engaging customers and inspiring employees, a powerful and clear brand purpose improves alignment throughout the organization and ensures consistent messaging across touchpoints" (*Harvard Business Review*, 2014). And this leads to *shared experiences*.

Shared Experiences

Experiences are the individual touch points, interactions and moments shared between the company and its stakeholders. They are the memories which are made, the lessons which are learned and the stories which are shared. They are how the company's purpose plays out in the world. Zappos, Rackspace and Starbucks – three very different companies which operate in three very different industries – serve as examples here.

In his book, Tony Hsieh (2010), the founder of online retailer Zappos, reflected that, "We decided a long time ago that we didn't want our brand to be just about shoes, or clothing, or even online retailing. We decided that we wanted to build our brand to be about the very best customer service and the very best customer experience. We believe that customer service shouldn't be just a department, it should be the entire company". Hsieh and the Zappos team realised early on that – in the dog-eat-dog retail industry in which billions of dollars are poured into advertising – remarkable customer service and customer experience can actually be a strategic differentiator and a driver for word-of-mouth. Zappos calls this "Delivering WOW Through Service" and it ranks as number one on the list of ten core values that drive the company. Indeed, Zappos became famous for its customer experience – elements like free shipping and returns, customer-service representatives who talk with customers for hours (whereas most companies minimise the time which representatives spend on the phone with customers by investing in statisticians to calculate the optimal call times for maximising margins), and even customer-service representatives who find merchandise for customers in a different retailer's store if Zappos does not have the product the customer wanted in its inventory. In opposition to many companies, Zappos even considers customer service a marketing expense instead of an operational expense. Zappos was founded in 1999. Just ten years later, Amazon.com acquired Zappos in a deal which TechCrunch reported was worth nearly 1 billion USD.

Rackspace, a company which provides managed hosting, stumbled upon a similar insight around customer service. In the early days of Rackspace, there was a customer call which went terribly. This sparked an entirely new approach for customer service which David Bryce, Rackspace's Vice President of Customer Care, coined as 'Fanatical Support™'. Realising that the incumbent companies which service information technology (IT) provide poor (if any) service, Rackspace decided to make Fanatical Support™ a strategic differentiator. IT and managed hosting might be considered boring by most accounts, yet Rackspace aims to be recognised as "one of the world's greatest service companies along with the likes of Nordstrom, Lexus and the Ritz Carlton" (Rackspace, 2014). Founded in 1998, Rackspace's focus on Fanatical Support™ and providing a remarkable customer experience has helped the company grow to 2 billion USD in revenues in 2015.

Zappos and Rackspace serve as excellent examples of delivering remarkable customer experience through service. But experiences are not limited to service alone. Starbucks shows us how experience extends to the bricks-and-mortar retail environment and even into the digital environment.

In 1981, Starbucks' CEO Howard Schultz visited Starbucks Coffee, Tea and Spice, and tasted specialty coffee for the first time. Up to that point in history, coffee in the United States was effectively a commodity item typically consumed as instant coffee, which was purchased at the grocery store. Mr. Schultz saw great potential in offering specialty coffee more broadly to American consumers who mostly did not have knowledge of, or access to, the product. Mr. Schultz joined Starbucks as a director of operations and marketing. Later in 1983, Mr. Schultz visited Milan, Italy on a coffee-buying trip. There he experienced the Italian espresso-bar culture for the first time. In Italy, espresso bars are found on virtually every corner and serve as a social centre point for Italians who start their day at their local bar, and who then connect with friends at that same location later in the day. Each espresso bar has its own character and community with baristas who are well-trained in brewing a variety of noteworthy coffees. Mr. Schultz saw the potential for bringing this culture to the United States.

Over time and through a test-and-learn approach, therefore, Mr. Schultz landed on the Starbucks experience which we all know today. Each store has its own character which is heavily informed by the local city – or even neighbourhood. Starbucks baristas are knowledgeable about the variety of specialty beans and brews which they offer. If you frequent the same location, baristas will often remember you and the particular brew which you order. Today, Starbucks also serves as a social centre in which you can meet with friends for conversation, hold business meetings, study or simply read a book comfortably.

Starbucks has also extended this experience into the digital realm. In store, Starbucks has moved away from offering wi-fi through AT&T, instead offering wi-fi through Google's superior Google Fiber. When a customer signs into its wi-fi, the customer receives access to music and other entertainment offerings which enhance the in-store experience. In mobile, the Starbucks Rewards™ application is a fan favourite: the application helps customers find the nearest Starbucks location, provides exclusive access to new music and integrates credit-card information so that you can purchase your coffee and earn rewards, all through the application. More recently, the application allows customers to order and pay ahead, thereby enabling them simply to pick up their coffee when they arrive at the location.

Starbucks has been hyper-focused on delivering remarkable, personalised experiences through both physical, in-store and digital channels. These experiences have created deeper connections which are shared between Starbucks and its stakeholders. And the effort has paid off. Starbucks' market capitalisation grew at a 24% compound annual growth rate (CAGR) in the five years from July 2011 to July 2016.

Shared Culture

Culture, in sharing the brand, is the behavioural alignment of purpose between the company and its stakeholders. Culture is the community that the company creates, the relationships that the company keeps, and the underlying rules for the community and those relationships. As Simon Sinek (2009) explained: "The goal is not to do business with everybody that needs what you have; the goal is to do business with people who believe what you believe." The people who believe what you believe enrol in your culture. So, whereas the company's shared purpose drives people's behaviour and the company's shared experiences reflect the behaviour, the company's shared culture *is* the behaviour (see Figure 10.1). Culture is how the company achieves its purpose. Perhaps most interestingly, when a brand has a strong culture which is built on shared purpose and experiences, the brand can solicit its stakeholders to participate in creating new, mutual value.

Once again, consider Starbucks. In March of 2008, Starbucks launched MyStarbucksIdea.com, a website in which a growing community of customers can share ideas for how to improve the Starbucks experience. Ideas have included new product offerings, community involvement, in-store experiences and improvements to the Starbucks Rewards™ application. Customers can then vote up or down on ideas which have been proposed by the community. Ideas which get a high volume of votes get implemented. Customers have contributed tens of thousands of ideas on the platform. But why do customers participate?

Figure 10.1. Shared Brand

Starbucks' mission statement is "To inspire and nurture the human spirit – one person, one cup and one neighborhood at a time" (Starbucks, 2016). Vision and mission statements are often lofty empty promises. They can be statements crafted by management consultants and MBA graduates as part of a best-practice process which is intended to align the company. These statements are sometimes supported by buzzwords like integrity and transparency, which are hung on walls and banners to serve as a rallying call to employees and customers. Enron's vision statement, for example, was "To become the world's leading energy company – creating innovative and efficient energy solutions for growing economies and a better environment worldwide". But, did this vision play out in the real world with its stakeholders – in the shared experiences of employees, energy providers, utility companies and financial markets? Not at all.

Meanwhile, Starbucks' mission statement does not appear to be an empty promise. Why? The answer might lay hidden in the 'About' section of its website:

> It happens millions of times each week – a customer receives a drink from a Starbucks barista – but each interaction is unique. It's just a moment in time – just one hand reaching over the counter to present a cup to another outstretched hand. But it's a connection. We make sure everything we do honors that connection – from our commitment to the highest quality coffee in the world, to the way we engage with our customers and communities to do business responsibly. From our beginnings as a single store over forty years ago, in every place that we've been, and every place that we touch, we've tried to make it a little better than we found it.

Starbucks is not just a coffee company: Starbucks is a connections company. That purpose about connections plays out in the experiences which Starbucks creates for its employees and customers. And when employees and customers experience this purpose, in-store or through digital and social channels, they want to belong to it, to participate in it. That is why customers participate in MyStarbucksIdea.com – they can create meaningful connections with Starbucks and other customers. They have a voice. They can be heard and get feedback. And maybe, just maybe, their idea might even be implemented by Starbucks, whether it is a product idea or simply an idea to support the customer's local community.

When stakeholders see that the company's actions reflect its purpose in the experiences which the company creates for stakeholders, the company builds trust and culture. And stakeholders buy into that culture. A strong, shared culture enables the brand to enrol its employees and customers to make the brand even better and stronger. This has a powerful network effect which protects and builds the brand's value over time. Starbucks' brand is so strong, for example, it has reduced price sensitivity. In times when the cost of its core ingredient, coffee beans, has increased, Starbucks has been able to increase the price of its coffee without losing customers. Indeed, consumers are so stuck on Starbucks that they are willing to absorb these cost increases.

Consider another company which has leveraged its brand and shared culture to enrol its community to build new value – Virgin. Virgin was founded as a record shop in 1971 by entrepreneur Richard Branson, out of an earlier magazine venture, *Student*. In 1972, Virgin expanded to become a recording studio and, in 1973, it became a record label, eventually signing iconic bands such as the Sex Pistols and Culture Club. But things really got interesting when, in 1984, Virgin launched Virgin Atlantic Airways. Suddenly, what started as a hip music company for young people became something more.

Like Apple, Virgin believes in disrupting the status quo. But whereas Apple has focused on disrupting the status quo through beautiful computing products, Virgin has focused on disrupting the status quo across a broad range of entrenched markets in which customers have endured poor experiences with the companies which serve them. Anyone can relate to the unpleasant experience of air travel with a typical airline. But from the moment you enter the Virgin check-in terminal (and certainly when you enter the plane), you feel the difference in atmosphere, care and attention to detail, all of which make for a remarkable experience. Over time, as Virgin launched new businesses such as Virgin Vodka, Virgin Cola, Virgin Trains and Virgin Mobile, the Virgin brand began to stand for more than any single product or industry in which it conducted business. The Virgin brand began to stand for *youthful fun* – delivered in "unique and exceptional customer experience" (Virgin Group, 2016b).

Today, the Virgin group of companies is essentially a branded venture-capital conglomerate. Its leadership team is comprised of financial and operational managers. And this team invests in entrepreneurs who align with the Virgin culture (brand) and who seek to create new companies which serve "geographies or market segments where consumers are underserved" (Virgin Group, 2016c). Indeed, Richard Branson and his team realised that they could extract more value from the Virgin brand by opening it up and sharing it with other talented entrepreneurs. The Virgin brand and its shared culture is so strong, in fact, that promising entrepreneurs from around the world have launched new ventures through the iconic Virgin masthead. Virgin Group's portfolio now consists of over 60 companies which leverage the Virgin brand, generating over 24 billion USD in revenue worldwide.

The Shared Brand Framework

Now that I have established the nature of a shared brand in today's modern digital world, how can digital marketers build (or transform) a brand successfully for this new environment? I propose the Shared Brand Framework, which suggests that the best brands are now designed to be shared and advances three guiding principles: 1. brands ought to be co-opted, 2. brands ought to be syndicated and 3. brands ought to be responsive.

The Co-opted Brand

Storytelling has always been a critical discipline for marketers and there is a fundamental, biological reason for this. As neuro-economist Paul Zak (2014) declared, storytelling enables us to direct human behaviour by changing brain chemistry through well-structured narratives. Freytag's Pyramid, for example, posits that good storytelling follows a dramatic arc which consists of five acts: 1. exposition, which introduces important background information to the audience; 2. rising action, which is a series of events that builds the plot, conflict and tension to a point of peak interest; 3. climax, which is a turning point in the story that twists the protagonist's fate, often in the opposite direction; 4. falling action, in which the conflict between the protagonist and antagonist unravels, typically with one winning over the other; and 5. denouement, or resolution, which resolves any remaining conflicts and tension, thereby ending the story.

From a neuro-chemical perspective, tension synthesises

the cortisol which focuses our attention and narrative synthe-sises oxytocin (or the 'moral molecule', as Mr. Zak dubbed it) which signals in our brains a sense of trust and empathy for the characters in the story. These neuro-chemical processes intimate two important implications for marketers. First, they explain why a company's stakeholders are drawn more to the company's transcendent purpose (the why) than they are to the company's functional purpose (the what and how). The former is communicated through stories, whereas the latter is communicated through lists and processes; the former has the potential to inspire trust, empathy and connection, whereas the latter is often dull. Second, the neuro-chemical processes create an opportunity for brands to breakthrough and capture their audience's attention through purposeful narratives and stories – especially in an era in which there is a tangible atten-tion deficit.

Great marketers, therefore, are great storytellers. Perhaps this is not a particularly ground-breaking concept; but in the modern digital world in which (I have proposed) the shared brand has become necessary, marketers must move from being storytellers to being story facilitators. Indeed, in the glory days of the adver-tising agency, the marketer's main role was to create. Picture Mad Men devising the content, producing the content and distributing the content through traditional, one-way media channels. But today, the company's audience is also telling stories about the brand, creating and publishing content online. Some stories might be brand enhancing and some might be detrimental to brand reputation. Some stakeholders might be brand advocates and some stakeholders might be brand detractors. Some information might be true, some information might be false – or somewhere in between. But the brand's ability to control the story is increas-ingly difficult. The best brands, therefore, are embracing this change, by allowing and enabling their digital stakeholders to create content in partnership with the brand.

As story facilitators, therefore, marketers plant the seeds of an idea into various stakeholder communities in such a way that they take ownership of the idea and create their own stories and content. The result is an amplification of the brand, because more content is created and more stories are told than the brand could ever hope to achieve alone.

The Coca-Cola Company is perhaps the best example of this notion of story facilitator. In 2011, for example, Coca-Cola launched its 'Content 2020' strategy which is focused on evolving "from creative excellence to content excellence". Observing the new democratisation of creativity and technology (which, as described earlier in the chapter, stemmed from Web 2.0), Coca-Cola realised that it needed to modernise its approach to storytelling. So Coca-Cola invented the concept of 'liquid and linked content development'. 'Liquid' means that its marketers (and agency partners) must create ideas which are so contagious that they cannot be contained. 'Linked' means that those ideas are aligned with Coca-Cola's business objectives, its individual portfolio brands and its consumers. From a process perspective, liquid and linked content development means that Coca-Cola 1. tells brand stories which create liquid and linked ideas, 2. these liquid and linked ideas provoke conversations and 3. Coca-Cola acts and reacts to these conversations 365 days a year.

As you can see, this shift in the storytelling approach involved a move away from the one-way storytelling (and distribution) which was discussed earlier in this chapter to dynamic story-telling, defined by Coca-Cola as "the development of incremental elements of a brand idea that get dispersed systematically across multiple channels of conversation for the purposes of creating a unified and coordinated brand experience".

To do this, Coca-Cola now develops a creative brief which reveals a "big, fat, fertile space at the heart". Traditionally, a crea-tive brief is a document which marketers – particularly advertising agencies – use to inform their creative team which is tasked with creating the brand's advertising ideas. Each brand and agency has a slightly different take on the creative brief, but it usually consists of some background business context (the business problem or objective, for example), background information on the target audience (demographics and psychographic profiles) and a singular insight around which the creative team can brainstorm in order to develop creative collateral. In its new approach to crea-tive briefs, Coca-Cola has shifted "from insights to provocations", the goal of which is to find ideas which provoke conversation. But what might a big, fat fertile space look like? Another iconic brand, Calvin Klein, provides an example.

As story facilitators, the marketer's role is not only to plant the seeds of an idea, but also to find the seeds of an idea in the behaviours which are already illustrated by an audience and then to shepherd a broader audience to engage around that behaviour. In 2014, Calvin Klein launched a new marketing program which it called #MyCalvins. The Calvin Klein brand is about being a cultural catalyst, but it had become known by today's younger generation as its parents' brand. So Calvin Klein set out to make the brand relevant to its younger target audience. Through social listening, Calvin Klein noticed that consumers were taking selfies of themselves wearing the iconic Calvin Klein brand logo and posting them on social-media channels. This became the seed of an idea for a bigger brand story: #MyCalvins.

Calvin Klein started by collaborating with social influencers such as fashion bloggers, giving them Calvin Klein underwear in exchange for them posting selfies of themselves in the underwear with the hashtag #MyCalvins. The program ignited engagement among consumers who began contributing their own selfies with the program's hashtag. Even celebrity Justin Bieber contributed a selfie to the program. Calvin Klein took notice and the two developed a formal partnership. Other celebrities such as Fergie and Kendall Jenner also joined the program.

In approximately the first eighteen months of the campaign, nearly 600 influencers from 31 countries reached over 469 million consumers globally and achieved some 23 million consumer social interactions. Calvin Klein's audiences on social channels also grew – its Facebook fan base grew by 2.2 million people, Instagram by 1.8 million and Twitter by 1 million. A quick hashtag search on Instagram shows that over 400,000 images have been contributed to the #MyCalvins program. Calvin Klein has always been a brand about image-making and provoking conversation, and this campaign certainly reflects that purpose.

As we learned from Coca-Cola and Calvin Klein, the co-opted brand embraces audiences' feeling of ownership over the brand by finding and seeding brand stories which are at the core of the brand's shared purpose. These stories enrol stakeholders into their culture, and drive stakeholders to participate and create their own brand stories and content extensions. This is word-of-mouth marketing on steroids and it is critical to a successful digital brand strategy.

The Syndicated Brand

Today, media items flow freely from one channel to the next. An article published by the digitally native online publisher Buzz-Feed might first be discovered not on its own website, BuzzFeed.com, but instead on channels like Facebook, Twitter or Snap-chat. The article which is first discovered on Twitter might then be retweeted or shared into someone's Facebook feed, thereby reaching another audience segment, where the article achieves more engagement and gets shared further into other people's Facebook feeds or Instagram or even Pinterest. The article might even be curated and commented on by another publisher like Mashable, in which case the syndication cycle begins again. So goes the nature of viral content. According to former *New York Times* Executive Director, Jill Abramson, the "Huffington Post and Flipboard often get more traffic from *Times* journalism than we do". The media industry has been turned upside down, as it struggles to find new, profitable business models.

With the accelerated growth of digital channels, it is easy for a brand to find itself offering disjointed messages and content across digital marketing channels – which is detrimental to providing consistent digital experiences that reflect the organisation's shared purpose. But as Collins and Branch discussed in Chapter 3, we live in a networked world. It is critical for marketers, therefore, to ensure that they focus on the correct channels, informed by where their target audiences engage, and that, while the story which is told in each of those channels is consistent, the content is native to the experience of the specific channel. The experience (and audience) is different in Facebook than in Instagram, or Twitter, or Snapchat. And so, marketers must understand the nuances between channels to know how to tell stories in formats which resonate with the audiences on each of those channels.

Audience intelligence can help inform which channels and content resonate with audiences. For example, the audience intelligence platform People Pattern enables marketers to create an online audience which fits a brand's target consumer profile, and then to analyse that audience's behaviours to uncover where they source and share content, around which topics, from which influencers and so on.

After marketers get a sense for which channels to employ, they must feel comfortable testing and learning and evolving on the platform, especially considering that digital platforms are always evolving and new channels are always rising. This test-and-learn evolutionary process must become institutionalised. Ultimately, the goal is to learn where and how the brand ought to live across digital channels to make the greatest impact. This means focusing on creating native content in each of those channels while simultaneously telling consistent stories across channels.

The Responsive Brand

The democratisation of content creation and publishing has only been accelerated by the maturation of social media. This has given rise to real-time content marketing, epitomised in the United States by Old Spice's 'The Man Your Man Could Smell Like' campaign in 2010 and Oreo's 'You Can Still Dunk in the Dark' tweet when the power went out during the 2013 Super Bowl. Now, it is important to note that 'real time' is relative. For consumer brands, where successful content-marketing efforts like these examples can hinge on creating content at the speed of the culture, 'real time' can mean instantaneously. But in B2B technology or service industry categories where engaging professional audiences does not rely so heavily on cultural moments of the zeitgeist, or in highly regulated environments such as healthcare where content must go through several rounds of medical and regulatory approval before being published, 'real time' probably means relevant time.

Irrespective of the temporal meaning of 'real time', marketing has shifted from a waterfall approach to content in which marketers spend months researching audiences, then testing creative concepts, and finally creating and deploying campaigns through advertising channels; instead moving toward an agile, test-and-learn environment in which marketers create small pieces of content in days (or hours), publish immediately and then see how the content performs 'in the wild' with actual audiences. With digital metrics, marketers can measure the results immediately and iterate on the content in the service of creating better engagement with audiences.

Consequently, marketing teams must be redesigned and organised to be responsive to audiences in real time. The *New York Times*, for example, first evangelised the notion of 'audience development' in its 2014 Innovation Report. Audience development considers three key disciplines: 1. discovery – how to package and distribute content, 2. promotion – how to call attention to that content and 3. connection – how to create a two-way relationship with audiences which deepens loyalty. Since this report, many other publishers and marketing agencies have created audience development departments. Indeed, Weed and colleagues (*Harvard Business Review*, 2014) highlighted three types of people who are now needed in marketing: 'thinkers' focus on data and analytics, 'feelers' focus on audience engagement and 'doers' focus on content and production.

While there is no single correct way to organise a marketing department for responsiveness – especially in a world in which team members' skill sets and expertise vary – what is needed are multi-disciplinary teams (and team members) that can glean insights from new forms of data, inform and create engaging content, and get that content out through the right paid, earned and owned channels. Exemplary leaders will take the time to organise their teams for responsiveness by getting the correct team members with the correct skills working together.

Conclusion

In our modern digital world, a brand is the shared purpose, experiences and culture which align a company and its stakeholders. Marketers who are aiming to succeed in this new world – a world in which their stakeholders are empowered yet distracted – must design their brands to be shared. Marketers must allow their brands to be *co-opted*, finding and seeding stories and ideas which align with the brand's shared *purpose*. Those stories and ideas must be *syndicated* across the channels in which the audience engages, and in formats which are customised and native to the *experiences* which are provided by each of those channels. New data can guide the way for identifying these ideas and channels. And marketers must organise their team for responsiveness, because audiences expect real-time engagement with their brands. Functional silos must be broken and teams redesigned, with a focus on placing the audience at the centre, and on creating remarkable content and experiences to build a shared *culture* which creates greater mutual value for the company and its stakeholders.

References

Advertising Age (no date) "The Positioning Era Cometh." Retrieved from: http://www.ries.com/wp-content/uploads/2015/09/Positioning-Articles002.pdf

AdWeek (2010) "How Old Spice Ruled the Real-Time Web." Retrieved from: http://www.adweek.com/news/technology/how-old-spice-ruled-real-time-web-102823

Airbnb (2014) "Belong Anywhere." Retrieved from: http://blog.airbnb.com/belong-anywhere/

American Marketing Association (2016) "Dictionary." Retrieved from: https://www.ama.org/resources/Pages/Dictionary.aspx?dLetter=BanddLetter=B

B Lab (no date) "What Are B Corps?" Retrieved from: https://www.bcorporation.net/what-are-b-corps

Drucker, P. (1954) *The Practice of Management*. New York, USA: HarperCollins Publishers.

Facebook (2016) "About Facebook." Retrieved from: https://www.facebook.com/facebook/info?tab=page_info

Godin, S. (2010) *Linchpin*. New York, USA: Penguin Group.

Google (2016) "Company Overview." Retrieved from: https://www.google.com/about/company/

Harvard Business Review (2014) "Why Your Brain Loves Good Storytelling." Retrieved from: https://hbr.org/2014/10/why-your-brain-loves-good-storytelling

Harvard Business Review (2016) "The Founder of TOMS on Reimagining the Company's Mission." Retrieved from: https://hbr.org/2016/01/the-founder-of-toms-on-reimagining-the-companys-mission

Hsieh, T. (2010) *Delivering Happiness: A Path to Profits, Passion, and Purpose*. New York, USA: Hachette Book Group.

Huffington Post (2013) "Oreo's Super Bowl Tweet: 'You Can Still Dunk In The Dark.'" Retrieved from: http://www.huffingtonpost.com/2013/02/04/oreos-super-bowl-tweet-dunk-dark_n_2615333.html

IBM Institute for Business Value (2013) "Reinventing the Rules of Engagement: CEO Insights from the Global C-Suite Study." Retrieved from: http://www-03.ibm.com/services/ca/en/documents/CSuite_CEO_EN.PDF

Ogilvy, D. (1985) *Ogilvy on Advertising*. New York, USA: Vintage Books.

Rackspace (2016) "Investor Deck Q1 2016." Retrieved from: file:///Users/davidfossas/Downloads/RAX%20Investor%20pres%20Deck%20Q12016%205-16-2016%20for%20website.pdf

Reuters (2014) "Bain Capital to Invest in Shoemaker TOMS." Retrieved from: http://www.reuters.com/article/us-toms-baincapital-idUSKBN0GK1ZZ20140820

Ries, A., and J. Trout (1972) *Positioning: The Battle for Your Mind*. New York: McGraw Hill.

Sinek, S. (2009) *Start with Why*. New York, USA: Penguin Group.

Starbucks (2016) "Our Mission." Retrieved from: http://www.starbucks.com/about-us/company-information/mission-statement

Stengel, J. (2011) *GROW: How Ideals Power Growth and Profit at the World's Greatest Companies*. New York, USA: Crown Business.

Stengel, J. (2013) "Stengel Grow Discussion Guide Questions Final." Retrieved from: http://www.jimstengel.com/wp-content/uploads/2013/12/Stengel-Grow-Discussion-Guide-Questions.pdf

TechCrunch (2009) "Amazon Buys Zappos; The Price is $928m., not $847m." Retrieved from: https://techcrunch.com/2009/07/22/amazon-buys-zappos/

TED (no date) "Simon Sinek: How Great Leaders Inspire Action." Retrieved from: https://www.ted.com/talks/simon_sinek_how_great_leaders_inspire_action#t-330408

Virgin Group (2016a) "About Us." Retrieved from: https://www.virgin.com/virgingroup/content/about-us

Virgin Group (2016b) "Our Brand." Retrieved from: https://www.virgin.com/virgingroup/content/our-brand-0

Virgin Group (2016c) "Our Senior Team." Retrieved from: https://www.virgin.com/virgingroup/content/our-senior-team

Washington Post (2015) "Starbucks' CEO Sent This Bizarre Memo Telling Baristas To Be Nicer Because of the Stock Turmoil." Retrieved from: https://www.washingtonpost.com/news/business/wp/2015/08/24/starbucks-chief-sent-a-bizarre-memo-telling-baristas-to-be-nicer-because-of-the-stock-market/

WWD (2015) "Calvin Klein Takes on Sexting, Tinder to Promote #mycalvins." Retrieved from: http://wwd.com/media-news/advertising/calvin-klein-tinder-mycalvins-10193692/

YouTube (2012) "Coca-Cola Content 2020 Initiative Strategy Video – Parts I and II." Retrieved from: https://www.youtube.com/watch?v=G1P3r2EsAos

YouTube (no date) "Rackspace Culture Story." Retrieved from: https://www.youtube.com/watch?v=5fPS1TUFiaQ

Zak, P. (2014) "Why Your Brain Loves Good Storytelling." Retrieved from: https://hbr.org/2014/10/why-your-brain-loves-good-storytelling

About the Author

David Fossas is Director of Brand at WP Engine and a marketing consultant and advisor to entrepreneurs through his firm, The Reciprocity Company. He has partnered with Fortune 500 and global brands such as Verizon, General Motors, Hewlett Packard Enterprise, Procter and Gamble and Clorox, to create and operationalise new digital and social marketing capabilities. He also enjoys collaborating with entrepreneurs at early and growth stage companies to create new market value. Learn more at http://reciprocitytheory.com. Follow him on Twitter at @dfossas. Contact him on email at david@thereciprocity.co.

Chapter 11

Designing Organisations for Holistic Digital Success

Shalonda L. Hunter

Introduction

The integration of digital technology in organisations has posed a difficult challenge for many companies. Indeed, leaders in start-ups and Fortune 100 companies alike have struggled, not so much with how to launch digital goods, services, channels or interfaces, but with how to integrate digital effectively throughout their organisations. This chapter examines how digital technology, as a strategic focus, can shape, and is shaped by, organisational design across business units and teams.

The chapter begins by explaining what is both a holistic and digital approach to organisational design. It then defines what is meant by each term, why they are important, how they are applied successfully and where they intersect and align with organisational goals. Finally, it introduces the Hunter Model for Holistic Organisation Design™, which outlines a framework that leaders can use to reach their digital technology goals in order to remain competitive, profitable and, most of all, relevant.

After reading this chapter you will be able to:

1. Create an effective digital strategy which can be executed easily throughout your organisation;

2. Collaborate with leaders throughout your organisation to bring new technologies to the marketplace; and

3. Update any outdated organisation design with a streamlined process to welcome both innovation and data-driven decisions.

Digital and Holistic

Traditionally, digital has often been regarded as the antithesis of analogue, referring to the technology which communicates continuous and indiscrete electronic signals as a series of discrete 1s and 0s. Today, however, with the insurgence of computers in business and everyday life, the term 'digital' has also come to encompass the processes or mechanisms by which things get done. Indeed, in their 2015 article "What 'Digital' Really Means", McKinsey partner Karel Dorner and co-author David Edelman make the case that digital is less of a *thing* and more of a *way*. I agree. To help cement this claim, they concluded that this more modern definition of digital ought to be viewed in terms of three possibilities: 1. creating value at the new frontiers of business, 2. creating value in the processes which execute a vision of customer experiences and 3. building foundational capabilities which support the entire organisation. These three possibilities, based on my experience, perfectly summarise how leaders within organisations ought to think about digital.

Consider examples from the summer of 2016, which brought some of the largest technology acquisitions in years. The first acquisition was Yahoo, once a web pioneer, which was sold to telecom giant Verizon for 4.6 billion USD. Not only was this acquisition viewed by many in the business world as the end of an era for the technology giant, but it was also highlighted by some in Silicon Valley as a clear case of how big companies can suffer from leadership and organisational strongholds which fail to listen to, and more importantly, respond to, changes in the market. The second acquisition was the purchase of LinkedIn, the world's largest professional social-networking platform, by Microsoft, a software and technology company. You might ask why a software and technology company decided to enter the social-networking industry. Closer inspection of this acquisition (and that of Yahoo) demonstrates how even well-established companies must shift their businesses as markets change. It also certainly alludes to the changes which digital has engendered in how people interact with their products. And hints at the reason why more and more organisations must integrate digital into how they conduct business – both internally and externally.

The focus in this chapter is not on distinguishing between various technologies which exist to facilitate digital. Instead, the focus is on how companies – from start-ups to established enterprises – can begin to digitalise their business. With this in mind, I designed the Hunter Model for Holistic Organisation Design™ to assist leaders to integrate digital holistically across the company.

What Exactly Is a Holistic Approach and Why Does It Matter?

Webster's Dictionary defines 'holistic' as "relating to or concerned with complete systems rather than with individual parts." It is about seeing the forest, rather than the trees. And when it comes to digital, leaders who focus on keeping digital functions and responsibilities in separate silos will cripple creativity, will eliminate marketplace competitive advantage and might even face the threat of extinction.

In 2011, digital-marketing thought leader and author Brian Solis's article in *Fast Company* magazine, "The Time Has Come For Holistic Business Strategy", made the case that businesses, not just teams, that do not make a shift in their organisation's structure toward digital will struggle mightily to exist in the marketplace of the future. Six years later, organisations are still grappling with some of the very same issues – but with more technological options, more competition and more online activities, in a more global economy.

In my experience, the challenge lays not with the adoption of digital, but with incorporating digital-centric leadership and capabilities throughout an organisation. Indeed, the philosophy and organisational structure of many companies leads to a situation in which the 'digital marketing team' has the single task of managing digital efforts. Often, this team reports to a single owner or management team. This situation leaves little room for collaboration with teams across the business and puts the great bulk of responsibility on digital marketing professionals to find solutions to problems which might be beyond their skill level or 'pay grade'. Inevitably, it will leave companies, both traditional and digital-centric, in danger of becoming irrelevant or, worse, extinct.

Holistic, digital-centric principles adopted by leading companies such as Facebook, Amazon, BMW and Google have allowed them to develop products, initiatives and game-changing technology that inspire innovation and creativity throughout their organisations. They take the digital-marketing process and its relationship with their other business units seriously.

Many other companies have also successfully made the digital transformation. Yet a key issue I see is that putting digital first in the decision-making process remains a challenge. Indeed, leaders across industries are struggling with questions such as:

- Who controls technology within the organisation? Is this a CIO, CTO, COO or CMO function?

- What are the roles and responsibilities of C-suite executives across the organisation?

- Who controls budget, priorities, human resources and new business?

- Is it more important to have highly skilled MBAs or start-up-trained talent?

- Which technological platforms will be used to execute strategies?

- What are the current digital capabilities? Do they exist in-house?

- Are teams collaborating to reach digital goals?

These questions are best considered holistically. Consider the following three examples.

Uber, the world's fastest growing and largest on-demand private car service, could not exist without a holistic digital strategy that incorporates its technology and digital marketing teams successfully. The technology works hand-in-hand with the customer relationship management (CRM) and social-media teams. How would Uber be able to serve its customers if it did not have a strong creative and technology team; a robust digital advertising plan; or a talent and retention plan that allows it to attract the best and brightest engineers, mobile team and drivers?

Gilt, one of the first luxury insider-access sale sites, provides daily deals on clothing, homeware, travel, dining and more. How could it pull this off day-to-day if it were not able to work across its social, IT and email marketing teams? How can sales and data analytics teams operate without collaboration? Which technology and team structure does it use to ensure that it is communicating with customers effectively across channels and devices?

Warby Parker, a mission-driven online eyewear company, launched its brand in 2010, transforming both the way in which consumers purchase prescription glasses and the price point at which stylish durable glasses are sold – 99 USD and under. What are its key performance indicators (KPIs) and how are they aligned with its strategic goals? How did it structure the roles and responsibilities of team members to create a seamless ordering process?

All three of these examples illustrate digital-centric companies, whose holistic approaches to organisation design have been able to disrupt their industries, generate competitive advantage and attract top talent. Similarly, their holistic organisation design has supported digital innovation, reinforced team structure and nurtured business model transformation.

The Hunter Model for Holistic Digital Organisation Design™

The Hunter Model for Holistic Digital Organisation Design™ (see Figure 11.1) serves as a guide for digital integration. This model outlines how leaders can focus priorities around strategies, teams and metrics, and how priorities can cross verticals. The simplicity of this model is intended to ensure that teams, and those who are responsible for specific business units, focus on the role which technology has on the effectiveness of the structure and on accountability.

Organisation design is a value-focused process that is built to guide leaders' attention around strategic priorities and critical operations of each business unit and product. Companies across industries utilise organisational design to drive strategy, accountability and collaboration, and to deal with the complexity of cost and capabilities. Creating a formula for success is neither simple nor easy to implement.

A new model for how companies can think about incorporating digital technology into organisation design is the Hunter Model for Holistic Digital Organisation Design™. As with all successful organisation design models, the Hunter Model for Holistic Digital Organisation Design™ delivers a simple and clear framework to incorporate digital strategy across business units. Organisations which want to remain relevant and have a competitive edge in the digital economy must ask themselves more than the basic strategic question "What are we trying to achieve?" It is important to ask "Where is our value?" and "Which mechanisms will be utilised?" Leaders ought to have a singular focus not just on how to streamline processes but also on which digital technologies will be applied to, and which services and capabilities will be needed for, each strategic goal.

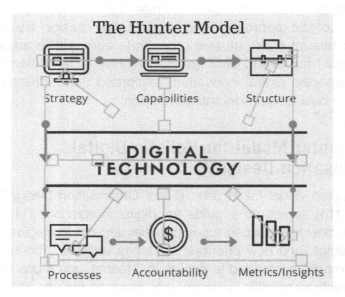

Figure 11.1. The Hunter Model for Holistic Digital Organisation Design™

Digital technology and capabilities are the two major elements of organisation design which keep a company competitive. When asked to re-evaluate their current processes, companies note that the ability to attract and retain specific talent is critical. This is how companies, in today's constantly evolving landscape, not only keep afloat but also set the bar higher as a key player within the industry for all others to follow.

The Hunter Model for Holistic Digital Organisation Design™ is a holistic framework for analysing digital organisations. The design policies for the model are outlined in six categories which are controlled by leaders and are heavily influenced by the choice of digital technology. The policies are the tools which leaders must utilise to integrate digital technology successfully throughout the organisation, and influence the selection of new talent and employee retention. The first and main policy is *digital technology*; this is the critical piece of the model. Not until an organisation understands fully which tools will be used to execute the vision and achieve company goals will it be able to successfully launch effective digital marketing initiatives, develop new technologies and sustain a competitive advantage. The second is *strategy*, which determines direction and outlines specific key performance indicators (KPIs) for each goal. The third is *capabilities*; these define which skills are available to and which missing from the team, and lists the current technological assets. The fourth is *accountability*, which delineates not only who has power and authority around the tasks that need to be performed, but also allows leaders to understand across functions where the digital marketing team fits into the workflow and structure beyond its traditional roles and responsibilities. The fifth is *structure*; this helps organisations and teams to realise the roles and responsibilities within the entire team and program. The sixth is *insights/metrics*; these are necessary for understanding how the digital program is performing across channels and where the audience lives online.

By opting to have technology as the focal point, the Hunter Model for Holistic Digital Organisation Design™ presents the importance of digital technology in modern organisation design. This allows leaders to shift their priorities from simple performance-related criteria to those of a design that integrates capabilities which can influence strategy and structure.

Technology and innovation are what will keep companies of the future alive. *How* leaders incorporate technology into their organisations' structures, and how they innovate, will keep companies moving forward internally. Rather than focusing on developing techniques for processes, rewards and streamlined sales, digital marketing professionals will need to begin to focus strategically on how to support accountability, structure and capabilities around technology in order to achieve competitive advantage and relevance. Sadly, for many companies, the lack of focus on these two components will inevitably lead to extinction.

For more than 30 years, the Star Model for Organisation Design (see Figure 11.2.) developed by Jay Galbraith has served as a guide for companies to follow for successful organisation design. Praised for its simplicity and universal approach, it was one of the first organisation models to shape how companies needed to create work across teams for effective accountability and structure. The Star Model was fundamental in introducing the notion that organisations are complex, and recognised that a need existed for functions to work together in order to ensure that success was comprehensive and competitive. The role of technology was not a consideration in this model, something that can be attributed to the time in which it was developed. The model has had many updates since its inception, but the original five policies have remained consistent. The first is strategy, which determines direction. The second is structure, which denotes the location of decision-making power. Processes are defined by the flow of information; they are the means of responding to information technologies. Rewards provide motivation and incentives for desired behaviour. And finally, the selection and development of the right people – in alignment with other core business policies – allow the organisation to operate at maximum efficiency.

Figure 11.2. The Star Model

Traditional organisation design models such as the Star Model have one main objective: to ensure that businesses keep moving as smoothly as possible. Efficiency, not effectiveness, was their main goal. Today's companies cannot afford to stay competitive and relevant with structure alone: they must understand and embrace technology, and follow a framework which not only aligns policies with one another, but which also puts digital technology at its focal point. In the Hunter Model for Holistic Digital Organisation Design™, team and project design fall into six categories, aimed at developing a corporate strategy and an organisation structure which support efficiency and effectiveness.

The Keys to Successful Holistic Digital Organisation Design

It is not easy to transform policies, structure and philosophies quickly within an organisation. Most companies, no matter the size or years in business, have 'their way' of doing business, and a process in place for how their leaders and C-suite executives are measured. Structure and business strategy are still a very necessary component of effective business planning. Indeed, as organisations become more complicated and larger, it will become even more important to ensure across verticals that coordination is in place.

The first challenge which many leaders face in activating their digital strategy is to understand where ownership of the specific task will live within their business structure. The second challenge is aligning the internal skill sets and capabilities with the new functions. When new functions or work are introduced, organisations tend to want to align internal skills with the current capabilities of team members. But the digital needs of today's marketplace might not fit within the current capabilities and team structure. As platforms and channels increase and become more complex, each function will need its own digital team and/or dedicated leader to manage and articulate the particular needs of the division and team.

Here are five key ways to incorporate holistic digital principles into the business unit structure of an organisation and team. These concepts are also incorporated in the Hunter Model for Holistic Digital Organisation Design™:

- *Rethink what you 'know'.* Leaders have a great deal of knowledge. This is what makes them experts in their respective fields. In order to learn from someone else or about how to improve systems, we must be open to new ideas and embrace change. What we know might already be old information. Simply staying current is no longer an option. We must stay ahead of the curve in order to innovate.

- *Attract players who understand the game.* Having the right staff members and leaders is not a new idea, but getting the best-skilled employees to execute your particular strategy is genius. Too many companies fail at getting the best and succeed at having the leftovers.

- *Re-organise.* There is no shame in cleaning out the clutter. It is as good for our closets as it is for our companies and teams. This is all a part of growth. When your business requires social media, paid search, mobile, web, IT and CRM, it is time to make sure that cross-unit decisions are being made. This is a safeguard to ensure that key performance indicators are aligned with strategic goals, and that the KPIs provide informed data to understand the opportunities to scale and learn more about what is missing.

- *Be confident.* Confidence is key to learning and embracing change. Technology is moving fast and a great deal of high-risk decisions will need to be made. Taking the opportunity to rush strategic planning will not get you there any faster. In my experience, leaders who understand how to balance the testing of new ideas get better results.

- *Build influencers.* You cannot go at it alone. Modern teams need to have leaders; and all of the skills which are needed might not be on your particular project. How do you bring them in? Utilise resources within and outside of your project or company, which can help you understand your project from a different perspective. Have you ever gone to a friend who is outside 'the machine' for advice? Just as we are cautious about what and with whom we share in our personal lives, we ought to follow that same cautious openness in the business world, as we build an influencer circle which has a similar mindset and passion to innovate.

Incorporating Principles to Transform Companies and Teams

The above skeleton presented how to integrate the values and ideas which can transform a company or team. But how do you know you are headed down the best road toward reaching your goals? To have a path for organisations and leaders to build business units that work across verticals to meet digital technology goals, five elements are needed: 1. create key performance indicators (KPIs) that hold leaders responsible; 2. focus on talent retention, not just acquisition; 3. plan for consumer-to-consumer (C2C) engagement; 4. do not go at it alone; and 5. utilise the data to count your wins and cut your losses.

1. Create Key Performance Indicators (KPIs) that Hold Leaders Responsible

Good leaders respond to two things: 1. performance and 2. profitability. If one of these two things is tied to their success or that of the organisation, people are watching. It is not an option for them to fail. If good leaders want to motivate their teams and support innovation, they will be more than willing to execute winning digital strategies and track metrics that matter. Leaders must inspire action, and KPIs tied to this can help spread the culture and mission simultaneously, thereby putting digital technology at the centre of the company.

2. Focus on Talent Retention, Not Just Acquisition

The greatest asset any company has is its employees. Companies which lead the competition and innovate typically have highly skilled employees and higher retention rates. Innovators who are able to drive change do so by being able to support and create cultures which have open, honest and creative environments, and by rewarding their employees' input and hard work. If organisations want to win and truly transform the way they do business, they will need to focus not only on getting the talent in the door, but keeping the talent in-house. Research has shown that for every employee a company loses, it takes a minimum of four-to-six months to replace and bring a new person up to speed. Can you imagine the productivity and creativity which is lost during this time period? Organisations must place value on their culture and ensure that they maintain the pioneering talent that they have already garnered.

3. Plan for Consumer-to-Consumer (C2C) Engagement

Watch out for word of mouth. Now more than ever, consumers take to social media and other websites to rate, praise and recommend companies. Though it may not seem like the kind of thing that fits with a holistic model of digital marketing, it is (see Chapter 4 by Collins and Branch). Organisations not only need to be ready to implement the best technology to track these conversations, but also must have these kinds of conversations in mind as teams plan for what kinds of insights and metrics will be aligned with KPIs and the ROI. The digital world is both qualitative and quantitative, and what is being measured needs to get organisations as close as possible to understanding the value of their brands.

4. Do Not Go at It Alone

Find consultants to execute your vision. The ability to recognise and lead consultants so that they are your partners is a valuable skill. In some cases, organisations bring consultants in piece by piece and do not give them an opportunity to understand the full scope of the project, metrics for success and sometimes even individual team members. Though they are not being paid to learn, consultants will need time and possibly some hand-holding to learn how your business works, and to get up to speed on how to meet your expectations and needs. A partnering firm or individual consultant can help to fill capability gaps which might exist, but they can also bring expertise gained from the wins and losses of their other clients which could strengthen additional digital (marketing) efforts.

5. Utilise the Data to Count Your Wins and Cut Your Losses

Inevitably, things do not always go as planned. There are times for recalibration, checks and balances. Most successful teams learn how to evaluate what did and did not work and why. It is key that a culture of sharing success be balanced with learning from losses. The infamous definition of insanity is repeating the same error over and over, thinking something will change. Organisations cannot afford to suffer from insanity. Whether it is not launching a product during a particular time of year, or keeping staff members who no longer have the skill set needed to be the innovative company which you envision, cutting losses is tough – but it must happen.

Conclusion

The solutions to any of these challenges are not simple. As we move more and more into a digital society, much of the transformation process will reveal itself in time. The Hunter Model for Holistic Digital Organisation Design™ provides a path to incorporate digital technology into organisation design. Traditional and new businesses which implement the six policies are on their way toward more highly skilled teams, improved competitiveness and stronger overall performance.

References

Dorner, K., and D. Edelman (2015) "What 'Digital' Really Means." Retrieved from: http://www.mckinsey.com/industries/high-tech/our-insights/what-digital-really-means

Galbraith, J. (2016) "The Star Model." Retrieved from: http://www.jaygalbraith.com/services/star-model

Godin, S. (2008) *Tribes: We Need You to Lead Us*. New York, USA: Piatkus.

Goel, V., and M. Merced (2016) "Yahoo's Sale to Verizon Ends an Era for Web Pioneer." Retrieved from: http://www.nytimes.com/2016/07/25/business/yahoo-sale.html?_r=0

Solis, B. (2011) "The Time Has Come For Holistic Business Strategy." Retrieved from: http://www.fastcompany.com/1719518/time-has-come-holistic-business-strategy

About the Author

Shalonda L. Hunter is a serial entrepreneur, and founder and Chief Strategist of Fast Lane Interactive, a digital marketing and solutions consultancy that helps companies drive profitability and impact in their digital marketing efforts. Shalonda has worked with global clients such as HBO, Marriott Hotels and Viacom, and with a variety of start-ups. Shalonda is a mentor and instructor at the Startup Institute in New York City. Shalonda holds a B.A. and an M.A. from the University of Michigan. She enjoys 1980s and '90s music. Follow her on Twitter at headfli@flitimes.com and at @digtialshalonda, and on Instagram at @flitimes.

Chapter 12

Social Utility – Useful Services, Applications and Content as Digital Marketing

Bryan Pedersen

Introduction

Digital marketing has given rise to countless new opportunities to message consumers and much of it has manifested itself in the form of the many new ways to place advertisements, both actively and passively to the browsing audience: banner ads, for example, site takeovers, Facebook news-feed sponsored stories, emails, pre-roll, post-roll and interstitial video ads. And of course, all of these new messages will follow you everywhere, thanks to advertisement retargeting. If you happen to break a shoelace and Google a replacement, you can be sure that you will be seeing all manner of shoe-fastening paraphernalia everywhere you browse for the next week – in your news feed, on digital banners and in video advertisements – all of which will claim to fasten your shoe better than you had ever thought possible.

That is not to say that inexpensive, targeted and retargeted digital messages are ineffective or that they do not have a place in the larger marketing paradigm. But there is also a new way to reach consumers through digital marketing that does not involve the digital hallmarks of faster, smaller and more frequent. It is an approach that does not feel like marketing at all. In fact, if done well, the consumer will seek you out for the value that you provide, assuming that the consumer has indeed chosen to engage with you and is open to receiving messages from the brand.

This approach is called *social utility* and it is aimed at the growing opportunity to engage those consumers by providing them with useful tools, services and platforms, rather than bombarding them with messages. It is a counterbalance to the ubiquity of digital marketing messages in an era of overwhelmed attention spans and is a way to pull in consumers by providing value first. After reading this chapter you will:

1. Understand the opportunity which social utility allows, by offering consumers something truly useful while keeping your brand top of mind;

2. Have looked at a number of brands that have created social-utility programs over the years; and

3. Possess a framework for implementing social-utility-based marketing programs of your own.

What Is Social Utility?

The Age-old Value of Utility

The idea of social-utility marketing is starting to pick up quickly as digital marketers look to the next big thing. But at heart it is simply the concept of providing something useful – something of utility – to consumers instead of marketing messages. This spans an enormous number of possibilities including, but not limited to: content, mobile applications, information, directions, customer service, weather, advice, tickets and tools. None of these is something new; indeed, they existed long before digital marketing became the dominant form of marketing that it is today.

Through the years, there have been numerous examples of utility as marketing. Soap operas are often cited as one of the earliest vehicles for advertising. They were highly targeted to the demographics of their day and age, meant to inform and entertain housewives who were the primary caretakers of the household. For decades, radio provided sponsored news and weather updates – brought to you by your favourite brand – long before you could look up such information on your smartphone. And supermarkets were and still are famous for creating circulars and coupons which help consumers with their weekly food-shopping decisions.

So what is different now? As marketers continue to seek more ways to stand out from competitors, they try new methods to be useful to consumers, just like those old examples. The difference is the ability for these methods now to be social in nature. They are able to spread incredibly fast not just because they are useful, but because consumers are now conditioned to share – and they expect to have their voices heard. People share more than 16,000 words per day and every hour there are more than 100 million conversations about brands (Berger, 2013). This is both an incredible opportunity and a daunting experiment in transparency.

All of this leads not only to an unprecedented way both to reach consumers and to provide value, but also to have those consumers help spread that usefulness to others, if done right. The social aspect means letting go of some control, but authenticity can have tremendous benefits, as we shall see in some of the examples in this chapter; and it is key to getting a social-utility program off the ground.

Five Thousand Messages a Day and Growing

The average consumer today is undoubtedly exposed to many more advertising messages than in decades past, and the number continues to grow with each passing year. An oft-quoted statistic in the media, in journals and among advertising professionals is that the average hovers somewhere around the five thousand mark (Hill Holliday, 2016). While there is some debate over the actual number, it is certainly a high number to process nevertheless – and that is without taking into account the enormous number of messages which consumers are also scrolling through on their own. The Facebook news feed is one of the most successful technology innovations of all time and the reason for the platform's enormous success. Other major social-media platforms have copied their *infinite scroll* format – allowing consumers to browse through stories indefinitely with a thumb flick. And even major media companies have started changing their websites and mobile apps to look more like the Facebook news feed. All this means that consumers are faced with a dizzying amount of information to process and that each little titbit of information is in competition with the others to stand out in the mind of the consumer.

One way of embracing this reality is to create more messages, specifically tailored to each platform on which they appear, thereby increasing relevancy and hopefully uptake. This is not incorrect and indeed is simply the reality of today's content requirement: proliferate across many channels in search of reaching consumers' hearts and minds. But as consumer attention spans continue to shrink, the question is whether or not all of these little pokes and prods from a brand add up to a truly engaging experience. In *Meatball Sunday*, bestselling marketing author, Seth Godin, writes about the changing landscape of marketing, arguing that there are no more big ideas in advertising messages due to the shifting and fragmenting of consumer attention (Godin, 2007). The lasting idea such as MasterCard's 'Priceless' campaign invented in 1997, well before most people were on the Internet, is a product of a bygone era. Godin argues that the product experience which is being offered must be the marketing itself, in an era when advertising messages are both ubiquitous and not trusted by consumers.

While there is some logic to that statement, not every brand will be the absolute best in its class at any given time. There is only one 'Car of the Year', only one wireless carrier with the best coverage and only one sneaker which is endorsed and worn by the NBA MVP. And while competitors might be close, it is difficult to rely solely on the product in this case.

But social utility is all about providing value to the consumer. In addition to helping the brand stand out in a crowded world of marketing messages, it also ought to work to make the product being sold even better, and in turn support Godin's hypothesis that the product itself is the new marketing. (See Chapter 15 by

Suwanjindar for a discussion of this new utility approach in the music industry, which was disrupted completely by the growth of the Internet and social file sharing.)

Consumer First

One of the simplest yet most important keys to creating a useful customer experience is by simply placing consumers first. It sounds like such an intuitive statement, yet it oftentimes gets lost in endless discussions around the product, pricing, market roll-outs and financial considerations. Then digital marketing quickly needs to drive enormous value by shepherding target consumers through virtual doors to the point of sale. After all those considerations are taken into account, it is easy to see why brands can sometimes forget the first rule of service – it is all about the customer.

When thinking about social utility – creating value as a form of marketing – a customer-first approach becomes that much more important. Brands need to be ever more considerate of how they are speaking to consumers if they are to engage in delivering them value, not just serving them marketing messages, especially in the age of social media and information sharing. A brand is only a step away from being called out for inauthenticity or pretending to deliver value to consumers, when in fact it is just a thinly disguised veil to gather sensitive data or target consumers for offers.

Aside from the public relations danger, returning to a customer-first approach is a lesson of which many brands need to be reminded time and again, as it relates to both marketing and products. In *Customers First: Dominate Your Market by Winning Them Over Where it Counts the Most*, author Bolivar Bueno (2012) writes about Burger King's strategy to win over 18–35-year-old males, the core customers of the fast-food industry. While McDonald's had been busy focusing on the experience which its customers got along with their orders, Burger King had decided to focus on its product. The problem with that approach was that the core customer did not care that much about the quality of the burger which they were getting. This led to a decrease in market share, with Burger King constantly changing its voice and positioning in an effort to right the ship. If one of the most recognised food brands in the world can misstep in its understanding of a consumer-first approach to its core business, it is easy for any brand to do so too – especially when rolling out new digital-marketing programs like social utility.

Methods and Considerations

Creating Your Own Utility Platform

Social media has created amazing new opportunities for brands to engage with consumers directly. Each new social platform that arises is a world unto itself, with its own medium – whether that be video, photos, longer-form blog posts, posts which disappear, and even live-streaming – or a combination of any of those media. Consumers on those platforms adopt their own voice and, in the case of hashtags and acronyms, even their own language. Each is its own microcosm and often the types of marketing initiatives that work on one platform will not necessarily work on the next. This is made all the more challenging when brands of all kinds proliferate on each platform, all competing for attention from consumers alongside their friends, pictures of their pets and, increasingly, high-quality targeted content from media organisations that specialise in tune-in and content uptake.

In his bestselling social-marketing book, *Jab, Jab, Jab, Right Hook,* Gary Vaynerchuk (2013) recounts how he finished the book on the day on which it was due to be sent to his editor – which was the same day on which Instagram launched a 15-second video feature:

> I went back to my hotel room and spent four hours looking at every Instagram video that I could find. And since then, my team at VaynerMedia and I, and all of the most progressive marketers in the world, have been scrambling to figure out the best way to storytell in fifteen seconds of video on a platform built for pictures. I can't think of a more fitting illustration of what kind of world we live in now.

That might sound daunting – because it certainly is.

And this is absolutely true when social-media marketing is taken as merely an offshoot of the platforms which are dominating the public consciousness at any one point in time. Vaynerchuk's book is just a few years old, and in the past few years, we have seen more change – the stratospheric rise of Snapchat capturing Millennial attention the world over, for example; Instagram's launch of Stories as a direct response or imitation; and Facebook's major push into video and live-streaming with Facebook Live. It becomes more and more difficult to keep up with consumer interest, and even more difficult to keep up with the platform changes in features, advertising products and targeting which they afford.

But if the idea of social marketing stops at each of the major social platforms' doorsteps, a digital marketer will forever be playing catch-up, adapting the latest features of each of those quickly evolving services, in an effort to out-message their competition. The social platforms and the content which a brand must provide are certainly parts of an overall digital marketing strategy, but just focusing on channels which are owned by others is not the only way to engage in social media with consumers. Indeed, it is very possible, aligning with the concept of social utility, to create your own platform.

Amex Open Forum is one of my favourite examples to use as a successful social-utility case study. It is also one of the earliest such examples, and helped Amex not only win the minds and hearts of small business owners, but also helped pave the way for their larger social-marketing initiatives. Launched way back in 2007, AMEX Open Forum was a place that allowed small-business owners to connect with one another to share tips and advice about running a small business and featured many forms of external content from recognised business leaders and valued publications. Another advantage of this platform was that it coincided with American Express's earliest forays into Twitter, when it launched a Twitter handle alongside the Forum launch.

This is noteworthy in its own right because American Express could have just as easily launched a Twitter handle which was focused on small-business owners, and followed it with attempts to develop useful content every day or multiple times per day, all contained within 140 characters. Imagine a tip on securing a loan, for example, a tip on cost-effective marketing or a tip on financial planning.

As time went on, AMEX would have likely run into the same issue which Vaynerchuk identified – the proliferation of more and more social platforms and other content media. Likewise, AMEX would have faced the challenge of developing new and fresh content everyday – content that could just as easily be consumed at any number of other financial and small-business information destinations.

Instead, AMEX invested in creating its very own social network – one that connects small-business owners across industries and countries, and acts as one of the very best resources for small-business owners to discuss ideas and get advice. The bonus is that all of this content and these discussions can then be repackaged for use on Twitter and other social-media platforms.

Over time, AMEX added in additional features to maintain audience interest, including offline events that allowed members to attend meet-ups and gatherings in their local business areas. AMEX has invited experts in different areas of business to create content and to answer members' questions. All the while, AMEX keeps promoting its small-business credit cards and other services to small businesses. Consumers continue to be drawn to this useful service and its success in converting customers even more effectively than targeted advertisements is clear. Ghazal Haque, a five-year veteran of AMEX, remarks that year after year OPEN Forum was the top lead generator for small-business credit cards.

It Is Content

Social utility is not just limited to creating useful social and content networks like AMEX Open Forum. In fact, content alone is often a utility in its own right and can be incredibly useful to consumers. As Goldring points out in Chapter 14, there are clear steps which a brand can take to create compelling content, ranging from introducing information, appealing to emotions and showing variety. The biggest key is continuing to put the consumer first by providing utility above all else, versus creating content which showcases the benefits of the product which the brand is selling. While this might sound counterintuitive from a marketing and business perspective, there is sound business strategy behind these approaches, as the following examples demonstrate.

One of the more well-known examples of a brand which embraces content as social utility is Lowe's 'Fix in Six' series. The campaign started on Vine and showed a series of home fix-it videos, utilising tricks and shortcuts which the average user could find sitting already within the home. This included removing a stripped screw with a rubber band, removing water stains with lemons and holding nails steady with clothes pins. In most cases, the videos featured no products from Lowe's and instead encouraged users to fix things around the house without making a trip to the second-largest home-improvement chain in the country. So how could Lowe's justify the campaign, other than merely as a positive branding exercise?

The answer lies in knowing the audience, knowing the channel and identifying a key part of the consumer journey that the brand is hoping to influence. Millennials were overwhelmingly the early adopters of Vine – on which the campaign ran – and attracting the next generation of homeowners was a key part of Lowe's strategy. Furthermore, knowing that people, especially Millennials, are intimidated by home repair proved a key part of the strategy in crafting this utility content. In an interview with Fast Company, Tom Lamb, CMO of Lowe's, relates: "Often people are intimidated by home improvement. It's not as easy as people make it look or maybe as it should be. They need someone to help them anticipate what's going on in their home and suggest some solutions." (FastCoCreate 2015) Put simply, the strategy was showcasing easy and useful home fix-its which did not even require a trip to the hardware store, all while connecting with Millennials for the day when they would need to renovate a kitchen, redo a bedroom or embark on a more challenging home fix-it project. And in the interim, Lowe's was still able to generate over 40 million loops on the new social video site.

An even more direct example of providing utility and useful

social content, seemingly at the expense of the services which the brand provides, is Best Buy's Geek Squad. The brand hosts a YouTube channel which has hundreds of videos showing users' tech-related, do-it-yourself fix-its which are often counter to the very services that Geek Squad provides to consumers. The content certainly works from an engagement perspective: the channel has millions of views on the videos which it has created. Geek Squad has undoubtedly created utility and popularity, but is it creating business value?

Geek Squad founder, Robert Stephens, thinks so, according to a story which was shared by Jay Baer, author of *Youtility: Why Smart Marketing is About Help Not Hype,* on his Convince and Convert website. At a conference which he attended, someone asked why Geek Squad was giving away free videos for potentially profitable services.

> Someone asked him a great question: "Let me get this straight Robert. You're in the business of fixing things?" "Yes," he nodded. [sic] "But yet, you have all these videos showing people how to fix things themselves. How does that make business sense?" "Well, our best customers are the people that think they can do it themselves. But even if they can, someday they'll be over their head, and who will they call for help? We're betting it's the company whose logo they looked at for 8 minutes when we gave them free video help."

(Convince and Convert, 2016)

Taking into account the ability to build a long-term relationship with a consumer through content is a central part of utility and social utility marketing. Goldring (Chapter 14) provides additional content marketing strategies and considerations.

Customer Service as Utility

Social utility need not include just the creation of new content and experiences for consumers. Indeed, that can be a daunting challenge for brands that embrace the idea of utility and customer first. Thinking back to the earliest examples of utility mentioned in this chapter – like old radio advertisements providing weather – offering simple information is a form of social utility and a great way to offer value to consumers. That information extends to one of the most direct connections between a brand and its consumers: customer service.

Today, customers not only appreciate but expect a great customer-care experience on social media. In her bestselling book, *The Social Business Imperative*, Clara Shih dedicates an entire chapter to social customer care, arguing that social has forever changed customer service. Now brands must respond immediately and authentically and they must be transparent (Shih, 2016).

The truth of this can be seen in both successes and failures. Delta Airlines is credited with being the first airline to embrace Twitter as a means of customer service. Launched in 2009, @DeltaAssist offered real-time assistance to customers by answering questions, handling flight delays and even helping to track lost luggage. Its use by customers has grown tremendously and it has since expanded beyond the Monday-thru-Friday, nine-to-six hours offered when it first launched to a 24/7 response, aligning with Shih's belief that the first rule of social customer care is response time.

To Delta, @DeltaAssist provides both operational and marketing value. Indeed, Shih notes that businesses can expect to service between four and eight times as many customers through social media than they could, in the same amount of time, by traditional methods like the telephone. This both decreases overhead costs and increases efficiency. But the brand also benefits by creating a valuable experience for consumers and by generating feedback. Delta likes to reference the thousands of positive tweets which thank its employees for the help and, because Twitter is an *open social network* – meaning that tweets are often publicly viewable – these tweets are all free and positive marketing messages for Delta, sent out into the world in real time.

Authenticity is Key

While producing a strong social care solution as part of a larger utility-based marketing strategy has many benefits, from both an operational and a marketing perspective, this area has many potential pitfalls. Because people who contact customer care often have a problem which needs solving, they are likely to be more upset than when engaging with the brand in other situations. And if the brand makes a major misstep on transparency, it can quickly go viral.

In 2013, for example, Bank of America made headlines when it was accused of using automated responses to customer-service complaints through social. Consumers and the media alike posted multiple tweets which seemingly offered the same responses to consumer problems. While Bank of America did in fact reveal that it has humans responding to those questions, it still appeared that it was following a script, with little understanding of the problems that consumers faced. The result is that the end consumer experience lacked authenticity and, rather than serving useful answers to its base of customers, Bank of America alienated them with generic responses that provided little value. This, of course, is counter to the main purpose of social utility – to find and offer value to consumers.

Positives and negatives aside, customer service as social utility remains an opportunity for most brands. A 2015 study by Brandwatch showed that just 46.6% of brands responded to @questions – or questions targeting a brand's Twitter handle directly. US brands also responded to questions on average three times slower than they did to generic comments (Brandwatch, 2015). This means that those brands are three times slower in providing actual value to consumers and much more likely to engage in banter. While it is nice to have your favourite brand respond to a generic comment, there is no utility there, unless it can help answer meaningful inquiries which a consumer takes the time to write.

Creating Social Utility Means Letting Go

Providing useful content, services and tools to consumers is inherently acceptable for most brands. Who could fault a destination where small businesses can get all the information they need to run their business more effectively, a source for short-form videos which help fix things around the house or a catalogue of great customer-service responses? The challenge for some brands, however, revolves instead around the social aspect of utility – letting go of control, particularly in highly regulated industries or industries which are viewed negatively by consumers.

The benefits, however, far outweigh the loss of control. Indeed, consumers have the ability not only to spread the utility which a brand provides, but also to create something which is authentic and in ways which the brand might not even have imagined to begin with. This certainly presents challenges on the regulatory front, but embracing utility and usefulness means placing the consumer first, as mentioned earlier, and then letting consumers take the brand to unexpected places.

In early 2013, I had the opportunity to work with Pfizer's senior global marketing team on a major social project which was entitled 'Get Old'. Pfizer, like most if not all pharmaceutical brands, was challenged when it came to public perception. It had less than a 50% favourability rating, according to social listening analysis and had just settled a major lawsuit around one of its products. All of that aside, Pfizer had bought into the concept of utility and was attempting to provide a useful resource for consumers on ageing. Pfizer could have easily taken the thinly veiled marketing approach and simply created a destination which listed all the common ailments that folks are likely to encounter at different stages of their lives, and then subsequently list the appropriate pharmaceutical solution (hopefully Pfizer-branded) to each ailment.

Instead, the brand embraced a consumer-first policy and usefulness, and decided to make a portal which allowed consumers to share experiences at each decade of their lives. The broad, overarching goal was to take away the stigma of ageing and in doing so Pfizer was able to uncover countless true stories of ageing in

America. The final outcome was three-fold in nature. It combined user stories, produced stories and helpful articles. Through our research, we concluded that people in America associated their age closely with decades – the thirties, forties, fifties and so on. More so, they felt that each decade brought a very different mindset and different challenges. So we organised the portal to centre around those decades and produced content which corresponded to these different phases in life. And we invited consumers to share their own experiences.

There is a proliferation of 'share your story' social-media campaigns at this time. But we felt that we were differentiating by truly organising around each decade and providing a useful resource for each of those decades with our produced stories and articles. When we opened the gates to users, we were shocked by the number of stories which did come in, and by the stories themselves. Thousands of stories were submitted in every decade, from the 1930s all the way up to the 1990s, each discussing the challenges which are associated with ageing – and in a very real and authentic way.

When most people think of pharmaceutical advertising, they imagine impossibly fit, happy and smiling citizens, oftentimes older, yet exhibiting an incredible youthfulness which alludes to the efficacy of the drugs which they are taking. The stories Pfizer received were anything but. Thousands of people talked about the difficulties which they faced with any number of ailments: hip replacements, diabetes, stroke recoveries, heart surgeries. But the amazing thing about these stories was that there was a consistent sense of positivity, even as they recounted debilitating disease. The folks who submitted those stories got up every day, they persevered and, through our utility portal, they connected with others who were going through the same trials. This was not a slick pharmaceutical commercial; it was social, it was utility and it was real.

The results from this experiment were incredibly positive for Pfizer. At last count, it had plans to expand this program into multiple countries around the globe, starting with Ireland and Japan – the country with one of the oldest populations in the world. It had also experienced a 20% increase in positive mentions according to social listening data and had created a useful offering for consumers, addressing the very real side of ageing, and both the challenges and hopefulness associated with it.

Imitate What Is in the Public Consciousness

For marketers who are challenged with ways to find useful and utility-based ideas with which to engage an audience, there are clues all around – and these need not come from the brand, industry or competitors. Often, there are exciting things which are happening all around, capturing the public interest, and marketers only need to keep an eye on the things with which people engage, either on their own or with a fee – a true sign that they are finding it useful and time-worthy.

In 2011, I had an opportunity to work with one of the biggest supplement companies in the world, Nature's Bounty. It approached my team with a great social marketing plan, the goal of which was to promote its new product, Met-Rx 180. The premise behind Met-Rx 180 was simple. Home-based fitness was taking off at the time, with products like P90X dominating the marketplace. As consumers of those fitness products know well, not only did P90X provide great fitness videos to which consumers could easily exercise in their own homes, but they also provided fitness supplements to go along with those videos. As one of the largest supplement providers in the world, Nature's Bounty wanted to create its own set of fitness videos, in order to promote its own supplement products. But it needed help in differentiating its product from P90X, which was already well-entrenched with consumers.

My team's solution was to look at one of the most popular leisure activities at the time – 'World of Warcraft'. This massively successful online multi-player game was generating millions of fees each month, and Business Insider (2015) listed it as the fourth-highest-grossing video game of all time, with 8.5 billion USD in revenues. It was clearly something which was capturing the public consciousness and something for which people were willing to pay lots of dollars.

The key behind the game's success was not only that it was an enjoyable video game with great gameplay and graphics, but also that it was a game which promoted social interaction. Players built up a virtual character alongside other teammates in groups, called 'Clans'. Along the way, players are rewarded with items which they can use in the game to make their characters even stronger; unlocking these rewards requires that groups work together. Taken another way, it sounds a lot like building up one's body in the physical world and unlocking supplements to get even stronger.

The final concept involved the creation of a fitness social utility which sat alongside the fitness videos of Met-Rx 180 and which allowed consumers to form teams (or clans) online so that they could embark on the fitness journey together. Along the way, they could invite their friends, track their progress through a variety of desktop and mobile applications, and receive supplement rewards from Nature's Bounty and Met-Rx for completing challenges and levels together.

The key to finding this social utility was looking at what was going on in the world around – that is to say, taking something which people were already paying to participate in – and adapting it to a very specific fitness audience that was accustomed to working out solo at home. And as anyone who has played an online multi-player game or enrolled in a team-based fitness regimen like Crossfit knows, it is the people who keep you coming back. Indeed, the social component is universal in its human appeal.

Putting It into Practice

After considering all the aspects of social utility listed in this chapter and recalling the examples, it is time to consider putting social utility into practice. The good news is that there are many different ways to initiate a social utility program, ranging from smaller-scale projects involving content to much larger initiatives like building an owned social network or application. The following sub-sections provide a framework for creating a social utility program, from initiation through to launch.

Research and Intelligence

The first steps of any good digital marketing program involve research and intelligence; creating a social utility program is no different. Marketers must unearth who the target consumer is and what he or she cares about, and of course, place the consumer first. Additionally, they must take a broader approach in their research and understand what else the target consumer cares about and how it relates to the brand which is being marketed.

As mentioned in this chapter, looking at what the broader culture is consuming is a great start. When my team pitched the idea of Met-Rx creating a fitness portal which was aligned with massively multiplayer online (MMO) games, 'World of Warcraft' was the most popular game at the time. Both internal decision makers and consumers, therefore, could easily see the corollary and perceive the value that Met-Rx was hoping to provide to fitness aficionados.

A useful tool in mining data and interests that are beyond traditional research methods is Facebook Analytics. If the idea behind social utility is to provide a useful tool or application, digital marketers can identify the other types of content or online applications with which consumers are engaging. As of today, it remains one of the most advanced tools available to digital marketers to target users by interest.

Another opportunity is to pay particular attention to the content which users are consuming on their own. This involves news, media, shared stories, YouTube videos and now Snapchat Stories and Instagram Stories, in addition to traditional media such as TV and movies. All of these data are available to marketers who are looking to create useful content for their audiences.

Finally, an often-overlooked place to gather intelligence is within a brand's internal departments. Indeed, thinking like a product manager is a useful step in rolling out any social-utility program. And there are no better resources than the employees within a company who spend their days refining the product or experience: they often understand intuitively what consumers are actually buying. Customer service is another area where there is often an enormous amount of information which can help fuel a useful service, or fill a void which has been affecting customers of the brand directly.

Find the Right Investment Level

Social utility might involve the creation of a useful service, application or experience for your brand's consumers. The usefulness can span an indefinite number of things that you can do for your customer and a number of different investment levels for a program. The AMEX Open program, for example, is among the most audacious instances of social utility. The brand set out to become the best resource for small-business owners by offering a dizzying array of produced content, expert speakers, external content, user-generated content, and ties to real-world events and meet-ups for their users. Pfizer's Get Old, on the other hand, was produced with a far more modest budget, with a very limited amount of produced content. Other than the website build, the majority of stories and utility came directly from the consumers themselves. It was simply about hitting upon an underserved need – in this case a place for Americans to be simultaneously realistic, but also proud about ageing through each decade of their lives. And while Lowe's 'Fix in Six' DIY tips were incredibly successful, there is a truly unfinished quality about them. They are well-crafted, but do not feel slickly produced – a testament to the platform authenticity. In an interview, the creative team responsible for the tips suggested that the cost of each video was not more than 5,000 USD.

The possibilities for social utility are numerous. Finding the right investment level, therefore, ought not to be the limiting factor for rollout. Lastly, do not forget the possibility of sharing costs internally. Great social care programs are both infrequent and efficient from an operations perspective. As noted in this chapter, Delta received great promotion through its @DeltaAssist Twitter handle, while also answering more requests than were possible through phone or email.

Think Like a Product Person

One of the true challenges of launching a social-utility initiative is the need to think like a product person – in addition to thinking like a marketer. Marketers want to induce a thought, an association or an emotion in a consumer's mind. They do this with creative messaging, well-produced pieces of content or alignment with events, celebrities or other things which their target consumer loves. Digital-focused marketers often take that a step further by looking to induce action immediately, because digital is always a click away from an online storefront, able to fulfil an order or drive the consumer to a track-able destination with every initiative.

While these still remain important ways of thinking about marketing when engaging in any type of utility-based marketing program, an equally important emphasis must be on thinking like a product manager. Because social utility is all about creating useful, shareable experiences for consumers, time must be spent on the consumer experience. Methods which prove useful in digital marketing, such as retargeting, need a thorough analysis to see if they are harming that consumer experience in any way.

Marketers in product-driven companies must often engage with product leaders and get sign-off for their marketing initiatives, particularly in entertainment and media in which they are selling fandom, not commodities as is in consumer packaged goods companies. And product leaders are notoriously protective of those fans. They will not compromise the user experience or run programs which are counter to what those fans know and expect, often at the expense of some new marketing initiative.

This mentality is essential to a successful social-utility program. Johnson and Johnson, for example, purchased Baby Center back in 2001 and helped foster one of the earliest and most successful social-utility platforms, which allowed moms across the globe to connect and find advice and tips on pregnancy, parenting and products. Importantly, in an age when many brands are trying to become media companies, Johnson and Johnson treats Baby Center as an independent entity. In turn, Baby Center claims that it reaches over 40 million moms across the world.

Make It Social

As mentioned in the beginning of this chapter, one of the key differences between utility marketing programs of today and those from the past consists of the abilities which digital and social afford. Through digital, marketers are able to create all manner of mobile applications, chat bots, online ticket ordering, connected home, augmented reality experiences and more for consumers. But making them shareable and connected to others in some way is one of the most valuable aspects of utility marketing today. As Bond notes in Chapter 5, the ability to convert advocates shifts the power balance even further from the old 80:20 rule of sales to something closer to 95:5. The social-utility programs of Delta, Lowe's and Pfizer were all examples of social-utility campaigns which were inherently social. Indeed, the content was shareable.

Consumers today not only want to share their experiences with brands (and they do so often), as noted by Seth Godin (Godin, 2007), but they also want to connect with others for the sake of connecting. Social media now makes up 20% of the time which US consumers spend on the Internet (Business Insider, 2015). That does not take into account the fact that many favourite pastimes are dominated by social interaction. The video-game industry is now larger than both TV and movies, and both the Playstation 4 and the Xbox One mandate online social subscriptions to access multi-player games. The two fastest-selling mobile games in history, 'Pokémon Go' and 'Clash Royale', both feature social gameplay.

Find Your Influencers and Early Adopters

After time is spent researching consumers, developing a consumer-first platform, identifying the right social-utility program, thinking like a product person and ensuring social functionality, it is time for rolling out the program. This book contains lots of digital marketing strategies and tactics to help generate interest in the utility that the program will provide. Hopefully you have done enough research to identify a need which your consumers have, so that the utility which you provide will be pulled in by consumers – and that it will not be just a marketing message that you will need to push outward in excess.

Like all things, however, traffic driving will be key. In the Pfizer example in this chapter, the company set aside money from the overall program to seed the stories on Facebook which it generated. This in turn drove traffic back to the portal and encouraged more users to share stories. Another tactic was to identify influencers around whom Pfizer could create stories and then highlight these stories to the audience.

All brands have brand champions and all new utilities have early adopters. Leveraging relationships with those specific people is key to success. These relationships can take many forms: additional support to content creators if the social utility solicits and shares information between users, for example; early access to new features if the social utility is an application which solves a consumer problem; or a way to incorporate user-generated content from power users if the social utility is about creating original videos. Finding the users who share the content most frequently, and having them star in the next video or pose the next topic, is a great way to reward and engage those users who are helping spread your utility further.

Lastly, do not forget the fans who you already have for your brand. Chances are, your brand has a social presence on the major social networks. There are numerous tools, both direct through those social networks and from external vendors, that help identify which users are most active, and offer a great way to create an internal focus group and solicit first-time users for your social utility.

The ROI Question

One of the key challenges to overcome when embarking on any utility and consumer-first approach to marketing is not only the resources which are involved in the creation of this service to consumers, but also the resources which are required for generating consumer uptake of the social utility itself – resources which alternately could be directed at generating consumer uptake of the products sold by the company. This is certainly a valid concern and something which needs a strong foundation in research and insights to answer. The good news is that when adopting the consumer-first approach to marketing and social utility, finding ways to engage consumers ought to be far easier than promoting the product itself. In fact, with the right research strategy, there ought to be more than a handful of different useful ways that a brand can employ within the boundaries of some kind of product alignment.

But as digital marketers, the onus is always on delivering ROI, especially because there are so many new ways of attribution which were previously unavailable in older marketing media like print, TV and outdoor display. With social utility, however, there simply will not be as direct a line of attribution as is available in other forms of digital marketing like Google Adwords. Utility programs often sit higher in the marketing funnel – and there are any number of ways to measure value, depending on the goal. In the case of @DeltaAssist, for example, Delta not only provided a useful service to its customers, but also generated a tremendous amount of positive open social-network mentions. And it helped retain loyal customers – customer satisfaction surveys, therefore, ought to play a large role in how Delta assesses this program.

Similarly, AMEX Open Forum generated a large number of leads for small-business credit cards through its social utility, because it advertises for the product directly on the site. Consequently, the ROI benefit is clear all the way down the marketing funnel to the point of purchase. Not all brands or social-utility programs have this luxury, however. Johnson and Johnson Baby Center does not sell its products on the site actively; on the contrary, it features thousands of baby-centric products not made by Johnson and Johnson, and advertising from outside companies. But Johnson and Johnson is able to mine an enormous amount of data from its utility marketing, helping it target its audience more effectively in other paid marketing efforts. And of course, there is the positive perception which the mothers who use the application everyday will have, when it is time to shop for something which Johnson and Johnson does indeed sell.

Conclusion

This chapter outlined the opportunity which digital media provides, specifically with respect to providing a useful experience for customers – that is to say, by letting utility be the marketing. As marketing messages and the media to deliver those messages continue to grow, and as consumer attention continues to fragment, digital marketers must find new ways to break through the clutter. Some marketers believe that big advertising ideas might be over. But this chapter is not about minimising the power of traditional or other digital forms of marketing. Instead, it is about looking forward to new digital marketing possibilities which provide useful services, applications and content.

The examples in this chapter illustrate just a handful of ways to provide both social functionality and utility to consumers. But opportunities will only expand as the field of utility marketing continues to grow and consumers find ever new and useful ways to use digital media in their own lives. Consider the 'Pokémon Go' craze, which is dominating people's attention across the globe in the form of an augmented-reality mobile application. 'Pokémon Go' became the fastest-selling mobile game of all time, allowing consumers to engage in an augmented reality experience by capturing Pokémon creatures out in the real world – in parks, shopping malls and even government buildings – viewed through their mobile screens.

Many marketers tried to figure out ways to leverage the success of 'Pokémon Go' into hyper-local activations for their businesses, by driving consumers to catch Pokémon outside their doorsteps, for example. I am waiting for the right brand to unlock the utility which is behind this phenomenon. Indeed, the game itself is undoubtedly fun, as its legions of fans can attest. But one of the core behaviours which it unlocks is getting people outside, moving about and hunting the real world for the virtual characters. It is as much exercise, socialising and exploring the real world as it is participating in a mobile game. And how many fitness, travel or countless other brands could find a way to offer that utility to their consumers?

References

Berger, J. (2013) *Contagious.* New York, USA: Simon and Schuster Group.

Brandwatch (2015) "Research: Brands Still Don't Listen to Customers on Twitter." Retrieved from: https://www.brandwatch.com/2015/01/research-brands-still-dont-listen-customers-twitter/

Bueno, B. (2012) *Customers First: Dominate Your Market by Winning Them Over Where it Counts the Most.* New York, USA: McGraw-Hill.

Business Insider (2015) "The 11 Top-grossing Video Games of All Time." Retrieved from: http://www.businessinsider.com/the-11-top-grossing-video-games-of-all-time-2015-8

Fast Company (2010) "What American Express's OPEN Can Teach Us About Social Media." Retrieved from: http://www.fastcompany.com/1669407/what-american-expresss-open-can-teach-us-about-social-media

FastCoCreate (2015) "How Lowe's Brought Social Savvy and a Sense of Humor to Home Improvement." Retrieved from: http://www.fastcocreate.com/3048021/behind-the-brand/how-lowes-brought-social-savvy-and-a-sense-of-humor-to-home-improvement

Godin, S. (2007) *Meatball Sunday.* New York, USA: Penguin Group.

Hill Holliday (2016) "The Myth of 5,000 ads." Retrieved from: http://cbi.hhcc.com/writing/the-myth-of-5000-ads/

Shih, C. (2016) *The Social Business Imperative.* Boston, USA: Prentice Hall.

Vaynerchuk, G. (2013) *Jab, Jab, Jab, Right Hook.* New York, USA: HarperCollins Publishers.

About the Author

Bryan Pedersen is the Group Senior Vice President, Digital Strategy at MMC, an Omnicom agency. Bryan has more than 15 years' experience in the digital media industry, specialising in content, influencer marketing, analytics, digital product development and paid media. Prior to joining MMC, he launched the social agency 3Degrees, working with clients like 20th Century Fox, WE tv and Simon G. Jewelry to create award-winning social, content and influencer programs. He has held various senior roles at companies including MTV Networks, Lagardère Group, Nielsen/ McKinsey Consulting and Edelman. He has also taught classes at NYU and Pace University on Digital Strategy and consulted with a handful of venture-funded start-ups. His offline world consists of finding time to play tennis every day and keeping up with his daughter, Natasha. Follow him on Twitter at @bryanpedersen. Contact him on email at bryan.pedersen@gmail.com.

Chapter 13

Ideological Capital, Networks and Social-media Strategies

Yotam Shmargad and Jameson Watts

Introduction

Social interaction has always shaped consumer behaviour. People look to their friends for shopping advice (Feick and Price 1987), they modify their food selections based on those sitting across from them at the restaurant (McFerran et al., 2010) and they choose clothing in anticipation of how others will react (Chan et al., 2012). Social-media platforms, like Facebook and Twitter, have placed social interactions front and centre in the minds of organisations. These platforms do not just let organisations monitor interactions between consumers; they also allow them to participate in these conversations like never before. In light of their new role as active participants, organisations need new frameworks which can help guide their interactions with consumers over social media (Mangold and Faulds, 2009; Kaplan and Haenlein, 2010; Kietzmann et al., 2011).

This chapter starts out with the assumption that online interactions between organisations and consumers represent a new kind of *sociality*. Indeed, even online interactions between people are often not social in a traditional sense. Social media let people broadcast information to large and diverse audiences (Shmargad, 2014). On Twitter, for example, even ordinary people can broadcast messages to hundreds of followers. When celebrities and politicians promote their movies and ideas over broadcast television, we do not usually refer to these activities as social. Likewise, organisations which broadcast content over social media ought to think of themselves as engaging in a new kind of social activity. People tend not to treat organisations like their friends, and organisations which pretend to be friends with consumers run the risk of coming off as disingenuous and creepy.

In this chapter, we present a framework to help guide organisations as they interact with consumers over social media. In the next section, we develop this framework, called *ideological capital*, and distinguish it from frameworks which scholars use to study social relationships. We provide a primer on network analysis and describe how organisations can collect and analyse social-network data. We then discuss how such data can inform an organisation's social-media strategy. We conclude with key takeaways. After reading this chapter, you will:

1. Appreciate the difference between what scholars mean by social and how companies ought to engage with consumers;

2. Understand the basics of network analysis and how companies can use it to analyse social-media data; and

3. Possess marketing strategies which organisations can use when interacting with consumers in an increasingly connected world.

Ideological Capital, or How Not to Be Social

Social relationships provide a host of benefits for people, including emotional and financial support in times of need (Wellman and Wortley, 1990). Social scientists refer to the benefits that are accumulated from social relationships as *social capital*, which relies on *trust* that good deeds tend to reciprocate (Coleman, 1988). From this perspective, it is clear that relationships between organisations and consumers are not social in a strict sense. This is not to say that organisations ought not to use social means to interact with consumers. Organisations often hire agents to generate buzz about their products (Godes and Mayzlin, 2009) and bots provide an automated way for organisations to engage with consumers through a social façade (Ferrara et al., 2016). These methods, however, ought not to serve as an organisation's primary marketing strategy. Instead, they ought to complement and reinforce the messages and content which the organisation disseminates.

How, then, ought organisations to think about their relationship with consumers when producing and disseminating content, and how ought they to assess the accumulated benefits which are gained through successful interaction? To capture these benefits, we borrow a concept from economics known as *ideological capital*. In an illuminating passage, Lin expands on this concept:

> The ability to produce [piety]... depends on an individual's ideological capital. When an individual's ideological conviction is strong, it implies that his ideological capital is large, and that the shadow price of producing piety is low.

> (Lin, 1989, p.11)

For Lin, ideological capital is related to a person's ability to produce *piety*. Piety, therefore, is to ideological capital as trust is to social capital. While piety can refer to religious belief, it can also be used more broadly to mean belief or devotion. Organisations might not be able to produce trust, at least not in the way in which trust is characterised in social relationships, but they can produce beliefs and devotion in the minds of consumers. Indeed, we argue that an organisation's social-media strategy ought to be oriented towards the production of piety, in this sense.

Three recent trends make ideological capital ripe for use by the marketing community: 1. the increasing focus of consumers on the *values* which organisations hold, 2. the emergence of *technology* which streamlines the dissemination of content, and 3. changes in the *structural* makeup of society into networks. In the remainder of this section, we discuss how these trends can inform marketers in the production, dissemination and assessment of their social-media content. First, we elaborate on expectations that consumers have about organisations' values and on how these ought to shape the messages which marketers produce. Next, we consider how marketers can use new media to disseminate messages and content which communicate their values to consumers. Finally, we outline how a deeper understanding of network structure can be used to construct metrics that assess an organisation's content marketing strategy. Table 13.1 summarises these aspects of our framework.

Values

Consumers increasingly care about the values that organisations hold. This is best exemplified by the rise of *cause marketing*, activities in which organisations engage that benefit society directly (Smith and Alcorn, 1991). For example, the shoe company TOMS gained international attention through its promise to give a pair of shoes to people in need for every pair that it sold (see Chapter 10 by Fossas for more about the campaign). Organisations can also express their values by aligning with certain political stances. Mark Zuckerberg, the CEO and public face of Facebook, helped to found FWD.us, a pro-immigration lobbying group. When Arizona was considering a bill which would let businesses discriminate against consumers based on religious grounds, the National Football League (NFL) sided with the LGBT community and issued a statement against the bill.

Table 13.1. Content Marketing through the Lens of Ideological Capital

Societal Trend	Content Activity	Marketing Decision
Values	Production	Messages
Technology	Dissemination	Media
Structure	Assessment	Metrics

In the case of TOMS, the value which was communicated was that of *equality*, whereas for Facebook and the NFL it was that of *inclusion*. The specific values that an organisation ought to communicate will depend on the nature of its products and services. An organisation that aligns itself properly with the values of its target audience will build ideological capital and, if truly successful, can become a thought leader in its industry. According to Lin (1989), organisations that achieve thought leadership will find it easier (and less expensive) to shape the beliefs of consumers. The ability to build ideological capital depends not just on the activities that an organisation chooses to pursue, but also on messages that communicate these activities and on the values associated with them. New technology can facilitate the dissemination of an organisation's messages and, consequently, the communication of its values.

Technology

When social-media platforms first started gaining prominence, they represented a new opportunity for marketers, simply because platforms were where consumers were spending much of their time. As these platforms (and the thinking around them) matured, however, they were increasingly viewed as new opportunities for engaging consumers. This is evident from the shift in how social-media activities are described, from *social media marketing* to *content marketing* (see Chapter 14 by Goldring). Figure 13.1 depicts trends in Google searches of these two terms. The y-axis of this chart captures the relative popularity of the terms, while the x-axis captures time. Social-media marketing took off in 2007 but plateaued in 2011. Content marketing entered the discussion in 2011 and the two terms are now equally popular.

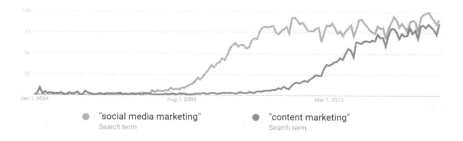

Figure 13.1. Search Trends for Social-media Marketing and Content Marketing

247

The shift in thinking is also characterised by a focus away from social-media *advertising* and towards social-media *posts* (see Figure 13.2). A post is content disseminated by an organisation through its *page* on social media. Consumers engage with an organisation's posts by liking, sharing or commenting on them. These also happen to be terms which Facebook uses to describe the various activities. Social-media platforms usually offer similar functionalities, albeit under different labels. On Twitter, for example, users favour, retweet and reply to a tweet, respectively. The set of consumers that engages with an organisation's content constitutes a social network. By analysing this network, organisations can construct metrics to assess how the content which they post contributes to the accumulation of ideological capital.

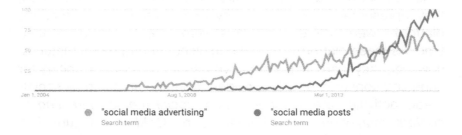

Figure 13.2. Search Trends for Social-media Advertising and Social-media Posts

Structure

Social-media platforms have facilitated the shift from a group-based society to a *network society* (Rainie and Wellman, 2012; van Dijk, 2012). In the past, people were defined by the community to which they belonged, and relationships largely depended on physical co-presence. As technology enabled communication across distance, people could belong to multiple communities and the makeup of society resembled more closely a network of people connected through their interactions, near and far (see Chapter 2 by Sawyer for more about society's increasing interconnectivity).

An analysis of the patterns of these connections, or a network's *structure*, can reveal deep insights about the ways in which society functions. For example, the structure of a person's network of social relationships can be used to assess the amount of social capital they have accumulated (Coleman, 1988; Burt, 1992).

A fundamental tension arises in the structural analysis of social capital between the benefits which accrue from a tight-knit, *dense* set of relations, and those which accrue from a loosely connected, *diverse* set. This tension between density and diversity is also likely to appear in the analysis of ideological capital. A dense set of hardcore believers can be easier for an organisation to mobilise, but a diverse set of retweeters can communicate the organisation's message to a broad audience. Indeed, dense networks facilitate the spread of behaviours more readily (Centola, 2010), while diverse networks are better-suited for disseminating information and content (Watts and Strogatz, 1998; Yoganarasimhan, 2012).

The tension between density and diversity might translate from social to ideological capital, but not all aspects of social capital are likely to carry over. For example, Burt (2007, 2010) shows that, while it is beneficial for a person to have a diverse set of social relationships, there is little to no benefit of *knowing* people with diverse relationships. In the dissemination of content, however, there is good reason to believe that knowing well-connected individuals can be beneficial. The successful spread of information is driven largely by broadcasts (Goel et al., 2015), and targeting opinion leaders can even help organisations sell their products (Iyengar et al., 2011). Indeed, the discovery of similarities and differences between social and ideological capital is a promising area of future research.

Network Analysis of Social-media Content

As we just discussed, when people interact online they form a web of connections that is called a *social network*. Platforms like Facebook and LinkedIn often encourage the formation of such connections with algorithms (Shmargad and Watts, 2016a). The interactions which constitute a social network, however, can also promulgate more organically. For example, email communications can also be formulated as a social network (Aral and Van

Alstyne, 2011). Regardless of the media which facilitate interactions, certain *patterns* of relations have predictable implications for behaviour. Accordingly, it is helpful to have a deep understanding of some fundamental network patterns before we introduce specific strategy recommendations.

Figure 13.3 illustrates a typical (albeit artificially small) representation of a social network. The circles symbolise social actors and the lines between these circles indicate the presence of a relationship between actors. In the language which is common to this area of research, we refer to these circles and lines as *nodes* and *edges,* respectively. The letter in the middle of each circle is simply a label for that particular node. When an edge exists between two nodes, they are said to be *tied*, or *connected*, to each other, such that nodes with many edges can be said to have many *ties* or *connections*.

Given this example network, we can make certain statements about its *structure*, or the way in which the various nodes and edges are organised. For example, we can say that node A has a relationship with nodes B, C and D, but not with nodes E or F. We might also observe that node C has the most ties to other nodes in the network, which places it in a *central* position relative to nodes A, B, D and E. Finally, we might notice that the nodes on the left side of the network appear to be somewhat more *interconnected* than those on the right-hand side and that Node E appears to form a *bridge* between different regions of the network.

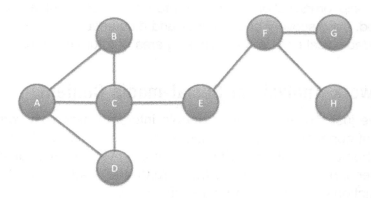

Figure 13.3. A Simple Social Network

Centrality, interconnectivity and *bridging* are examples of the types of patterns which scholars typically use to understand and predict the behaviour of networked actors (Watts and Koput, 2014). In the marketing literature, *centrality* is the most commonly utilised concept, because central actors are often vital to the diffusion of information about new products (Tucker, 2008; Iyengar et al., 2011). Consequently, the practice of influencer marketing has focused on basic measures of centrality, like the number of followers that a person or organisation has on Twitter. The concepts of *inter-connectivity* and bridging, however, also have implications for digital marketing (Shmargad and Watts, 2016b). To illustrate this, we depict two organisations (X and Y) and their connections to consumers in Figure 13.4. In X's network, consumers C_1 and C_2 are not themselves connected, whereas consumers in organisation Y's network have an existing relationship.

One could think of this type of arrangement in the context of a platform like Facebook in which customers (or interested people) have *liked* an organisation's page. An alternative is to consider the people who liked, shared or commented on a particular piece of content which the organisation posted. In organisation X's network, consumers are not connected or, in Facebook's vernacular, *friends* with each other. The organisation's ties, therefore, act as bridges into potentially distinct consumer communities. In contrast, all of those in Y's network are interconnected.

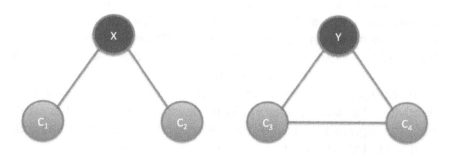

Figure 13.4. Example of Two Organisations with Different Types of Networks

Given these two distinct types of networks, ought organisation X to have a different digital marketing strategy than organisation Y? As we shall see shortly, the answer is almost certainly yes. But before we consider why this is the case, let us dive into the details of how an organisation can analyse the social network of consumers who interact with them on social media to infer whether it is more like X or Y.

From the previous example, the primary difference between the networks of organisations X and Y lies in the answer to the question, 'Are the consumers who interact with me connected to each other?' We can answer this question by counting how many connections exist between these consumers and dividing this by the number of relationships which could exist. This definition describes a continuum between networks which are *diverse* (low interconnectivity, many bridges) and those networks which are more *dense* (high interconnectivity, few bridges). Though not covered in detail here, various tools can help marketers analyse the networks of their customers. For example, Netvizz and Mentionmapp can be used to analyse consumer networks that are formed around specific content.

Figure 13.5 depicts three networks, each with four nodes (one organisation and three consumers) and differing levels of interconnectivity. In each one of these networks, the number of possible connections between the consumers is three. This can be generalised to networks of any size using the equation $n*(n-1)/2$, where n is the total number of nodes in the network (not including the organisation). In X's network, there are no edges out of a possible three, and so it has a density of 0%. In Z's network on the right-hand side of Figure 13.5, all three possible edges are present; it has a density of 100%. Broadly speaking, diverse networks have more bridges, whereas dense networks have greater interconnectivity. Our task, therefore, is to develop strategies that work best for organisations with diverse networks, and strategies that work best for organisations with dense networks.

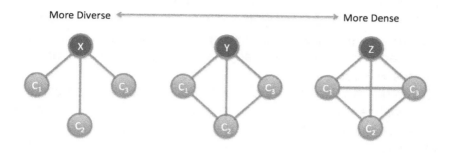

Figure 13.5. The Continuum between Diversity and Density

Social-media Strategies for the Connected Consumer

Consider the following comment that was posted to Facebook's community discussion forum on 30 September 2015:

> I don't mind if my comments and 'likes' on the political pages that I support are viewed by others who also follow the same pages as I do, but wtf are all my comments and random 'likes' doing automatically showing up in my regular friends news feeds? Not only do I feel that this violates my privacy, but it is also pissing my regular friends / gaming buddies off to the point where I am getting un-followed / un-friended. Your decision to change FB to do this is flawed. I want to be able to air my political views without having FB ram them down everyone I knows throat. That isn't social networking. That's social harassment. Fix it please.

> (Facebook, 2015)

When an organisation encourages Facebook users to engage with its content, it often does so with the explicit intention of spreading that content to other users of the platform, to increase awareness of its brand or cause. Facebook aids them in this endeavour by broadcasting to a user's friends when they engage with an organisation (when they like or comment on the organisation's page or posts, for example). As we can see from the comment above, however, aggressive sharing policies are not always well-received.

The knowledge that their activities can be shared without consent has led to a change in the way in which consumers behave on social-media platforms. For example, Bernritter and colleagues (2016) show that not-for-profit organisations are easier for people to endorse on social media than for-profit organisations. This occurs because endorsements (likes on Facebook, for example) are used to signal a consumer's values, and not-for-profit organisations tend to encompass a more socially agreeable set of values. In a related study, Watts and Shmargad (2015) show that people are less willing to use a digital gifting service when there is a greater risk that friends of the recipient can see gifts which are being exchanged.

So how does knowledge of a person's social network help us avoid these types of conflicts? The answer depends on the type of interaction in which organisations are engaging. When engaging in *outbound marketing* (paid advertising, for example) organisations ought to use targeted content for customers in diverse networks, and broad-themed content for customers in dense networks. On the other hand, when engaging in *inbound marketing* (content creation like posts on a social-media page, for example) organisations ought to use broad-themed content for diverse networks, and content which is targeted to the values of the community for dense networks.

We summarise these strategies in Table 13.2. The key difference between the different marketing activities is in the level of publicity which is associated with them. For outbound marketing strategies, consumers have some control over whether or not their engagement is made public. For example, a click on an advertisement is not broadcast automatically to a person's social-media connections. For this reason, organisations can create targeted (narrow) advertisements when consumers are more diverse. Because consumers tend not to be connected in a diverse network, they are less likely to find out about messages which do not target them (and which may conflict with their values).

Table 13.2. Content Marketing Strategies by Network Type

	Diverse Network	Dense Network
Outbound Marketing	Targeted to Customer	Broader
Inbound Marketing	Broader	Targeted to Community

To illustrate, consider a product like the Toyota Prius, which has two key benefits: 1. low fuel cost and 2. low carbon footprint. While many customers care about both of these benefits, it is also easy to imagine a group of individuals for whom cost savings are more important than the environment. Indeed, some individuals might even have a negative attitude towards products that purport to address environmental concerns. When consumers are not themselves connected, as in a diverse network, there is less of an opportunity for interactions that highlight these competing emphases. In contrast, consumers in a dense social network are much more likely to compare product claims. If these claims are perceived to be in conflict, then discussion between consumers can undermine a brand's credibility. For this reason, organisations ought to craft more general outbound marketing campaigns that are consistent with the values of the group.

For inbound marketing campaigns (posts on a social-media page, for example), the logic flips. Creating content on a blog or Facebook page invites public engagement by consumers. When consumers are in a diverse network, they are usually different from each other and some in the network might view a given person's public engagement negatively. This concern is clearly what motivated the complaint highlighted at the beginning of this section. Inbound marketing efforts to diverse networks, therefore, ought to avoid specific product claims that have the potential to conflict with the worldview of consumers. Dense networks, by contrast, are often indicative of ideological homogeny (McPherson et al., 2001). When organisations target a dense network with inbound marketing content, messages which are communicated at this homogenous community can be safer and more effective. Because consumers in a dense network tend to share a similar worldview, there is less potential for conflict arising from public engagement.

Conclusion

The rise of social media means that consumers are now more connected than ever before. But organisations that use social media to interact with existing and future customers ought to understand their limitations. The first step is to recognise that interactions with consumers are not necessarily *social*, in the traditional sense. Typically, consumers do not trust organisations in the same way in which they trust close family members and friends. Nonetheless, organisations can engender a certain degree of belief in their message, or commitment to their causes, through the dissemination of useful or compelling digital content – a process which culminates in the accumulation of *ideological capital*. This practice has matured under the label of *content marketing*, as organisations have concluded that the phrase 'social-media marketing' overemphasises the amount of meaningful social interaction that occurs. Instead, organisations focus on ideological capital to realise value in subsequent interactions with consumers, and perhaps even the eventual conversion of an interested person into a committed believer and customer.

The practice of digital marketing is fraught with risk. When consumers are heavily connected to one another, many of their interactions with organisations become visible to those in their social network. For some, this is a welcome signal of their identity and an invitation to promote themselves to the world. For others, the indiscriminate sharing of engagement activity can feel like an invasion of privacy. By understanding the structure of an organisation's consumer network, digital marketers can craft content that fits the privacy expectations of their audience. We summarise our recommendations in Table 13.2. The key difference between inbound and outbound marketing is the degree of control which consumers have over the publicity of their engagement. Because consumer control is higher for outbound digital marketing campaigns (paid banner ads, for example), content can be more targeted, but only for consumers in diverse networks. For inbound campaigns (blog posts, for example), consumers in diverse networks will respond better to content that has a low risk of offending those people in the network who might have different worldviews. This occurs because invited engagement is often publicised indiscriminately by platforms like Facebook, Twitter and LinkedIn.

There is still much to learn about the connected consumer. We hope that our focus on social networks and network analysis, however, provides insights that can help organisations craft better digital marketing campaigns in the future. While the tools that facilitate the type of analysis which we recommend are plentiful, new methods and tools are constantly on the horizon. By using the framework of ideological capital, however, along with the social-network-analysis methods which were presented in this chapter, you ought to feel comfortable crafting strategies using any of the current or emerging technologies that are available to modern-day marketers.

References

Aral, S., and M. Van Alstyne (2011) "The Diversity-Bandwidth Trade-off." *American Journal of Sociology*, Vol. 117, No. 1, pp.90–171.

Bernritter, S., P. Verlegh and E. Smit (2016) "Why Nonprofits are Easier to Endorse on Social Media: The Roles of Warmth and Brand Symbolism." *Journal of Interactive Marketing*, Vol. 33, pp.27–42.

Burt, R. (1992) *Structural Holes: The Social Structure of Competition*. Cambridge, USA: Harvard University Press.

Burt, R. (2007) "Secondhand Brokerage: Evidence on the Importance of Local Structure for Managers, Bankers, and Analysts." *Academy of Management Journal*, Vol. 50, Iss. 1, pp.119–48.

Burt, R. (2010) *Neighbor Networks: Competitive Advantage Local and Personal*. Oxford, England: Oxford University Press.

Centola, D. (2010) "The Spread of Behavior in an Online Social Network Experiment." *Science*, Vol. 329, Iss. 5996, pp.1,194–7.

Chan, C., J. Berger and L. Van Boven (2012) "Identifiable But Not Identical: Combining Social Identity and Uniqueness Motives in Choice." *Journal of Consumer Research*, Vol. 39, Iss. 3, pp.561–73.

Coleman, J. (1988) "Social Capital in the Creation of Human Capital." *American Journal of Sociology*, S95–S120.

Facebook (2015) "Question." Retrieved from: https://m.facebook.com/help/community/question/10100978574740558/

Feick, L., and L. Price (1987) "The Market Maven: A Diffuser of Marketplace Information." *Journal of Marketing*, Vol. 51, pp.83–97.

Ferrara, E., O. Varol, C. Davis, F. Menczer and A. Flammini (2016) "The Rise of Social Bots." *Communications of the ACM*, Vol. 59, Iss. 7, pp.96–104.

Godes, D., and D. Mayzlin (2009) "Firm-Created Word-of-Mouth Communication: Evidence From a Field Test." *Marketing Science*, Vol. 28, Iss. 4, pp.721–39.

Goel, S., A. Anderson, J. Hofman and D. Watts (2015) "The Structural Virality of Online Diffusion." *Management Science*, Vol. 62, No. 1, pp.180–96.

Iyengar, R., C. Van den Bulte and T. Valente (2011) "Opinion Leadership and Social Contagion in New Product Diffusion." *Marketing Science*, Vol. 30, Iss. 2, pp.195–212.

Kaplan, A., and M. Haenlein (2010) "Users of the World, Unite! The Challenges and Opportunities of Social Media." *Business Horizons*, Vol. 53, Iss. 1, pp.59–68.

Kietzmann, J., K. Hermkens, I. McCarthy and B. Silvestre (2011) "Social Media? Get Serious! Understanding the Functional Building Blocks of Social Media." *Business Horizons*, Vol. 54, Iss. 3, pp.241–51.

Lin, J. (1989) "Economic Theory of Institutional Change: Induced and Imposed Change." *Cato Journal*, Vol. 9, Iss. 1, pp.1–33

Mangold, W., and D. Faulds (2009) "Social Media: The New Hybrid Element of the Promotion Mix." *Business Horizons*, Vol. 52, Iss. 4, pp.357–65.

McFerran, B., D. Dahl, G. Fitzsimons and A. Morales (2010) "I'll Have What She's Having: Effects of Social Influence and Body Type on the Food Choices of Others." *Journal of Consumer Research*, Vol. 36, Iss. 6, pp.915–29.

McPherson, M., L. Smith-Lovin and J. Cook (2001) "Birds of a Feather: Homophily in Social Networks." *Annual Review of Sociology*, Vol. 27, pp.415–44.

Rainie, H., and B. Wellman (2012) *Networked: The New Social Operating System*. Cambridge, USA: MIT Press.

Shmargad, Y. (2014) "Social Media Broadcasts and the Maintenance of Diverse Networks." *Proceedings of the Thirty Fifth International Conference on Information Systems*.

Shmargad, Y., and J. Watts (2016a) "Strangers You May Know: Social Surveillance and Intimacy Online." *iConference 2016 Proceedings*.

Shmargad, Y., and J. Watts (2016b) "When Online Visibility Deters Social Interaction: The Case of Digital Gifts." *Journal of Interactive Marketing*, Vol. 36, pp.1–14.

Smith, S., and D. Alcorn (1991) "Cause Marketing: A New Direction in the Marketing of Corporate Responsibility." *Journal of Consumer Marketing*, Vol. 8, Iss. 3, pp.19–35.

Tucker, C. (2008) "Identifying Formal and Informal Influence in Technology Adoption With Network Externalities." *Management Science*, Vol. 54, Iss. 12, pp.2,024–38.

Van Dijk, J. (2012) *The Network Society*. London, England: Sage Publications.

Watts, J., and K. Koput (2014) "Supple Networks: Preferential Attachment by Diversity in Nascent Social Graphs." *Network Science*, Vol. 2, Iss. 3, pp.303–25.

Watts, J., and Y. Shmargad (2015) "Social Visibility and the Gifting of Digital Goods." *Proceedings of the 2015 ACM on Conference on Online Social Networks*, pp.49–58.

Watts, D., and S. Strogatz (1998) "Collective Dynamics of 'Small World' Networks." *Nature*, Vol. 393, Iss. 6684, pp.440–2.

Wellman, B., and S. Wortley (1990) "Different Strokes From Different Folks: Community Ties and Social Support." *American Journal of Sociology*, Vol. 96, No. 3, pp.558–88.

Yoganarasimhan, H. (2012) "Impact of Social Network Structure on Content Propagation: A Study Using YouTube Data." *Quantitative Marketing and Economics*, Vol. 10, Iss. 1, pp.111–50.

About the Authors

Yotam Shmargad is an Assistant Professor and the Director of Undergraduate Studies in the University of Arizona's iSchool. He received his Ph.D. in Marketing from the Kellogg School of Management in 2014. In his research, he analyses how social media alter the properties of users' social networks, and the impact this has on how products and information spread. In his increasingly sparse spare time, Yotam makes music and video mashups under the YouTube pseudonym *thesickish* – a slangy portmanteau of the words sick (meaning good) and ish (meaning stuff). Follow him on Twitter at @thesickish. Contact him on email at yotam@email.arizona.edu.

Jameson Watts is an Assistant Professor of Marketing in Willamette University's Atkinson Graduate School of Management. He received his Ph.D. in Marketing from the Eller College of Management in 2015. In his research, he looks at how differences in social structure affect consumption practices. When Jameson isn't jumping on the trampoline with his kids, he likes to surf, mountain bike and ski (sometimes all in the same day). Follow him on Twitter at @jamesonwatts. Contact him on email at jwatts@willamette.edu.

Chapter 14

The Past, Present and Future of Digital Marketing Content

Deborah Goldring

Introduction

Content marketing emerged in the early twenty-first century as a unique strategy for engaging hard-to-reach consumers. Indeed, marketers began encountering increasingly fragmented media, digital ad blocking, resistance from consumers on the use of interruption advertising, and lack of brand loyalty. Early content marketing approaches included the creation and publishing of blog posts and other product information which was findable via search engines and sharable on social media. Content marketing grew into a strategy of co-creating value to enable customer–brand engagement and to foster greater brand awareness, lead generation, sales conversion and customer relationships. Content grew rapidly beyond blog posts, however, to a plethora of text, graphics, audio and video communication which needed to be managed with sophisticated content management systems (CMS), and required curation and maintenance by content managers and strategists. Content marketing platforms grew as fast as the new media platforms were being created.

The life cycle of content marketing appears to be following

either a growth-slump-maturity model, in which a rapid accept-ance of the strategy is followed by some disillusionment and then a phase of disengagement, or a cycle-recycle pattern in which, following a decline, there is a secondary continued – albeit slower – growth (see Figure 14.1). Content marketing appears to be on the downslope of acceptance due to its saturation and only the future will tell if this marketing strategy will continue to be an important messaging tool for marketers. Whichever turns out to be the case, content marketing appears to be decreasing in popularity.

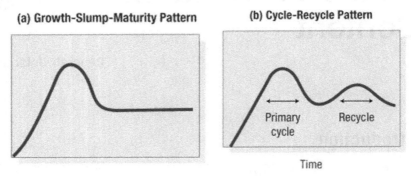

(a) Growth-Slump-Maturity Pattern   **(b) Cycle-Recycle Pattern**

Primary cycle   Recycle

Time

Figure 14.1. Life Cycle Patterns for Content Marketing
Source: Kotler and Keller (2011)

Given the importance of content in both social media and search engine marketing, this chapter argues that digital content marketing can continue to provide marketers with an impor-tant tool for driving traffic, and for generating conversions – if the content emphasises quality over quantity. Content provides prospective and existing customers with a reason to visit your site. Social media provides a mechanism for informing prospec-tive and existing customers about your brand. Done correctly, therefore, content marketing excels at increasing traffic, offers multiple opportunities for conversion and enables relationship engagement. How marketers use this increased traffic from content marketing to generate revenue depends on their skills in creating high-quality, effective content.

This chapter begins with a review of the historical development of content marketing. It continues into a discussion of the key elements of effective digital marketing content, grounded in marketing theory. Finally, it concludes by speculating on how digital marketing content is evolving to leverage new marketing strategies.

After reading this chapter, therefore, you will:

1. Understand content marketing as a marketing communications tactic;

2. Appreciate the conceptual foundations of content marketing within the integrated marketing communications mix;

3. Possess a framework for creating effective, valuable content; and

4. Have an idea where content marketing is headed in the future.

Digital Marketing Content in the Historical Context – The Past

Content marketing is the process of creating, distributing and promoting customer-focused messages that facilitate branding, sales and the customer relationship process. These customer-focused messages are distinct from the media platforms on which they are distributed, and distinct from related promotional strategies such as advertising and publicity. The creation of high-quality, effective and engaging content has been a significant challenge for marketers.

Content marketing is not new. Indeed, although it is a current trending practice of marketing managers, it has been a successful activity for decades. Consider the Pan Am in-flight magazines of the 1940s, the Betty Crocker cookbooks of the 1950s and the four-colour brochures, product demonstration videos and info-mercials of the 1980s and 1990s. One of the first empirical studies of marketing content (Vrendenburg and Droge, 1987) identified the importance of printed and mailed magazines and newsletters in the information search and purchasing process. These company publications were useful and memorable sources of information to a group of surveyed industrial buyers. This marketing material was seen not as propaganda, but as valued information. Moreover, tracking and measuring the effectiveness of these printed pieces of sales collateral which were written by copywriters was difficult to discern and attribute, and most marketing departments were not held accountable for the return on investment of brochures and newsletters.

The modern era of content marketing began with the groundbreaking work of Hoffman and Novak (1996) who introduced a then-revolutionary new medium – the hypermedia computer-mediated environment. Indeed, they described a new typology of an interactive medium in which dynamic content flowed from a brand through a medium to consumers, which then led to interactivity between consumers via other consumers back through the medium. They also identified three important characteristics of this new medium: the interconnectedness of brands and consumers, media feedback symmetry and equality, and temporal synchronicity – meaning that the experience occurred in real time.

Contemporary Content Marketing – The Present

More recently, Pulizzi and Barrett (2009) started the conversation on content marketing as a new digital marketing communications tactic with their book *Get Content Get Customers*, and with the formation of the Content Marketing Institute in 2010. Halvorson and Rach (2012) believed in the less-is-more philosophy, in which content is only valuable if it meets an organisation's objectives and its consumer's needs. By 2012, however, marketers were producing an overabundance of webinars, podcasts, blogs, videos, e-books, infographics and other content to engage with their customers (Handley, 2012). The number of how-to books on creating and distributing content exploded. There seemed to be no discernible decrease in marketing's love for content marketing. In 2016, there were nearly 500 content-marketing consulting firms around the world, according to the directory of the Content Marketing Institute.

The leading book authors in content marketing are primarily practitioners rather than academicians, perhaps due to the rapid growth of the practice and to the demand for straightforward pragmatic advice based on experience and real case studies. Table 14.1 contains a curated list of books that focus either exclusively or primarily on the challenges of creating digital marketing content.

While there is no question that these authors have made a strong case for content marketing as a valid practice, there is always a degree of risk when managers depend on consultants who have an interest in the subject matter on which they write and which is not always supported by evidence-based scholarly research (Abrahamson, 1996). This chapter seeks both to confirm some of these authors' perspectives and to identify ways in which marketers can develop more effective content marketing through the understanding of well-tested marketing theories.

With the growth of new digital media such as social platforms and applications, and the growth in the power of mobile phones, digital content marketing has moved to the forefront. Printed marketing collateral has transformed into interactive websites and micro-sites. Copywriters are now working alongside content specialists and content curators. Owned media, such as websites, blogs, email and social platforms, are giving brands additional control over their messages. Pull media outflanks push media.

Table 14.1. Influential Books on Digital Marketing Content

Year	Author(s)	Book Title
2009	Joe Pulizzi and Newt Barrett	*Get Content Get Customers*
2011	Jon Wuebben	*Content Is Currency: Developing Powerful Content for Web and Mobile*
2012	Christina Halvorson and Melissa Rach	*Content Strategy for the Web*
2012	Ann Handley and Charles Chapman	*Content Rules: How To Create Killer Blogs, Podcasts, Videos, E-Books, Webinars (and More) That Engage Customers and Ignite Your Business*
2014	Joe Pulizzi	*Epic Content Marketing: How to Tell a Different Story, Break Through the Clutter, and Win More Customers by Marketing Less*

Year	Author(s)	Book Title
2014	Ann Handley	*Everybody Writes: Your Go-To Guide to Creating Ridiculously Good Content*
2015	Sonja Jefferson and Sharon Tanton	*Valuable Content Marketing: How to Make Quality Content Your Key to Success*
2015	Ardath Albee	*Digital Relevance: Developing Marketing Content and Strategies That Drive Results*
2015	Robert Rose and Carla Johnson	*Experiences: The 7th Era of Marketing*
2016	Carmen Simon	*Impossible to Ignore: Creating Memorable Content to Influence Decisions*

New media platforms have enabled marketers to communicate brand value via relevant and informative content which has become a force in both business-to-consumer (B2C) and business-to-business (B2B) channels. Nearly three-quarters of B2C marketers and about 90% of B2B marketers use content marketing as a means of engaging with their customers (Content Marketing Institute, 2016). B2C marketers favour Facebook, while B2B marketers prefer to use LinkedIn. There are key differences in the objectives for content marketing, with B2C marketers identifying sales, loyalty and engagement as the primary objectives, and B2B marketers looking for lead generation, sales and lead nurturing as the primary objectives. All marketers agree that producing engaging content and measuring content effectiveness are their key challenges. Gauzente and Roy (2012) found that for digital advertising, messages with informational content outperform messages which are primarily persuasive, reflecting consumers' desire for less sales-oriented messages. Content marketing can fill this gap.

In terms of Search Engine Optimisation (SEO), content has replaced off-page SEO (backlinks, for example) as an important component of search-engine algorithms. Frequently updated content has a positive impact on organic rankings in search-engine results pages (SERPs). According to Neil Patel, co-founder of KISSmetrics, this algorithmic change, from backlinks to content, was a direct result of the proliferation of 'black-hat' SEO practices which sought to game the search-engine system by using surreptitious font colours or sizes, or excessive or inappropriate keywords, without providing useful and relevant content or websites.

Indeed, there are important differences which distinguish content marketing from traditional marketing communications practices. Advertising is the paid, mass-media, non-personal communication of persuasive information about a product that is offered by an identified brand. Advertising attempts to convince consumers to take some action with respect to a trial or purchase of a product offering. The existing marketing literature has studied the effects of advertising in the form of paid media such as television, radio, magazines, newspapers, digital and direct advertising. Publicity of public relations (PR), another promotional tactic, is the unpaid, non-personal communication of information about products through the editorial channels of journalists, bloggers and influencers. Content marketing has some overlap, although there are significant differences in terms of message goals, message interaction and time horizon. Table 14.2 summarises the differences between advertising, publicity and content marketing.

Table 14.2. Differences between Advertising, Publicity and Content Marketing

	Advertising	Publicity/PR	Content Marketing
Media Placement	Paid	Earned	Owned (mostly)
Sponsor Identification	Yes	No	Yes
Perceived Credibility	Low	High	Medium? (future research)
Message Control	Yes	No	Yes
Message Strategy	Push	Pull	Pull
Message Goal	Persuade	Influence	Engage
Direction	One-way	One-way	Two-way
Time Horizon	Short-term (campaign)	Short-term (campaign)	Long-term (ongoing)
Audience	Prospects	Influencers	Customers

Digital marketing content is primarily distributed on owned media, not paid media. Owned media include corporate websites, email accounts, corporate blogs, twitter accounts and YouTube accounts. These owned media platforms are not a form of advertising because they are controlled and managed by brands. Content marketing is a tactic defined by transparent sponsorship identification, message control, the capability to enable feedback and sharing. The message content emphasises informative rather than interruptive messages, using a softer, less 'salesy' approach (Truong and Simmons, 2010).

Digital Marketing Content Strategies and Tactics

Content marketing must be recognised as a new tool in the marketing communications mix that ought to be tightly integrated into, and consistent with, advertising, publicity, sales, direct marketing and so forth. Efforts to measure the activities encompassed by integrated marketing communications (IMC) have been elusive, but may be summarised by the following: unified communications for consistent message and image, differentiated communications to segmented customer groups, data-driven communications for tangible results, and relationship-building communications with existing customers (Lee and Park, 2007).

Effective digital marketing content starts with understanding the objective of a campaign. Van den Putte (2006) identified nine message strategies that can be mixed and matched to the needs of the target market, according to one or more of the following phases of the buying process:

- Awareness (using novel methods to gain top-of-mind brand awareness),

- Likability (providing entertaining content to obtain a positive attitude toward the brand),

- Information (communicating relevant, new or improved, functional advantages),

- Emotional (associating brands with feelings, usually in product use situations),

- Identity (convincing consumers that the brand matches their self-identity),

- Social (convincing consumers that the brand can communicate their social identity to others),

- Stimulus response (creating an immediate, usually rational, response),

- Self-efficacy (persuading consumers that the brand can make something which is difficult easier to perform), and

- Variation (showing novelty or new uses for brand to prevent boredom).

Related marketing communication strategies include creating message objectives, establishing a credible message source, selecting media channels and acting on feedback. Message objectives are based on the brand value proposition and competitive positioning. These objectives relate to the overall communication and sales strategy, and include attitude toward the brand and revenue goals. Objectives also include engagement, behavioural intention or purchase intention.

The new framework for media channels includes paid, owned and earned media (POEM). Paid media comprises traditional advertising media. Owned media includes company-branded websites and blogs. Earned media is the response to marketing activities in the form of shared content, user-generated comments or product reviews. Specific media platforms constantly evolve and change, and marketers must test their messages for a sustainable content marketing strategy. Table 14.3 summarises the POEM framework.

Investing in content marketing is good for the bottom line. Digital marketing content has a positive and significant effect on consumer behaviour, in terms of consumer spending and cross-buying behaviour, and works synergistically with television advertising and email marketing (Kumar et al., 2016).

Content marketing thrives on an understanding of the inbound marketing concept, popularised by Hubspot (www.hubspot.com), of publishing content on social-media platforms to enhance organic search-engine listings that link back to non-sales messages which attract, engage and delight (Halligan and Shah, 2014). Recent research has attempted to classify the types of non-promotional messages which are found on Facebook, the dominant social-media platform (Coursaris et al., 2013). These broad categories of message types might provide some hints on which type of marketing content is most successful, specifically for social media. The categories include:

- Corporate brand awareness (posts which build corporate reputation),

- Corporate social responsibility (posts which show the company's involvement in social causes),

- Customer service (posts which help customers use the product or notify them of issues),

- Brand engagement (posts which build brand connections or communities through interactions), and

- Brand awareness (posts which create recognition and recall of the brand).

Table 14.3. Summary of the POEM Framework

Media Type	Definition	Channels	Target	Purpose
Paid	Company buys media space from a third party to promote its product and services	Advertising, direct mail, sponsorships, product placement, paid search, events	Strangers	Buys attention
Owned	Company uses or creates its own channels and content to communicate information about products and services	Corporate and product websites, social-media channels (YouTube, Facebook, Instagram), content-sharing sites (Slideshare), blogs	Customers	Builds relationships

Media Type	Definition	Channels	Target	Purpose
Earned	Customers, the media and other stakeholders engage with and share information about a company's products and services	Social-networking sites, editorial coverage, user-generated content	Advocates	Drives conversations

While there have been calls for the generation of more and more content, recent surveys of marketers now point to a saturation point, where there is too much content that is not being read, downloaded, shared or acted upon. One of the biggest challenges on which marketers agree is how to produce and publish effective content; there is less agreement in the content marketing community, however, on what effective content really means.

Content effectiveness depends on both the information and the media on which it is distributed. Information richness theory (Daft and Lengel, 1984) identifies two tasks of content: to reduce ambiguity and uncertainty (called equivocality reduction) and to provide an appropriate amount of communication (called information sufficiency). Media richness theory (Daft et al., 1987) refers to the capacity of a medium to facilitate shared meaning, based on the content timeliness, content richness, content accuracy and content adaptability of the information communicated in the medium.

Conversational Content

Effective digital marketing content is based on fostering a two-way dialogue that is open and authentic, and that invites and encourages opportunities for further interaction. This interaction also ought to consider adapting the content and linguistic style of the recipient to enhance communication success (Ludwig et al., 2013).

Conversations are characterised by honesty, non-manipulation, recognition of uniqueness, mutual confirmation and openness to another's point of view (Varey, 2003). Based on relationship marketing, which recognises the beneficial interactions between buyers and sellers, marketers ought to listen more deeply to customers and focus less on the sales transaction. Initiating this conversation with content can result in a real and meaningful dialogue that generates value for buyers and sellers – and it is difficult for competitors to copy (Varey and Ballantyne, 2005).

Customer-centric Content

Customers can find nearly any information that they need to make a purchasing decision by searching for content on the Internet. Marketers who are invested in effective content ought to position their brand messages carefully to be less promotional and more informational. Engaging content is not about what the company does or makes; it is about solving customer problems or answering questions which the customer finds important (Parise et al., 2008). Brand-developed content ought not to be about the brand, but about how the product benefits the customer. Content ought to reflect what customers need and want, and the features and benefits they find most important. While the brand is responsible for communicating the value proposition, the customer is in control of when, where and how they want to activate communication with the seller (Schultz et al., 2012).

Content Which Tells a Story

Narration refers to "symbolic actions that have sequence and meaning for those who live, create, or interpret them" (Fisher, 1984, p.2). Great stories are memorable and trusted, have an immediate 'hook' and appeal to the senses (Godin, 2009). Both content and advertising can be in narrative form. Narrative processing, however, imposes high cognitive demands, which makes storytelling ideal for content about brands (Chang, 2009). A good story is more likely to be repeated in traditional word-of-mouth communication or in online social media (Mangold and Faulds, 2009). Digital marketing content, therefore, is all about storytelling, which includes identifiable characters, imaginable plot and authenticity (Van Laer et al., 2014). Chapter 7 by van Laer and Lurie has more discussion of storytelling.

Engaging marketing content tells a believable story about a company's brand. Content that tells a story helps customers make sense of a brand's identity and is the 'relational glue' which influences the customer's relationship with the company (Kodish and Pettegrew, 2008). Stories help customers make sense of the brand's efforts, values and goals. Research has found that consumers who are exposed to the brand story are more willing to pay more for a product, and that brand stories can create and reinforce positive brand associations, brand attitudes and purchase intentions (Chiu et al., 2012; Lundqvist et al., 2013).

Quality Content

Quality content means that the message is accurate, understandable, memorable and relevant. The work of Barnes and Vidgen (2002) provides us with the dimensions of content quality. Their Information Quality (IQ) measure is comprised of four dimensions: 1. intrinsic quality, 2. contextual quality, 3. representational quality and 4. accessibility quality. Intrinsic quality is the inherent quality of the information itself, such as believability, accuracy, objectivity, credibility and unambiguousness. Contextual quality relates to the relationship which the information has to the task at hand and includes relevancy, timeliness, completeness and information quantity. Representational quality is the way in which the content helps to provide consistent, understandable and interpretable information. For example, a product demonstration would be of higher quality presented as a video rather than as a numbered textual list. Finally, accessibility quality is the ease with which information is findable and available. Chapter 12 by Pedersen provides several examples of companies that have provided useful, customer-centric content.

Informative Content

Informative messages are more likely to attract attention to a brand and to help customers in the buying process (MacKenzie et al., 1986). Content that emphasises honest, descriptive information about a product is more effective when consumers are searching for information online because they might be expecting subtler persuasive attempts (Gauzente and Roy, 2012). This is similar to Bond's claim in Chapter 5 that marketing might be most effective when content does not look like marketing. Marketing content, whether in print or on the web, is more explanatory than advertising and customers consciously expect to process content more attentively (Gallagher et al., 2001). Consequently, advertising is persuasive communication *to* customers while content is informative communication *with* customers.

Informative marketing content enables customers to learn more about a company and its brands, and also invites them to engage in further interactions, including sharing their own information about searching for, trying or using the product. Informative content helps to reduce risk and uncertainty in the buying process.

Content Message Success Factors

Content marketing has reached a tipping point in terms of both the sustainability of content development and media distribution. Headlines question whether there is content overload, content clutter or, worse, content chaos. There seems to be a growing disparity in content quantity, content quality, and content actually downloaded and read. Reach on social media has been declining. So how will brands find the equilibrium between an excess supply of content and reduced demand? How do brands manage excess content? What is the marginal value of adding another content campaign? Is pay to play, such as sponsored content, the best strategy – meaning that push communication has trumped inbound? Will brand-owned media result in a loss of brand strength? What does the evolution of brands into media mean for the customer and the editorial capabilities of the brand? Can high-quality content be maintained?

Research on these questions is limited. One view, however, is that marketers ought to reverse the fragmentation of marketing communications – digital versus non-digital, web marketing versus mobile marketing, owned media versus paid media and so on. Baetzgen and Tropp (2015) identified eight critical success factors for marketer-generated content:

1. Content quality (messages must be professional, authentic and original),

2. Non-advertising appeal (messages ought to weigh more heavily as information or entertainment, not as persuasion),

3. Product involvement (the higher the product involvement, the greater the positive effect on the brand-owned media, although low-involvement products can still achieve success),

4. Relevance for consumer (consumers' needs, wants and desires ought to be addressed),

5. Frequency (regular, fresh content must be created and managed),

6. Brand fit (both the content format and the media channel must be appropriate for the brand – a B2B white paper on LinkedIn that is aimed at impacting brand image, for example),

7. Reach (brands must reach a significant number of consumers to have a multiplier effect), and

8. Brand strength (brands need not develop a reputation and establish themselves as a media property in order to be successful).

Fundamentally, content marketing is grounded in the marketing concept – our product exists to meet the needs of consumers... that is to say, to fulfil existing consumer wants/needs instead of creating these wants/needs. Content marketing provides B2B and B2C customers with the information that they seek, when they want it, and how they want it delivered.

What's Next for Digital Marketing Content – The Future

Content marketing is experiencing some headwinds and tailwinds. There seems to be an overabundance of content and a decrease in engagement with content. Quantity has outmanoeuvred quality in many cases, to the detriment of results. Every year tools change and evolve, which constantly challenges marketers to keep up and manage an ever-growing stream of messages and platforms. The traditional website is not always the hub of inter-actions with your customers, and consequently marketers must find customers on whichever platform they are seeking brand information.

On the other hand, content marketing is a strategy that is seem-ingly here to stay, sought after by consumers who are hungry for relevant, functional brand information that can help them make purchase decisions (Ashley and Tuten, 2015). Marketing content can be customised for a variety of social-media platforms and can provide the value which customers appreciate. Long-form blog posts can co-exist with six-second videos. While there has been a cat-and-mouse game of blocking advertising on social media and mobile platforms, content marketing enables marketers to get their messages through the obstacle course of ad blocking.

Another evolution of content marketing is the dominance of mobile devices for accessing brand information and conducting commerce. It is not enough to be mobile-optimised; marketers must think in terms of creating content specifically designed for mobile platforms, because this is the device on which shoppers are converting sales in greater numbers than desktops. Mobile users are increasingly seeking video content, which presents additional challenges for content marketers. Integrating video into written content works well as long as the video is prop-erly embedded, works in multiple operating systems and web browsers, and enhances rather than detracts from the brand's message.

New social media, apps, and the increased fragmentation of media, combined with the proliferation of content, are making it more difficult to be found on search engines. Use of long-tail keywords is becoming increasingly important. But again, the increased use of video provides challenges for using search-engine marketing as a means to attract traffic. Well-written, concise video descriptions are required. Future changes in search-engine algorithms are difficult to predict, as is the search-engine landscape. Will content remain an important part of the organic search-engine results page (SERP) equation or will its influence diminish for some unforeseen variable of importance?

There are at least two evolving practices on the horizon for content marketers. One is leveraging content marketing with influencer marketing. The other is to steer content marketing into content-driven commerce. Leveraging content marketing with influencer marketing enables the brand message to be amplified by a third party who has the freedom to recommend a brand or not. This helps to solve the growing gulf between content output and customer engagement. While marketers are free to pump out their own content on their own platforms, there is an opportunity cost. Marketers, therefore, will need to consider using paid media or paid influencers to amplify their messages. By working with targeted influencers, marketers can provide their content and co-create content with influencers in exchange for some type of incentive or compensation.

Content-driven commerce might indeed be the ultimate goal for content marketing. Content can be used throughout the sales cycle to attract prospects, convert them into customers, facilitate order processing, enable retention and engender loyalty. Content that attracts customers includes blog posts, articles and short videos. Content that converts includes incentives, promotions, product guides and catalogues. Content that facilitates orders includes ordering and shipping messages. Finally, content that retains customers includes instruction guides and product update information. Current content creation and distribution platforms would need to be integrated into enterprise-based e-commerce systems and offer a seamless and consistent experience.

Finally, there are visionary predictions about how content marketing will look, considering the dynamic nature of the digital landscape. Hennig-Thurau and colleagues (2010), who called the new media environment "multidirectional, interconnected, and difficult to predict" (p.313), identified several of these challenges on which brand managers need to reflect continuously. For example, how does consumption of digital marketing content on new media channels impact the consumption patterns of traditional media? What is the demand for marketing content on new media? What is consumers' willingness to pay for content? How ought companies to react to critical content or hijacked campaigns? And finally, how are existing brand relationships affected by digital marketing content? Content marketing has drawn the attention of marketers because it has disrupted how relationships are developed with customers. Customers are more in control and have become active partners with brands to interact with and amplify marketing messages. But this also comes with increased complexity in measuring brand image and message effectiveness.

Conclusion

Although the digital landscape is constantly changing, the one constant is that great content generates optimal search-engine results, and hence traffic to a website or other targeted landing page. Content marketing is a practice that is maturing and has permanently changed the way in which marketers contribute to both brand-building and demand-generation. Content marketing can raise brand awareness, engage prospects at various phases of the buying process, and keep customers committed and loyal to the brand after purchase. When marketers have a greater understanding of how targeted, relevant and authentic marketing content fits into a comprehensive content-marketing strategy, they can manage the content creation, distribution and promotion process more efficiently, and begin to measure the communication and sales effects which content marketing promises. In conclusion, here is some final advice for content strategists, analysts and curators: 1. provide helpful content first and more subtle calls to action, 2. develop authenticity over time, 3. keep in mind the importance of building a trustworthy brand, 4. be well-informed on how your content marketing activities fit into other marketing communications programs, 5. aim for worthwhile content which is useful for your customer, 6. listen and understand your customer, 7. publish the right content for the right media (owned or paid), and 8. commit to relevant and achievable metrics (Holliman and Rowley, 2014).

References

Albee, A. (2015) *Digital Relevance: Developing Marketing Content and Strategies That Drive Results*. New York, USA: Palgrave Macmillan.

Abrahamson, E. (1996) "Management Fashion." *Academy of Management Review,* Vol. 21, Iss. 1, pp.254–85.

Ashley, C., and T. Tuten (2015) "Creative Strategies in Social Media Marketing: An Exploratory Study of Branded Social Content and Consumer Engagement." *Psychology and Marketing*, Vol. 32, Iss. 1, pp.15–27.

Baetzgen, A., and J. Tropp (2015) "How Can Brand-Owned Media Be Managed? Exploring the Managerial Success Factors of the New Interrelation Between Brands and Media." *International Journal on Media Management*, Vol. 17, Iss. 3, pp.135–55.

Barnes, S., and R. Vidgen (2002) "An Integrative Approach to the Assessment of E-Commerce Quality." *Journal of Electronic Commerce Research*, Vol. 3, Iss. 3, pp.114–27.

Chang, C. (2009) "'Being Hooked' by Editorial Content." *Journal of Advertising*, Vol. 38, No. 1, pp.21–33.

Chiu, H.-C., U.-C. Hseih and Y.-C. Kuo (2012) "How to Align your Brand Stories with Your Products." *Journal of Retailing*, Vol. 88, Iss. 2, pp.262–75.

Content Marketing Institute (2016) "Benchmarks, Budgets, and Trends – North America." Retrieved from: http://contentmarketinginstitute. com/wp-content/uploads/2015/09/2016_B2B_Report_Final.pdf

Coursaris, C., W. Van Osch and B. Balogh (2013) "A Social Media Marketing Typology: Classifying Brand Facebook Page Messages For Strategic Consumer Engagement." *Proceedings of the 21st European Conference on Information Systems,* Paper 46, pp.1–12.

Daft, R., and R. Lengel (1984) "Information Richness: A New Approach to Managerial Information Processing and Organization Design." In B. Staw and L. Cummings (eds). *Research in Organizational Behavior.* Greenwich, USA: JAI Press, pp.191–233.

Daft, R., R. Lengel and L. Trevino (1987) "Message Equivocality, Media Selection, and Manager Performance: Implications for Information Systems." *MIS Quarterly*, Vol. 11, Iss. 3, pp.355–66.

Fisher, W. (1984) "Narration as a Human Communication Paradigm: The Case of Public Moral Argument." *Communication Monographs*, Vol. 51, pp.1–22.

Gallagher, K., K. Foster and J. Parsons (2001) "The Medium is Not the Message: Advertising Effectiveness and Content Evaluation in Print and on the Web." *Journal of Advertising Research*, Vol. 41, Iss. 4, pp.57–70.

Gauzente, C., and Y. Roy (2012) "Message Content in Keyword Campaigns, Click Behavior, and Price-Consciousness: A Study of Millennial Consumers." *Journal of Retailing and Consumer Services*, Vol. 19, pp.78–87.

Godin, S. (2009) *All Marketers Are Liars*. New York, USA: Penguin Group.

Halligan, B., and S. Shah (2014) *Inbound Marketing: Attract, Engage, and Delight Customers Online*. Hoboken, USA: Wiley.

Halvorson, K., and M. Rach (2012) *Content Strategy for the Web*, 2nd Edition. Reading, USA: New Riders.

Handley, A., and C. Chapman (2012) *Content Rules*. Hoboken, USA: Wiley.

Handley, A. (2014) *Everybody Writes: Your Go-To Guide to Creating Ridiculously Good Content*. Hoboken, USA: Wiley.

Hennig-Thurau, T., E. Malthouse, C. Friege, S. Gensler, L. Lobschat, A. Rangaswamy and B. Skiera (2010) "The Impact of New Media on Customer Relationships." *Journal of Service Research*, Vol. 13, Iss. 3, pp.311–30.

Hoffman, D., and T. Novak (1996) "Marketing in Hypermedia Computer-mediated Environments: Conceptual Foundations." *Journal of Marketing*, Vol. 60, Iss. 3, pp.50–68.

Holliman, G., and J. Rowley (2014) "Business to Business Digital Content Marketing: Marketers' Perceptions of Best Practice." *Journal of Research in Interactive Marketing*, Vol. 8, Iss. 4, pp.269–93.

Jefferson, S., and S. Tanton (2015) *Valuable Content Marketing: How to Make Quality Content Your Key to Success*. Philadelphia, USA: Kogan Page.

Kodish, S., and L. Pettegrew (2008) "Enlightened Communication is the Key to Building Relationships." *Journal of Relationship Marketing*, Vol. 7, Iss. 2, pp.151–76.

Kotler, P., and K. Keller (2011) *Marketing Management*, 14th ed. Upper Saddle River, USA: Pearson.

Kumar, A., R. Bezawada, R. Rishika, R. Janakiraman and P. Kannan (2016) "From Social to Sale: The Effects of Firm-Generated

Content in Social Media on Customer Behavior." *Journal of Marketing*, Vol. 80, Iss. 1, pp.7–25.

Lee, D., and C. Park (2007) "Conceptualization and Measurement of Multidimensionality of Integrated Marketing Communications." *Journal of Advertising Research*, Vol. 47, Iss. 3, pp.222–36.

Lieb, R. (2012) *Content Marketing*. Richton Park, USA: Cue Publishing.

Ludwig, S., K. de Ruyter, M. Friedman, E. Brüggen, M. Wetzels and G. Pfann (2013) "More Than Words: The Influence of Affective Content and Linguistic Style Matches in Online Reviews on Conversion Rates." *Journal of Marketing*, Vol. 77, Iss. 1, pp.87–103.

Lundqvist, A., V. Liljander, J. Gummeru and A. van Riel (2013) "The Impact of Storytelling on the Consumer Brand Experience: The Case of a Firm-Originated Story." *Journal of Brand Management*, Vol. 20, Iss. 4, pp.283–97.

MacKenzie, S., R. Lutz and G. Belch (1986) "The Role of Attitude Toward the Ad as a Mediator of Advertising Effectiveness: A Test of Competing Explanations." *Journal of Marketing Research*, Vol. 23, Iss. 2, pp.130–43.

Mangold, W., and D. Faulds (2009) "Social Media: The New Hybrid Element of The Promotion Mix." *Business Horizons*, Vol. 52, pp.357–65.

Parise, S., P. Guinan and B. Weinberg (2008) "Marketing: The Secrets of Marketing in a Web 2.0 World." *Wall Street Journal*, Vol. 252, No. 141, R4.

Pulizzi, J., and N. Barrett (2009) *Get Content Get Customers: Turn Prospects into Buyers with Content Marketing*. New York, USA: McGraw Hill Professional.

Pulizzi, J. (2014) *Epic Content Marketing: How to Tell a Different Story, Break Through the Clutter, and Win More Customers by Marketing Less*. New York, USA: McGraw-Hill Education.

Rose, R., and C. Johnson (2015) *Experiences: The 7th Era of Marketing*. Cleveland, USA: Content Marketing Institute.

Schultz, D., M. Block and K. Raman (2012) "Understanding Consumer-created Media Synergy." *Journal of Marketing Communications*, Vol. 18, Iss. 3, pp.173–87.

Simon, C. (2016) *Impossible to Ignore: Creating Memorable Content to Influence Decisions*. New York, USA: McGraw-Hill Education.

Truong, Y., and G. Simmons (2010) "Perceived Intrusiveness in Digital Advertising: Strategic Marketing Implications." *Journal of Strategic Marketing*, Vol. 18, Iss. 3, pp.239–56.

Van den Putte, B. (2006) "A Comparative Test of the Effect of Communication Strategy, Media Presence, and Previous Purchase Behaviour in the Field of Fast Moving Consumer Goods." In S. Diehl and R. Terlutter (eds). *International Advertising and Communication: Current Insights and Empirical Findings*. Wiesbaden, Germany: Deutscher Universitätsverlag, pp.89–105.

Van Laer, T., K. de Ruyter, L. Visconti and M. Wetzel (2014) "The Extended Transportation-Imagery Model: A Meta-Analysis of the Antecedents and Consequences of Consumers' Narrative Transportation." *Journal of Consumer Research*, Vol. 40, Iss. 5, pp.797–817.

Varey, R. (2003) "A Dialogical Foundation for Marketing." *Marketing Review*, Vol. 3, pp.273–88.

Varey, R., and D. Ballantyne (2005) "Relationship Marketing and the Challenge of Dialogical Interaction." *Journal of Relationship Marketing*, Vol. 4, Iss. 3/4, pp.11–28.

Vrendenburg, H., and C. Droge (1987) "The Value of Company Newsletters and Magazines." *Industrial Marketing Management*, Vol. 16, Iss. 3, pp.173–8.

Wuebben, J. (2012) *Content is Currency: Developing Powerful Content for Web and Mobile*. Boston, USA: Brealey.

About the Author

Deborah Goldring is an Assistant Professor of Marketing at Stetson University's School of Business Administration in DeLand, USA. She received her Ph.D. in Marketing from Florida Atlantic University in 2011. In her research, she explores the impact of brand associations, influencers and content marketing on behavioural intentions. She also has over 20 years of experience in marketing leadership with B2B companies. Deborah loves hot Florida weather and hates blue cheese. Follow her on twitter at @debgoldring. Contact her on email at goldring@stetson.edu.

Chapter 15

Conversing through Content – The Intersection of Social Media and Digital Media in Music

Ed Suwanjindar

Introduction

The rise of social media could be attributed to many factors: the natural evolution of how we communicate, our desire to be connected with one another following advances in technology (ubiquitous Internet access and powerful mobile devices), and the influence of personalities and celebrities whose use of social media as their primary outlet for communication helped to popularise it.

Musicians are among the most-followed figures in the world of social media. While they constitute an industry, their core value proposition has only recently begun to reach consumers on a large scale. In its early days, social-media content consisted of text, web links and images. Now, however, the social-media experience serves as an interactive platform between artists and consumers.

The purpose of this chapter is to explore how the worlds of social media and digital media are converging, specifically in the context of music. After reading this chapter, you will:

1. Appreciate how musicians are harnessing the enthusiasm of their audiences on social networks to drive the consumption of their music;

2. Understand the role that technology companies (social media and digital platforms) play in the dynamic between artists and the digital-media business;

3. See the tools, programs and incentives that companies offer to artists and, additionally, how they cater to artists through various platforms;

4. Witness how these companies benefit from such activity; and

5. Perceive how all this affects customers and fans.

By examining this confluence of social-media virality and digital content consumption, we can see that the combination of forces is part of the inevitable transformation of our mode of communication. Words and pictures will no longer suffice as we, and the artists whom we follow, take the conversation to content.

Artists, Social Media and Digital Media

What do Shakira, Eminem, Rihanna, Justin Bieber, Michael Jackson, Taylor Swift, Bob Marley and Katy Perry all have in common? At first glance, it is obvious – they are musicians. But these eight people also each have one of the twenty most popular 'pages' on Facebook.

The nature of the posts which they make on their profiles varies from the mundane (Taylor Swift often posts birthday wishes to close friends, for example) to the sensational (Swift also uses the same page for defence and rebuttal in her ongoing feud with Kanye West). Beyond the glimpse into their lives which many artists offer to their fans and followers, they exist on social media for another reason – to make money.

In the case of these artists (and many others like them), the massive audiences and targeted fan engagement that are afforded by these platforms offer a valuable channel to further their business interests. Katy Perry, for example, has the smallest audience of the artists who are mentioned above with a formidable 71+ million fans!

As the music industry has evolved from physical formats to downloads and streaming, the promotion and marketing of music has also evolved. Although traditional avenues for promotion such as radio are still relevant, today's most successful popular musicians have taken to social media to publicise their newest releases. In its early days, promotion via social media took the form of text posts which announced the availability of new music to fans. Most of these posts simply included web links to the distributor of choice: iTunes, Amazon, or physical retailers such as Target or Wal-Mart, for example. In comparison, today's artists can offer new releases directly to their fans through posts. In this way, social media acts as a single boundary between fans and musicians, so that fans can feel that much closer to their artists.

Consider a recent example from pop superstar Justin Bieber. To promote 'Cold Water', a new Major Lazer track on which Bieber was featured, Justin Bieber's Facebook profile re-posted from Major Lazer's account (see Figure 15.1). The post included both a link to purchase or stream the track, and also a short video snippet featuring audio from the track, along with the track's lyrics. The post was then pinned to the top of Justin's profile. Additional promotional impact could then be applied with this post, including paid advertising on Facebook.

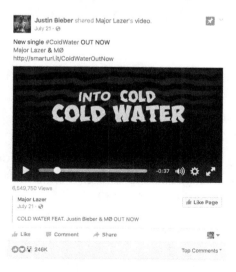

Figure 15.1. Justin Bieber Retweet

This way of doing business is becoming increasingly stand-ardised in today's music industry. While many who market and promote music on social media might still only post links and photos, the savviest marketers know that it is more effective to put new forms of digital content onto social-media accounts. In another track featuring Justin Bieber – this track from DJ Snake – Bieber's profile posts a link to the song on Spotify (see Figure 15.2). As a result of a product integration between Spotify and Facebook, the link automatically 'unpacks' itself into a music player within the post. As with the previous example, this type of post is consider-ably more interesting to a fan than a web link and can be used to spur consumption of the music as opposed to simply promoting it.

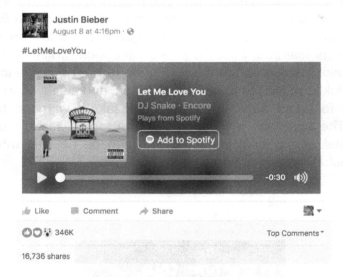

Figure 15.2. Justin Bieber Spotify Link

The interplay between digital media and social media can also be seen on Twitter. In the example in figures 15.3 and 15.4, Rihanna tweets an image as a teaser for her upcoming music video. The following day, she posts again, but this time uploading a clip from her music video in the tweet.

Facebook, Twitter and other social-media platforms like Insta-gram and Snapchat offer various ways of integrating digital media content within social media. While there is still money to be made in promoting web links, more innovative marketers are bringing digital media assets into the world of social media and betting that the subsequent virality results in positive commercial outcomes.

Figure 15.3. Rihanna Twitter Teaser

Figure 15.4. Rihanna Twitter Video Upload

Social-media Companies and Artists

The social-media companies that benefit from the engagement and activity of artists and fan bases have a somewhat tenuous relationship with them, because the primary business model of each of these companies is advertising, whose revenue seldom flows back into the hands of artists. Consequently, there has always been some degree of discord between the social-media companies and the music industry.

Nevertheless, artists and social-media companies have found ways in which to work together, in an arrangement which is somewhat mutually beneficial – even without a share in advertising revenue. Artists benefit from having easy access to hundreds of millions of potential fans via platforms on which users spend a great deal of time; social-media companies benefit because the activity that occurs on their platforms provides ample opportunities to monetise audiences further through both incremental visits and the data about their users. Music provides indications of interests, demographics and more, which can be very useful to social-media companies. Many companies have taken steps to make their platforms more commercially appealing, using extensive analytics and advertising tools. As a result, social-media companies are investing in several aspects of their businesses.

Dedicated Staff

Despite the range of job titles, the main task of staff members at social-media companies is to interface with the artistic community and its representatives. These employees meet regularly with artists, management firms and record labels, discussing anything from keeping the artists abreast of new features to negotiating for exclusive promotions or content.

Sharing Best Practices and Case Studies

In addition to these boundary-spanning staff members, the social-media companies have also created resources for artists to help them develop their presence in a given social-media environment.

For example, Facebook has a website entitled 'Tips for Musicians and Bands' that is intended for artists to use – and share.

Music and Content-focused Product Features

As mentioned previously, social-networking platforms (Facebook and Twitter, in particular) have recently invested in products and engineering to construct features specifically aimed at artists. Another great example of this is Facebook's enabling of 'Simple Music Stories', a feature which allows any links to Apple Music or Spotify to be expanded automatically into a music playback experience (see Figure 15.5, for example). Similarly, Twitter's implementation of the 'audio card' displays a link to Spotify or Soundcloud as a full-screen music player in a single tweet.

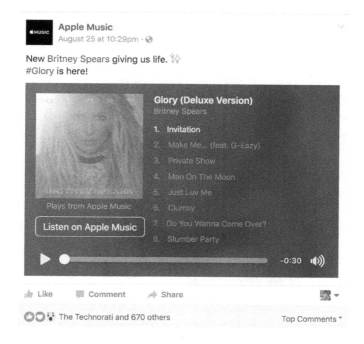

Figure 15.5. Automatic Playback Feature

Thanks to the deliberate products of social-media companies, incorporating digital and social media is becoming more efficient and accessible. By releasing features that enhance consumption of artists' content, artists now have ample reason to invest in social-media platforms. Additionally, these products provide digital-media distribution companies with material to help boost paid advertising, and fans have the convenience of click-to-play on their own accounts.

Impact on Fans

And the result? It turns out that fans engage at a lower rate for more commercial content, but there remains considerable virality in the responses to posts. For example, fans of One Direction hang on every word that is uttered – or typed. But you can see that the response to the availability of their newest album on iTunes is considerably lower than to general 'banter' from individual members – although you can see that the engagement is still quite considerable when compared with other commercial activity on Twitter. Also noteworthy is that posts from individual members often have as much – and sometimes more – impact on Twitter than posts from the collective band.

Figure 15.6. Louis Tomlinson Tweet

Figure 15.7. One Direction Album Tweet

Conclusion

Although we are still in the early days of transitioning from text and images to fully fledged digital-content experiences on social media, the genie cannot be put back into the bottle. In short, digital content has become not only the topic of conversation between artists and their fans, but now constitutes the very conversation itself. Furthering the evolution is the fact that all the key players in the industry are taking part. Indeed, more and more artists are making digital media a core part of how they interact with fans. Consequently, social-media companies will continue to build features which enable this phenomenon – and because they are motivated by traffic, engagement and media spending. Fans will soon *expect* to consume music that is promoted by their favourite artists within the promotional format of digital media itself.

About the Author

Ed Suwanjindar serves as a Strategy Advisor at Spotify. Formerly, Ed was the Director of Marketing for the Apple Music and iTunes business at Apple Inc, with responsibility for consumer marketing for the Apple Music subscription business, iTunes Music, Movies and TV Stores, and iBooks, and for leading the consumer marketing team for the world' s #1 digital music and entertainment destination across marketing programs and channels (Advertising, Social Media, Content Marketing, Email, Affiliate Marketing, Partnerships and Business Development). Prior to working at Apple, Ed played key roles in the mobile, search and entertainment businesses at Microsoft. He resides in Maui where he spends time photographing sunsets and swimming with turtles when not entrenched in digital media. Follow him on Twitter at @ edsuw.

Chapter 16

Using Technology for Smart Localisation

Francesco Rocchi and Eric Watson

Introduction

Globalisation has opened new frontiers of growth. For ambitious companies, more and more markets are within reach, goods are easier to distribute and services can be provided easily worldwide. The UN estimates the growth rate in international trade for 2016 to be 50% higher than that for gross world product. Meanwhile, the web provides a perfect infrastructure to internationalise, both in terms of distribution and marketing, with billions of customers potentially reachable from anywhere in the world.

According to a Forrester study (O'Grady, 2016), global cross-border B2C e-commerce will more than double over the next five years, reaching 424 billion USD by 2021. Cross-border sales will take an increasing share of online commerce, rising from 12% in 2015 to 15% in 2021.

Simply having a website, however, does not ensure that international customers will automatically buy a product or become aware of the existence of a company. Every market has different needs that must be addressed and the web itself has specific needs from a technical standpoint when it comes to international websites. This chapter, therefore, will analyse the most important issues to take into account in creating an international website, and the potential solutions to these issues. The focus of the chapter will be on the site itself; other forms of localised digital and offline marketing will be considered out of scope for this chapter.

The first section includes a summary of the long-term debate in international marketing regarding standardisation vs adaptation, and a description of the role of technology in finding a balance between the two approaches. In the second section, a general practical approach to creating an effective international website will be introduced. Sections three, four and five will detail both the need and the solutions for linguistic, cultural and technical localisation. Finally, there will be a discussion on the potential future developments of localisation.

After reading this chapter, you will:

1. Appreciate the issues which are related to globalising the website of a company;

2. Comprehend the role of technology in content localisation; and

3. Become familiar with real-world success stories of localisation and their applications.

Globalisation, Standardisation, Adaptation, Localisation

In international marketing literature, the trade-off between standardisation and adaptation has been one of the most discussed and controversial topics for over 50 years. It started with an article by Erik Elinder (1961) regarding the standardisation of advertising and later became a relevant matter in the 1980s, after Theodore Levitt declared that every marketing effort that is put in place by multinational companies in an increasingly globalised world ought to be standardised. In 1986, Philip Kotler took an opposing view to the argument, and the debate between standardisation and adaptation took off.

Over the next 30 years, several studies tried to prove one position over the other. Most of them were able to obtain results in specific contexts, explaining which characteristics of a product, company or market made standardisation more suitable than adaptation, or vice versa. Cavusgil and Zou, for example, showed how only companies with international competence could adapt their marketing strategy successfully (Cavusgil, 1994; Cavusgil and Zou, 2002). Numerous authors focused on the kind of differences or similarities between markets that made adaptation or standardisation preferable (Roth, 1995; Lim et al., 2006). Other authors focused on more specific components of the marketing mix, such as pricing (Sousa and Bradley, 2008; Samiee and Roth, 1992). Several theories were used to explain the behavioural differences or similarities between the two approaches – from semiotic theory (Alden et al., 1999), which explained the relevance of verbal and visual meaning perception, to institutional theory (Shoham et al., 2008), which concluded that standardisation can only be partial, due to a need for legitimisation.

Finding the Optimal Balance

A company's decision to have a localised marketing strategy (in terms of products, communication, prices, etc.) can be a daunting one. And indeed there are good reasons for standardisation and adaptation marketing approaches. In favour of standardisation is the notion that a company can employ the same marketing techniques across a range of different markets, thereby providing efficiency for production. It also allows managers to standardise processes, instead of duplicating work functions and reusing marketing and communication materials. Furthermore, consistent communications (websites, brochures, brand standards, logos, packaging, etc.) help promote non-discriminatory treatment and are less confusing for customers. A customer who sees that the American version of a website is different from the Argentine version, for example, might think that the company is limiting options to buy the best products at the most affordable price.

On the other hand, adaptation is usually considered valuable for customers, especially when different countries have different cultures and needs. Offering food with the same amount of spice on the Swiss and Moroccan markets would probably not produce the same results. Companies can also make customers feel special by providing access to something that is not available anywhere else. Regulatory and logistical limits can also force companies to localise their marketing efforts, whether or not they want to.

Situations vary between companies and consequently each situation requires a different approach. But the question remains: what is the optimal balance that, given the current conditions in different markets, will allow for the best results? Consider Coca-Cola, for example, which has historically maintained a universal product when possible. On the other end of the continuum is Procter and Gamble which adopts a different strategy for each product. In some cases, the brand changes, in some cases the communication campaigns are local and other times the product itself differs among countries. In between Coca-Cola and Procter and Gamble are companies like McDonald's, which has standardised processes despite differences in products and marketing communications. Much of the menu is the same across the globe, but pricing varies drastically and many restaurants offer local options (wine in France, for example, or the lobster sandwich in Eastern Canada).

It is impossible to provide a universal rule that is valid for every market and industry, but a company in today's world must address the issue of whether localisation is optimal and, if so, how and to what extent it will be implemented. Invariably, this question begs another question – what is the most effective and efficient way to provide the necessary localisation?

The Impact of Technology

Throughout history, technology has always contributed to shifting production, consumption and marketing habits. Populations with the most developed technology thrived and those populations that discovered agriculture were able to settle, create cities and rule over their neighbours. The ability to write was leveraged to increase wealth and gain supremacy over larger and larger areas. The Romans were a prime example of this: their legions established sovereignty throughout Europe and the Mediterranean, thanks to superior technology (bridges, roads, fleets, etc.). Similar developments took place throughout the Industrial Revolution, which transformed England into the first global superpower, and more recently between high-technology companies.

The more technology evolved, the smaller the world became. In the nineteenth century, for example, only a small fraction of the population could conceptualise the rest of the world; by the end of the twentieth century, the relatively inexpensive cost of flying allowed people to travel and experience the world. And billions of people can now speak a language other than that of their native society.

Currently, the Internet allows an ever-increasing number of users to access information and products from remote countries. How does this impact the amount of localisation that companies require? On the one hand, it is possible to argue that globalisation is standardising the tastes of customers. This is partly true for certain products and segments of the population: across the world, people view the same show on Netflix or purchase the same pair of Nike shoes. On the other hand, these same products still have some degree of localisation (dubbing in the case of television shows, for example, or different packaging in the case of shoes) and more markets are now within reach that cater to different tastes and needs. No longer is the globe-trotter millionaire the only customer who can purchase abroad: clusters of the population with strong local roots can order whatever they prefer from Amazon or Alibaba. A start-up in Nairobi can get in touch with a vendor in Seattle. Consequently, it is necessary for companies to rethink their positioning, generate awareness for themselves in both their home country and in any other market which they deem fit, and create the conditions to serve customers with the right approach.

While technology expanded the need for localisation, it also helped fulfil it. Websites are an easily accessible showcase and account for more and more of the total customer spending. The US Census Bureau published data which show that more than 8% of total retail sales are now from e-commerce. Even for brick-and-mortar companies, online is key – Google's research shows that 76% of people who do a local search show up to a store within a day and 28% of the searches result in a purchase. Furthermore, most of the preliminary information gathering before a purchase occurs online.

In the past, research to find a product was offline and mostly local, but the web now allows everybody to be in touch with potential suppliers from any area of the world in minutes. For suppliers actually to be considered available and relevant, therefore, they must have an online presence that provides for customers outside of their home market. Technology can ease the processes of translation and localisation, which were traditionally slow and completely manual but are now supported by more and more sophisticated tools.

Conquering a New Market Online: A Practical Approach

When a company separates marketing teams for each market, it is easy to create different content, infrastructure and websites. But when there is only a centralised website or when there is a stronger need for online consistency, it is necessary to explore other solutions. The first solution is to create dedicated local minisites with only a fraction of the information that is available on the original site. This can be achieved for a majority of companies, but is inherently an inferior experience for international customers, despite the customisation.

Conversely, it is possible to create parallel versions of the original site, each of which is translated into the necessary language. This makes possible an international experience that allows for the same content as the original experience. But for many companies, this translation is difficult and expensive, and it involves no customisation of content.

An intermediate option is the creation of an original website alongside the use of proper technology – such as the right CRM modules or a proxy – to generate mirroring versions that are automatically translated by humans or a machine. In this case, it is also easier to generate customisations for each of the sites in order to adapt them to the local context. This solution isn't necessarily optimal for every company, but it does elucidate the importance of not underestimating the planning necessary for the creation of an effective international website.

Whichever approach is taken, every digital marketer ought to consider three main dimensions of localisation:

1. Linguistic localisation (making the site accessible to local visitors in their own language),

2. Cultural localisation (adjusting the site based on local culture and preferences), and

3. Technical localisation (providing a technical structure which drives traffic to the site through optimal SEO which is tailored specifically to the local market).

In each of these dimensions, it is necessary for digital marketers to define the optimal approach for their sites. Each of the dimensions will be different and will entail a slightly different solution. If a site fails to accommodate for the local in terms of language and culture, and is not technically optimised for its home country, it will never reach its full potential.

Linguistic Localisation

While English remains the dominant second language of the world, most consumers still have not adapted to it. Based on Common Sense Advisory research (DePalma et al., 2014), 75% of website visitors prefer to shop in their own language and 72% are more likely to buy from a site that offers a native-language experience. We have seen this same phenomenon time and time again, even in regions that have a very high level of English proficiency. In Scandinavia, for example, an e-commerce retailer saw its revenue jump by over 62% in the first year after translating its already high-performing website to Swedish. While Swedish customers were able to speak and understand English offline and were comfortable reading it online, a significant number were not prepared to make purchases on a site that was not in Swedish. It benefits a global brand to take this into account, by increasing global sales on a website, and understanding its customers better.

Marketers are proficient at marketing their brands to their primary-market audiences. Indeed, they are fluent in their native language, they understand the culture tacitly (because they are usually natives themselves) and are sensitive to consumer behaviours (because they are also local shoppers). Marketers take this nuanced market knowledge for granted... when at home.

There is no one solution to promoting brands in global markets, however. Being fluent in the local language is relevant from both a marketing and a legal perspective. Even small errors in localisation can lead to disastrous outcomes. Consider the Dutch advertisement with a child pointing to an ice cream cone with the text "Mama, die, die, die". In Dutch it means "Mama, this one, this one, this one", but has a completely different meaning for an English speaker.

There are plenty of other examples where linguistic misunderstandings have repercussions. Recently, a large sport apparel firm had to translate its website's sales section to Italian and used the word 'Saldi' instead of 'Offerte', without realising that in Italy 'Saldi' is a term which is restricted legally to a specific seasonal discount. In this case, not only did the misuse of the term potentially violate local laws, but it was also a clear indication to customers that the brand was not 'speaking their language' – and that the shopping experience which they were having was not optimised for them.

In-country Localisation

In some cases, it can be a legal requirement to provide double-language services. For example, for a brick-and-mortar company in Quebec, the store's signage and corporate website must be available in French and English. It is not always a legal constraint, however, that drives the decision to have a separate strategy for targeting specific international segments among the residents in a country. The growing Hispanic market in the USA is leading to more and more companies creating Spanish-language versions of websites and also customised campaigns. One of the major US-based telecom companies recently created a custom promotional banner that featured international calling plans prominently on the Spanish site. To ensure that only relevant users saw these banners, they were additions which were exclusive to the Spanish site. Revenue increased by 117% while the banner was online.

Companies might also consider servicing minority populations alongside traditional target audiences. In Canada, for example, there are now nearly 1.5 million people of Chinese heritage who live in the country. That is more than 10% of the total population in some provinces that carry more purchasing power than the national average. These citizens rarely expect that a mainstream Canadian website will be in Chinese. But when presented with a clear and welcoming option to experience a site in their native language, website conversions and engagement increase dramatically. On a Canadian commercial bank website, the number of Chinese visitors who opted for the version of the site in their own language tripled that of the same visitors choosing the English version.

Cultural Localisation

If a website cannot connect with consumers in a meaningful way, they tend to shop elsewhere. International brands that are entering local markets, in particular, face this challenge from local brands that understand and speak to the customers in that market (see Chapter 6 by Baazeem for more on cultural localisation in developing countries).

International brands must adapt to this challenge with more than linguistic fluency. A kind of social- and data-based cultural fluency is absolutely critical for success. Understanding the market from a cultural perspective allows brands to avoid embarrassing misunderstandings which can ruin their reputation in the local market. Pairing this with data fluency creates insightful analysis for how the brand is performing in the market, and suggests ways of connecting with local customers further and maximising returns to the site.

Even large companies with significant resources devoted to marketing can make catastrophic errors when they do not consider the local customers' perspective. Walmart bailed on Germany in 2006 after eight years in the market, at the cost of around 1 billion USD. Observers hypothesised that the company's ethos of high-volume sales and low prices did not resonate with German culture. The Home Depot took it on the chin for about 160 million USD when it closed shop in China. Commentators speculated that this was due to how Chinese consumers associate do-it-yourself home-improvement projects with poverty, not an enjoyable hobby. An attention to detail and a commitment to cultural fluency make all the difference between failure and success in new international markets.

Even the most culturally aware and detail-oriented marketer must be careful, however, because well researched and logical efforts to connect with local customers can have unintended consequences. An American electronics retailer conducted a test for television in which the English-language site showed a scene from an American Football game, while the Spanish-language version of the site showed a scene from a soccer match. While the visual and messaging might have been relevant for a customer in each market, performance on the Spanish-language site actually dropped during the test. What the company discovered was that users on the Spanish-language site were toggling back and forth between the English and Spanish sites, and after they realised that the images they were shown were different, they discontinued their shopping on the Spanish site. It was hypothesised that customers believed that the Spanish site was a sub-par model of the same product on the English site. The takeaway is clear – testing ought to be carried out on even the most well-intentioned and planned campaigns to ensure the desired results.

Payment Methods

For e-commerce clients, perhaps the most critical way to create a localised experience is to support local payment methods. Unlike American consumers, not all (or even most) global consumers are comfortable using credit cards for their online shopping. And even in a country where the use of credit cards is widespread, there are strong preferences for one method of payment versus another. In the Netherlands, for example, there are cases of websites with revenues from purchases through iDeal (an e-wallet platform particularly common in the country) that are three times higher than purchases using credit cards.

Providing the right payment options is key, but it is not sufficient unless user experience is implemented correctly. A UK-based apparel retailer entered the online German market and began paid search campaigns to support its new site. Conversion rates were much lower than expected, however, and the campaigns were unprofitable. After a brief audit of user experience of the site, the reason became clear: although the company offered all the locally relevant payment methods for Germans, they had only displayed them at the bottom of the checkout funnel. German users who landed on the site were led to believe, based on the information in the website's footer and the product pages, that only Credit Card and PayPal were acceptable payment methods. This was not ideal for Germans, who prefer bank transfers for international transactions. After the appropriate changes were made, the site exploded: the conversion rate increased by almost 200% and the company was able to turn back on its paid search campaigns.

Technical Localisation

Technology has two different roles in localisation. The most intuitive role is to make it easier for companies to translate and customise content. The other is to attract and direct each visitor to the correct version of the site.

Technology as a Supporter of Localisation

When a website is created or goes through a re-platforming process, it is key to take scalability for different markets into account and to pick a solution that allows for localisation and customisation. The traditional translation model consists of recreating the same website in several different languages, manually translated. The more modern model allows instead for scalability, often through proxy technology.

Proxy technology works by storing translated versions of the original content and using them to serve a translated version of the same website to visitors who request it by visiting the local URLs. This process is managed automatically, and new content can easily be added and sent to translators, thereby increasing efficiency. It also allows for technical tools to promote organisation and for the efficiency of the translation process itself. Examples of this include the creation of translation memories that automatically reuse the same content wherever it is repeated, and stronger integration of specific glossaries and style guides by marketing efforts to preserve and adapt the voice of the brand. Moreover, the ability to maintain constantly updated versions of all the websites is guaranteed through crawlers which automatically report updated content on the original site, thereby leading to translation in the span of a few hours. This ensures that localised versions of a website are always accurate representations of the original experience.

Customising local versions of a website is usually a lot of work for companies – especially for marketing departments that do not have direct access to the site and, consequently, must rely on IT to make most changes. Simply customising a local version of a website can be a difficult technical task.

If the platform is already established and cannot be changed, proxy-based technology is a potential solution to the issue, because it makes it easier to implement changes which are targeted to localised versions of a website, without the need for heavy implementation or changes to the current structure of the original website. Furthermore, it makes it easier to perform A/B testing on different versions of the content in order to determine which performs better, thereby optimising user experiences and conversion rates.

A clear example of how websites can be customised easily using such a technology comes from a UK-based online retailer. It created a localised US site in American English (this kind of linguistic localisation can help generate trust and credibility despite the usually low number of differences between different 'dialects'), but it had to overcome an almost total lack of awareness among the US customers. After a promotional campaign to support the launch, the website was analysed to identify the most important 'trust badges' (the elements which visitors in a certain market must see in order to trust a company), which were subsequently included only in the local version. The results were remarkable: in less than a week, this trust messaging increased checkout rates by 27%, resulting in nearly 200,000 USD of additional revenue.

Technology as a Tool to Optimise Traffic

If there is more than one version of a website, each specifically catered to a single market, it is key to drive each visitor to the one specifically created for him or her. This can be accomplished in two key moments. When a customer is looking for specific content through a certain engine, the correct version of a website must show up. Similarly, after a customer is already on the site, it must be easy to navigate towards the appropriate version.

Search engines attempt to offer the most relevant website to users based on their 'judgement'. The challenge, therefore, is to understand how this judgement works and to help search engines recognise the role of each version of the site. Each search engine has a different approach to understanding the geographical and linguistic nature of a website. Baidu, for example, requires a specific licence for Chinese versions of sites and has two different verification processes. But there are some general rules that tend to apply to all search engines:

- The language of the pages' content,

- The language of the URLs,

- The language of meta tags,

- The geo-localised tags (hreflang), and

- The webmaster tools localisation for that specific search engine.

While eventually most search engines are able to 'discover' the authority of the differing sites, there are ways to shortcut this process and help generate greater returns more quickly. An agency which is proficient in SEO, with a specific focus on international sites, goes a long way towards making a site effective. But technology can also make the process more efficient. Indeed, after making content translation easier, technology can provide basic assistance in applying translation to other elements of a site.

URLs and meta tags are often ignored by translation agencies, but savvy SEO experts know that they must also be taken into account. Technology makes it easier to recycle the work that was done in translating the content and apply it automatically to both URLs and meta tags (hidden snippets of code which are aimed at describing the page content for search engines).

Inside the website code, there is another category of tags that is aimed at describing the geographical and linguistic nature of a page specifically. These tags, called hreflang, indicate country and language of the page, and state the equivalent URL in every other language for the same site. For example, the description of a specific product will have an almost identical page in French and English on a site, and the search engine must understand that they are correlated, in order to establish one page's authority – and probability of being shown in search-engine results. Each page can have hreflang tags with the list of all the equivalent pages in other languages, or the complete list can be part of the website's sitemap – an xml file which search engines use to find their way in a website and understand its hierarchy and structure. Through the appropriate tools, it is possible to automatically generate sitemaps connecting all the pages of an international website, making life easier for both the search engine and the website creators. Finally, there is a human component in making sure that the webmaster tools (the set of tools provided by each search engine, such as Google Search Console) are properly set in order to provide all the possible localisation signals.

The sum of all these optimisations has been seen to increase performances dramatically for local versions of websites, in some cases doubling the number of impressions on search engines and with positive effects on conversion rates, due to better experiences for the visitor on the website. Even when websites that serve different countries are not translated into different languages and have no relevant difference in content, it is still useful to apply all the solutions described above, because search engines are less compatible with duplicated content and might assign a ranking penalty if they notice exact copies of the same site – consider, for example, a company that serves Spain, Mexico and the Hispanic market in the USA each with the same version of the website but with separate shipping options and different CCTLDs or subdomains (es.companyname.com, companyname. es and es.companyname.mx).

Technology as a Tool to Channel Traffic

Once a search engine has a clear picture of the specific potential visitor each version of a website is designed for, it will probably direct most of the traffic correctly. But there is still the possibility that somebody will execute a search in English despite being more comfortable speaking Spanish, or directly type a .com URL without knowing that a .fr version of the same site exists. In this regard, it is key to have an optimal international user experience, which requires making the visitor aware that alternate versions of the site exist, thereby making it as easy as possible to switch from one site to another.

Technology also provides solutions for this. The most common solution is what is called country-based hard redirect. Depending only on the visitors' IP locations, visitors will be steered to a specific version of a website. This approach has two pitfalls, however. First is that it is possible that the hard redirect makes the user experience worse because some customers might not like being precluded from visiting the website in another language or denied access to a foreign country catalogue. The second pitfall is legal and it affects mostly websites in Europe (although it is not limited only to European companies). The EU proposed a new piece of legislation recently concerning geo-blocking, which will prevent companies from hard redirecting visitors to a specific local version of a website.

More modern technologies deal with redirection in a less intrusive and more flexible way. Based on a series of signals that they detect from the visitor (IP location, browser language preference, etc.), some tools are able to suggest only to a subset of customers an alternate experience in the language that they might appreciate more, whilst leaving them the freedom to decide on their own. Furthermore, the tools will remember customers' preferences and redirect them automatically to the best version at every future visit.

The Future of Localisation

Localisation is still a developing concept and as such will undergo changes in the future. As the practice of entering multiple markets through translation becomes the standard, the challenge of connecting with relevant cultures within those linguistic spheres will grow. Rather than simply offering a Spanish site that targets the Spanish-speaking world, it will become critical for companies to customise their messaging and brand to *specific* Latin markets. Similarly, targeting Canada with a Canadian site will become less important than targeting French and Chinese Canadians with unique experiences that are tailored to them.

As the appeal of international markets grows, we expect that companies will face more pressure to integrate these different dimensions of the localisation process. Rather than having to coordinate a Content Management System with product feeds, translation platform and SEO tasks, markets will increasingly bundle these offerings together in powerful packages included in the CMS itself or in the communication tools.

Technological shifts will largely underpin this movement, increasing the ease with which these aspects can be bundled together and addressed more efficiently. More and more, companies will be able to achieve the desired balance between standardisation and localisation, defining it more precisely through better knowledge of each market – whether internal to the company or outsourced to vendors. At the same time, the digital aspects of localisation will increasingly be integrated with the offline aspects, in terms of both integrated campaigns and co-creation of local expertise.

Conclusion

The optimal balance between localisation and standardisation is a struggle which companies have confronted for decades, and it will continue to be part of fundamental discussions in business. Notwithstanding the logistical factors that allow companies to sell abroad, there are multiple decisions in a company's journey to enter a market with a localised approach. Translation of content allows for a wider reach and higher effectiveness, which is becoming more important due to the rising percentage of non-native speakers in most of the Western world.

Translation is a necessary foundation for a localised market-place or showcase, but it is usually not enough. A knowledge of local culture and customs is necessary to enhance an approach's effect and, in some cases, to avoid legal and PR problems. With increasing globalisation, technology also eases longstanding difficulties of localisation and standardisation. For companies looking to create localised websites, technology can go a long way in helping a site's customisation and the optimisation of its performance.

References

Alden, D., J. Steenkamp and R. Batra (1999) "Brand Positioning Through Advertising in Asia, North America, and Europe: The Role of Global Consumer Culture." *Journal of Marketing*, Vol. 63, Iss. 1, pp.75–87.

Cavusgil, S., and S. Zou (1994) "Marketing Strategy-Performance Relationship: An Investigation of the Empirical Link in Export Market Ventures." *Journal of Marketing*, Vol. 58, Iss. 1, pp.1–21.

DePalma, D., R. Stewart and V. Hegde (2014) *Can't Read, Won't Buy: Why Language Matters on Global Websites.* Lowell, USA: Common Sense Advisory Research.

De Nale, R., and D. Weidenhamer (2016) *US Census Bureau – Quarterly Retail E-ceommerce Sales 2nd Quarter 2016.* Retrieved from: http://www.census.gov/retail/mrts/www/data/pdf/ec_current. pdf

Elinder, E. (1961) "How International Can Advertising Be?" *International Advertiser*, Vol. 2, pp.12–16.

European Commission (2015) *Digital Single Market – Geo-Blocking.* Retrieved from: https://ec.europa.eu/digital-single-market/en/ geo-blocking-digital-single-market

Kotler, P. (1986) "Global Standardization – Courting Danger." *Journal of Consumer Marketing*, Vol. 3, Iss. 2, pp.13–15.

Levitt, T. (1983) "The Globalization of Markets." *Harvard Business Review*, Vol. 61, Iss. 3, pp.92–102.

Lim, L., F. Acito and A. Rusetski (2006) "Development of Archetypes of International Marketing Strategy." *Journal of International Business Studies*, Vol. 37, Iss. 4, pp.499–524.

O'Grady, M. (2016) *Forrester Research Online Cross-Border Retail Forecast, 2016 To 2021 (Global).* Retrieved from: https://www.forrester.com/report/Forrester+Research+Online+CrossBorder+Retail+Forecast+2016+To+2021+Global/-/E-RES133597

Roth, M. (1995) "Effects of Global Market Conditions on Brand Image Customization and Brand Performance." *Journal of Advertising*, Vol. 24, Iss. 4, pp.55–75.

Samiee, S., and K. Roth (1992) "The Influence of Global Marketing Standardization on Performance." *Journal of Marketing*, Vol. 56, Iss. 2, pp.1–17.

Shoham, A., M. Brencic, V. Virant and A. Ruvio (2008) "International Standardization of Channel Management and Its Behavioral and Performance Outcomes." *Journal of International Marketing*, Vol. 16, Iss. 2, pp.120–51.

Sousa, C., and F. Bradley (2008) "Antecedents of International Pricing Adaptation and Export Performance." *Journal of World Business*, Vol. 43, Iss. 3, pp.307–20.

Think with Google (2016) *How Mobile Search Connects Consumers to Stores, Think With Google.* Retrieved from: https://www.thinkwithgoogle.com/infographics/mobile-search-trends-consumers-to-stores.html

Zou, S., and S. Cavusgil (2002) "The GMS: A Broad Conceptualization of Global Marketing Strategy and Its Effect on Firm Performance." *Journal of Marketing*, Vol. 66, Iss. 4, pp.40–56.

About the Authors

Francesco Rocchi is a Global Growth Strategist at MotionPoint Corporation, a tech company that focuses on localisation of digital efforts. He manages relationships with universities for research purposes and conducts data analysis for product management. He also leads the performance improvement initiative for some of MotionPoint's largest clients. Francesco holds a Master of Business Administration from the University of Michigan in Ann Arbor, USA, and a Master Degree in Marketing Management from

Sapienza University in Rome, Italy. His current research interest is on the use of data to support local performance in international markets. Find him on LinkedIn at francescorocchi. Contact him on email at fraroc@umich.edu.

Eric Watson is also a Global Growth Strategist at MotionPoint Corporation; he manages the development of analytics and business intelligence systems for aggregating, managing and reporting data. Eric holds a Master Degree in Finance from Yonsei University in Seoul, South Korea. He previously served as the editor in chief of the *Yonsei Journal of International Studies*. His current research interest is the development of new manufacturing technologies, and the new national policies which are necessary to encourage their efficient and egalitarian adoption. Find him on LinkedIn at ericwwatson. Contact him on email at ewatson@motionpoint.com.

CPSIA information can be obtained
at www.ICGtesting.com
Printed in the USA
LVHW080956040919
629894LV00013B/176/P